edited by M.Breheny, P.Congdon · London papers in regional science 20 · a pion publication

growth and change in a core region:

the case of South East England

p Pion Limited, 207 Brondesbury Park, London NW2 5JN

British Library Cataloguing in Publication Data
A CIP catalogue record for this book is available from the British Library.

ISBN 0 85086 134 9

Contributors

J Barlow — *Centre for Urban and Regional Research, Faculty of Social Science, University of Sussex, Falmer, Brighton BN1 9QN, England*

M Breheny — *Department of Geography, University of Reading, PO Box 227, Reading RG6 2AB, England*

A Champion — *Department of Geography, University of Newcastle upon Tyne, Newcastle upon Tyne, NE1 7RU, England*

P Congdon — *London Research Centre, Parliament House, 81 Black Prince Road, London SE1 7SZ, England*

A Evans — *Department of Economics, University of Reading, Whiteknights, Reading RG6 2AA, England*

P Hall — *Institute of Urban and Regional Development, University of California at Berkeley, Berkeley, CA 94720, USA*

C Hamnett — *Faculty of Social Sciences, Open University, Milton Keynes MK7 6AA, England*

D Hart — *Department of Land Management, University of Reading, Whiteknights, Reading RG6 2BU, England*

A Hooper — *Department of Land Management, University of Reading, Whiteknights, Reading RG6 2BU, England*

R Lee — *Department of Geography, Queen Mary College, Mile End Road, London E1 4NS, England*

C Mason — *Department of Geography, University of Southampton, Southampton SO9 5NH, England*

J Mohan — *Department of Geography, Queen Mary College, Mile End Road, London E1 4NS, England*

D Palmer — *Confederation of British Industry, Centre Point, 103 New Oxford Street, London WC1A 1DU, England*

P Pinch — *Department of Geography, Polytechnic of North London, Holloway, London N7 8DB, England*

S Pinch — *Department of Geography, University of Southampton, Southampton SO9 5NH, England*

S Rogers   Planning Department, East Sussex County Council,
                        Southover House, Southover Road, Lewes BN7 1YA,
                        England

A van Delft   National Physical Planning Agency, PO Box 90618,
                        2509 LP The Hague, The Netherlands

A G van der Knaap   Economic Geography Institute, Erasmus University
                        Rotterdam, PO Box 1738, 3000 DR Rotterdam,
                        The Netherlands

R Vickerman   Eliot College, The University of Kent at Canterbury,
                        Canterbury CT2 7NZ, England

S Witt   Coalfield Communities Campaign Secretariat, Barnsley
                        Metropolitan Borough Council, Barnsley Enterprise
                        Centre, 1 Pontifract Road, Barnsley S71 1AJ, England

Contents

Part 3 Strategic planning

Growth and Change in a Core Region: The Case of the South East of England

M BREHENY
University of Reading
P CONGDON
London Research Centre

1 Introduction

For two decades or so, much of the research in the United Kingdom devoted to questions of regional development has focused on the economically depressed north and west. The priority has been to understand the causes and consequences of uneven spatial development in these regions. Although it has always been acknowledged that to understand such uneven development both disadvantaged and advantaged areas have to be studied, the latter have been relatively ignored. More recently, however, as the South of England has become more buoyant still, and as the 'North–South divide' threatens to get wider, attention has begun to focus on growth regions. This increased interest arises both from a desire for a better understanding of the nature of uneven regional development, through knowledge of the functioning of a 'core' region, and from interest in a number of internal features of the South East: for example, the decentralisation of population and jobs (Gordon, 1987), the nature of the burgeoning service sector (Marshall, 1988), the appearance of 'high-tech' concentrations (Hall et al, 1987), and the contrast between the growth of strategic issues and the weakening of strategic planning (Breheny, 1987).

These issues should not be of interest only to UK readers. The South East is regarded as an example of a 'core' region, occupying a dominant position, economically, politically, and culturally, within a capitalist economy which exhibits distinct and enduring uneven development. Other such 'core' regions exist in other parts of the world. Thus the South East of England is an interesting case study of a phenomenon that should be of widespread interest. It does, of course, have peculiar features, as we shall see, but it also has features that if understood in this case will improve our understanding of the phenomenon generally.

This focus on the South East as a core region comes at a time when some researchers are suggesting that the role of such regions might be changing. For some time now, such regions have been viewed as fulfilling a distinct place in an international spatial division of labour, in which transnational companies divide their functions spatially in order to maximise their trading conditions. Thus, at the one extreme a separation has tended to emerge between the company headquarters, located in the originating country, and the production plants, located in peripheral, low-cost locations. Between these extremes, other locations might fulfill

an intermediate role. For example, within, say, Europe or South East
Asia, a capital city region might function as headquarters for North
American and Japanese companies, where administration, marketing, and
possibly some research and development is carried out. According to
this view, the South East of England functions both as a global headquarters for British transnationals and as an intermediate, European base
for companies headquartered elsewhere; contributing to uneven
development intranationally and internationally.

The view now is that this form of functional separation is beginning
to break down. For a variety of reasons, including increased competition
and changing technology, the emphasis has now switched from mass
production to flexibility. Thus, the way to gain relative advantage is no
longer to outproduce your competitors, but to be able to respond more
rapidly to changing market conditions. A desire for flexible production
systems is matched by the need for a flexible labour force; flexible both
in terms of numbers—hence, more subcontracting—and in terms of skills.
This perspective of a new 'regime of flexible accumulation' (Harvey, 1987)
has many supporters (for example, see the set of papers edited by Scott
and Cooke, 1988) but some detractors (Amin, 1989).

For our purposes, the interesting question—within the broader one of
how core regions tick—is how this perspective, if it has some validity,
will affect core regions. Will they lose, maintain, or gain on their existing
dominant positions? Research to date is rather inconclusive on this
question, but does point to the likelihood of increased spatial agglomeration.
Many of the features of flexible production imply the need for tighter
spatial organisation within and between firms. The outcome may be a
reconcentration of production in core industrial countries (Schoenberger,
1988). In turn, we might expect the core regions of those countries—
with their established advantages—to benefit. Thus, the South East of
England may be the beneficiary of these profound changes in capitalist
industrial structures.

We might continue our deductions still further by suggesting that within
the South East it is the outer area, which has been the real focus of
growth, that will in turn continue to gain from these changes. If we move
our attention from the external role of the region to intraregional issues,
then we must focus on the decentralisation of people and jobs from
London to the outer parts of the region and beyond as a major issue.
Since about 1940 London has been the net loser of people and jobs,
and the outer parts of the region the net recipient. Furthermore, over
time the areas receiving the highest growth rates have been further and
further out, to the point where now the focus of growth is on those
counties immediately beyond the regional boundary; that is, to the
periphery of what is now called the 'Greater South East'. Despite this
clear process of decentralisation, or even deurbanisation according to
some researchers, there is some evidence in the 1980s of small gains in

the metropolis. This has generated a debate as to whether there is a genuine 'return to the city' (see Champion and Congdon, 1987; Gordon, 1987).

It is the rapidly growing outer parts of the South East that have been the beneficiaries of postwar industrial restructuring. While many other parts of the country, including London, suffered the deindustrialisation of the 1970s and 1980s, many of the outer parts of the region were relatively immune. With some exceptions, this area was not heavily industrialised, and hence did not have to overcome this legacy as the new industries sought new locations. Thus, towns like Wokingham, Newbury, and Cambridge have found themselves being industrialised for the first time, as they have become the focus of 'high-tech' industries. Hall et al (1987) have found that the major concentration of high-technology industry in the region, indeed in the country, is in a 'Western Crescent' to the west of London. They also found that although some of this activity can be explained by looking at the core role played by the South East in the world economy, localised factors, particularly the presence of defence research establishments, were also important.

Although high-technology industries have been significant in the growth of the outer South East, their contribution to job growth has been very modest. Of much greater significance has been the growth of the service sector, particularly the producer service sector. In percentage terms, the growth of the service sector has been as high in the depressed regions as in the South East. However, the South East has for some time had a greater share of its employment in the service sector than other regions. Thus, a similar percentage rise in all regions gives the South East a much higher absolute growth. Although London retains a strong financial sector, much of the growth in the service sector has been in the outer parts of the South East. Part of this growth arises from the decentralisation of some headquarters from London. Outer areas of the region such as Bournemouth have been favoured, along with Bristol, which is beyond the South East region but is very accessible. Growth has also come from decentralisation not of headquarters but of 'back offices', housing large numbers of clerical staff in cheaper locations, while a small number of staff remains in the headquarters in London. This dramatic growth of the service sector has prompted research into not just its economic effects, but also into the social and cultural features of the new 'service class' (Thrift et al, 1988).

Although many of the characteristics of the South East region at the end of the 1980s are consistent with the ethos of the Conservative governments in power since 1979, it would be wrong to assume that the government has intervened directly in the region. Indeed, the land use planning system has not been spared from the general deregulation of the public sector. Strategic planning in particular has suffered, with regional plans and metropolitan authorities already abolished and structure plans set to follow suit. Coupled with a general antiplanning philosophy and a belief in the ability of the private sector to resolve development issues, these changes have diminished our capacity to assess strategically the trends discussed above and the major, undeniably strategic, developments projects such as the Channel Tunnel, Stansted Airport, and many more. Valiant efforts are being made by SERPLAN (London and South East Regional Planning Conference), which represents the local authorities of the region, but their policy statements are little more than platitudes in the absence of statutory backing and a strategic planning 'infrastructure'. Thus, the consequences of all of this growth are occurring largely by accident not design (Breheny, 1987).

Because of this renewed interest in the South East, papers were commissioned by the editors for a theme on 'Growth and Change in the South East' at the annual conference of the British Section of the Regional Science Association, held in September 1988 at the University of Sussex, Brighton, England. These papers form the basis of this collection. All of the papers, except the one by Evans, were presented at that meeting. Evans acted as a discussant during the theme sessions and produced his paper after the conference.

The papers are presented here in three parts: economy and employment, population and housing, and strategic planning.

2 The book
2.1 Part 1 Economy and employment
The economy of the South East is more buoyant now than for some years, and a distinct set of trends indicative of overheating have emerged in the labour market. As a result of interactions between job and housing markets, the ramifications of economic growth can also be seen more widely; for example, in house price inflation (see part 2). The height of the recession, marked by rapid increases in unemployment and reduced production in some economic sectors (such as manufacturing and construction) occurred in the early 1980s. Unemployment continued to increase slowly in the mid-1980s to reach a peak in 1986, but since then there has been an improvement in employment and unemployment in the South East at slightly above the national average. A recent report on prosperity in local labour markets in Britain (Champion and Green, 1988) found the areas of top-performing local labour markets lie in an arc around London from west to north. The slower growth of other parts of the region means that overall the job growth rates are lower in the South East than in adjacent regions of the 'Greater South East': the South West, East Anglia, and the East Midlands. However, the South East accounts for 35% of total jobs in Britain, and the net gain in jobs during the period 1981–86 of 328 000 exceeded the combined absolute growth of other expanding regions (272 000).

The rate of growth in gross domestic product (GDP) per head and in average earnings in the region has exceeded the national average, and if anything, the gap in average prosperity between the South East and the rest of the nation has widened over recent years (Egginton, 1988). Average incomes in the richest region, the South East, are now (in 1987) 44% higher than those in the poorest British region, Wales, and 53% higher than those in Northern Ireland (CSO, 1988). London incomes are on average even higher; for example, 57% more than those in Wales. The growth and prosperity of the South East economy and of the 'Greater South East' has led many commentators to point towards the economic imbalances and potential social and political results of a widening North – South gap (Green, 1988; Martin, 1988).

The nature of revival and growth in the South East is sharply differentiated by economic sector and by locality within the region. The greatest gains in employment have been concentrated in the service sector, especially in banking, insurance, and finance. The growth in such 'producer' services has been the main factor in the economic revival of London, where stability in total employment since 1983 is in contrast to heavy job losses during the 1970s (see Congdon and Champion, this volume). During the period 1981 – 87 a gain of 154 000 jobs in financial services in London offset a net loss of 204 000 jobs in other sectors, including 164 000 in manufacturing alone.

The decline in jobs in the South East outside London (that is, the rest of the South East—the ROSE) was relatively small in the recession years and a recovery here was apparent as early as 1983. Between 1983 and 1987, employment in the ROSE grew by 9.1%—from 3 667 000 to 4 000 000, whereas in London the growth in the same period was by only 1.6% (from 3 462 000 to 3 517 000). Growth of financial services in the ROSE has been a major component of overall growth in employment (169 000 jobs out of a total increase of 322 000 in the period 1981 – 87), and the growth rate of this sector (59% over the period) far exceeds that of London. Decentralisation of producer services from London to other urban centres in the South East has been the subject of a number of studies (Gillespie and Green, 1987; Jones Lang Wootton, 1988).

2.1.1 *Intraregional contrasts*
The divide between the main metropolitan centre and the rest of the region is not the only one of significance in economic terms. There are wide differences in growth and prosperity between counties in the South East outside London. Indeed critiques of the North – South divide stress that intraregional variations in indicators of prosperity are considerable (Green, 1988). The most prosperous and high-growth counties are located to the north and west of London, though it may be noted that criteria for assessing such differences are not necessarily consistent. The highest levels of GDP per head in 1984 were in Berkshire, Hertfordshire, and

Hampshire, whereas the highest rates of job growth in the period 1981 – 84 were in Buckinghamshire, West Sussex, and Surrey. The lowest unemployment levels (in December 1988) were in Berkshire, Buckinghamshire, Oxfordshire, and West Sussex. The definition of the less prosperous counties is far from clear cut and such counties are not homogenous. Thus the evidence points to lower average earnings, slower employment growth, and higher unemployment in districts located in the 'Lower Thames Corridor' of Kent and Essex. However, these counties also contain areas of high-status commuter belt (for example, in west noncoastal Kent) with below average unemployment.

There are several factors underlying these intraregional differentials, including the location of high-growth producer services or jobs in high-technology manufacturing as against those in more traditional manufacturing or port jobs; these locational patterns may in turn be linked to factors such as the siting of government defence establishments, especially in the case of high-technology employment (Breheny, 1988). However, differences in average GDP or income per head also reflect the residential segregation of different income groups: average costs of housing in Essex and Kent are lower than those to the west of London and attract more middle-income migrant households (Barlow, this volume). The influence of peripherality associated with national frontiers and accessibility to the main national transport routes has also been implicated in the relatively low economic performance of counties such as Kent (Vickerman, this volume).

There is some evidence that intraregional differentials in unemployment rates and employment growth have been narrowing over time, with the difference in annual average rates of job growth smaller in the period 1981 – 84 than in 1971 – 81 if 'high-growth' counties (Berkshire, Buckinghamshire, Hampshire, and West Sussex) are compared with the remaining 'low-growth' counties (SERPLAN, 1988a). There are also some indications that a simple concentric model of economic growth is losing its applicability, given the economic revival of London and that the highest rates of job growth in the region in the period 1981 – 84 were in travel-to-work areas immediately beyond the Greater London boundary.

The contrasts in growth and prosperity within the region, between both London and the ROSE, and between the east and west of the region, have been a major influence on economic policy. Thus a policy of fostering economic growth in general, regardless of location, was most appropriate in the recession years, whereas now the emphasis has shifted to easterly revitalisation. This is particularly so in view of the disequilibrating consequences for the national and regional economy of excess growth in certain subregions. Concern about the consequences of employment decentralisation from the metropolis, and especially of high job losses in inner London, have led to an abandonment of planned job decentralisation to new and expanded towns and to the inception of developments for inner-city jobs, such as in the Docklands area of East London (Congdon and Champion, this volume).

There is much uncertainty over the future course of these intraregional differentials and thereby the more wider North-South gap (Vickerman, this volume). For example, the Channel Tunnel and the Single European Market may tend to improve prospects of the eastern part of the South East but worsen the competitive position (and increase the peripherality) of the 'north' of Britain. Similarly, pressures on the housing and labour markets and transport infrastructures of more prosperous subregions may encourage diversion to the east or decentralisation of firms to adjacent growth regions such as the South West or East Anglia.

2.1.2 Stress in the labour market

The economic revival since the mid-1980s has been associated with labour shortages, especially of certain types of skilled labour, though extending to some less skilled jobs, and with concentrations of shortage in certain local labour markets. Thus Beresford and Craig (1988) have highlighted the labour problems of eleven districts in the South East (in December 1988) where unemployment was below the 3% level which represents a minimal frictional turnover. The labour shortages apply to both manual and nonmanual jobs and extend to sectors such as manufacturing where overall the sector is still in decline. Deficiencies are most marked in computing and electrical occupations, in finance and accountancy, and in the construction industry where there are particular problems in recruiting craft employees in the current building boom. There are also many unfilled vacancies in low-skilled jobs often associated with 'secondary' labour markets and part-time workers such as married women. Recruitment difficulties are one source of the wage inflation in the private sector, and of losses of staff in the public sector to the private sector (Mohan and Lee, this volume).

A considerable number of researchers have investigated the role of housing markets in the amplifying of labour shortages in growth regions. In the past the focus was on the extent to which residence qualifications for local authority housing inhibited migration by manual workers to regions where jobs were available (Hughes and McCormick, 1981). Most recently, the focus is to what extent migration by all social groups is inhibited by large interregional differentials in house prices (Forrest, 1987). Such differentials impede the classical market response, such as migration from high-unemployment areas in the North to low-unemployment areas in the South East.

Moreover, demographic trends point to a worsening of labour supply problems (the 'demographic timebomb' as it has been described by a government minister). The supply of young people entering the labour market is expected to decline in the 1990s, an echo of the very low fertility levels of the 1970s (NEDO, 1988; Palmer, this volume). This again may effect disproportionately certain sectors such as the health service whose recruitment of nurses has been primarily among new entrants to the labour force. On the other hand, the increase in labour demand and the problems of skilled labour supply may have beneficial effects such as increasing the incentives for firms to offer more training or to draw on alternative sources of labour supply such as married women reentering the job market.

Shortages of labour, high costs of land and housing, and other problems such as the extent to which the transport infrastructure can handle increased freight and commuter traffic, may also have an effect on employment location, both within and between regions. Pressures for decentralisation from London to the rest of the region, or beyond the region to the adjacent 'Greater South East' have increased (Jones Lang Wootton, 1988; Palmer, this volume). There may even be an increased tendency toward international relocation, for example, to Northern France, where land costs are considerably cheaper than those in South East England (Vickerman, this volume).

Palmer's paper is a general overview of the labour market and of economic pressures in the South East from the point of view of employers. The nature of recruitment problems in the current prosperity are discussed, and their extent by standard region and by skill level is assessed. Possible causation is discussed, not only in terms of economic demand, but with respect to training policies by both government and firms. The possibilities of skill mismatch are also highlighted, as in cases where the jobless lack the skills in demand or are in different locations to where job opportunities exist. Such mismatch may be associated with housing market factors; differentials in housing cost impede not only movement into high-cost areas but reverse moves from high-cost to low-cost areas. The expected impact of demographic factors in the amplifying of labour shortages is discussed; for example, the decline in new entrants is expected to be greatest in London.

Future infrastructure developments in the region may also exacerbate labour shortages, both during their construction and in the longer term. Examples are the Canary Wharf project in London's Docklands, the expansion planned at Stansted Airport, and the fixed-link Channel Tunnel. The contradictory pressures placed on companies in the South East, as a result both of such changes and of the relaxation of national frontiers in the Single European Market, are evident. Thus the Channel Tunnel and Single Market increase pressures on firms to remain in or relocate to the South East, whereas labour costs and shortage, planning constraints, high house prices, and inadequate transport facilities tend to encourage location away from the region.

In their paper Mohan and Lee focus on skill and labour shortages in the public sector of the South East, and particularly in the health sector.

There is evidence that, as pay in the private sector has been inflated by increased housing and transport costs and by skills shortages, recruitment and turnover problems in the public sector have worsened. This is not necessarily a concomitant of core region growth, as it partially reflects central government policies towards the size of the public sector. Thus public-sector employers have been subject to budget cuts and constraints and are faced with inadequate resources to respond with pay increases to labour shortages. Central government has opposed 'catching up' awards for public-sector workers, though the recent pay award to nurses is a belated recognition of the problem. Problems of labour supply in public services are compounded by the demographic contraction in natural increase in the labour force, because such services have in the past relied heavily on recruitment from new entrants to the labour force.

Mohan and Lee consider these issues in a wider theoretical framework: the South East is regarded as a core region, and public services recognised as a dynamic element in the growth of core regions. Thus, the more developed a regional economy in terms of market services (a reflection of 'core' status) the more important are nonmarket services as producers and consumers. In their chapter they consider the responses of public-sector employers to labour shortages, especially among nursing and clerical staff; for example, increased resort to temporary staff from private agencies, attempts to attract back former staff (for example, by offering child care facilities to married women returnees), and help with mortgages for housing. These measures are either an attempt to diversify labour supply or to meet the basic problem of the low pay of nurses and similar workers in relation to escalating costs of housing.

More broadly, employers' responses have included a slowdown in aggregate employment growth through recruitment, especially among support staff as opposed to those staff involved directly in patient care; and also a move towards competitive tendering for such support or ancillary services. Both strategies have been related to central government pressures for greater cost efficiency. They can be placed within wider evidence of 'flexible labour processes' with privatisation and amateurisation producing a two-tier wage and labour market structure. Combined with the encouragement of private-sector medicine by central government, these trends are seen by Mohan and Lee as threats to the future universality of health care provision in core regions.

2.1.3 *Changes in spatial relationships*
One of the most persistent trends in South East England has been the decentralisation of people and jobs from London to outer parts of the region. Although this trend may have been evident for much longer, it is generally identified as a postwar phenomenon, with the focus of growth in each successive decade being further out from the capital. The latest

focus has been at the very edge of the standard region, and, indeed, beyond it in the neighbouring counties of the South West and East Anglia —often referred to as Britain's 'Sunbelt'. Much of the growth has been in areas—typically market towns—that were not previously industrialised. Thus, our case study of a 'Sunbelt' town—Southampton—is interesting because it is something of an exception: an industrialised port city, with all of the associated problems of deindustrialisation, but now benefitting from its 'Sunbelt' location.

The paper by Mason, Pinch, and Witt has two main objectives: a detailed analysis of industrial change in a town that has particular features not previously identified in studies of the 'Sunbelt', and a comparison with other 'Sunbelt' localities, such as Reading and Bristol. They begin their paper with a review of 'Sunbelt' literature, highlighting attempts to explain growth, but argue in favour of exploring local diversity and of broadening the scope from the high-technology focus of earlier studies. They provide a detailed economic profile of the Southampton city-region, giving broad sectoral analyses and evidence of particular changes at the corporate level. Of particular interest here is the nature of service-sector change in Southampton. Although the town has benefitted from substantial growth in the service sector, the sources of such growth are very different from those in Reading and Bristol. Whereas both of these towns have been the recipients of the decentralisation of 'back' offices from London, and in the case of Bristol relocation of headquarters, Southampton has not benefitted in this way. Its service-sector growth has come largely from local expansions and subregional reorganisation.

Traditional patterns of job decentralisation, and the west-east contrast may, however, be altered as a result of the planned Single European Market and fixed Channel link. In his paper, Vickerman investigates the particular effects of improved links between the South East and the European Community, both as a result of the Single European Market in 1992 and the Channel link planned for completion in 1993. The focus is on the impact of these developments on peripheral subregions as defined in terms of national frontiers. Such subregions may suffer an 'economic shadow' effect in the presence of trading restrictions across national boundaries. Within the South East, those subregions to the east of London have fared relatively badly in terms of their economic development, and have lagged behind in the development of high technology and producer services. Despite British membership of the European Community and increased traffic through the Kent ports, several districts within Kent continue to suffer above average unemployment. Both Kent and frontier subregions of continental countries (such as Belgium) may be seen to exhibit a 'transport corridor' effect whereby improved through-links do not necessarily induce economic gain.

Vickerman goes on to consider the costs resulting from the present frontier restrictions, and the potential gains for the South East that may result from their removal and from the fixed link. Any gains may be offset by the inability of the present (or indeed planned) transport network to cope with the anticipated increase in freight and passenger traffic, and also by the competitive locational advantage of the more centrally placed continental subregions.

2.2 Part 2 Housing and population

The South East has accounted for half the total increase in national population in recent years, even though its share of the nation's total population is only a third. This is a major contrast to the 1970s when there was a net population loss from the region, due especially to heavy net migration from the capital. Shifts in intranational and international migration (as opposed to natural increase) have been the major component of this revival, with the South East and especially London gaining from a move towards a net gain through international migration. The population of London is now virtually stable, a sharp contrast to the 1970s (reviewed in Robert and Randolph, 1983). Within the South East outside London there are signs that the focus of growth has shifted to the outer periphery (the 'outer South East') and that the outer metropolitan area adjacent to London is making smaller contributions to the regional population total.

The continued growth of the South East outside London, and the population revival in the metropolitan centre are both projected to continue into the future (DoE, 1988). This has particular implications for the planning and provision of housing. There are a number of indications of stress in the housing market which can be related to such population shifts, to the economic prosperity of the region and associated intraregional imbalances, and to mismatches between the demand and supply of housing.

In the broadest sense the problem of matching supply and demand is apparent from the upward revision of household numbers projected in the region in the latest central government forecast. The 1985-based projections are significantly higher than the previous 1983-based set in this biennial series: for example, 226 000 more in the entire region over the period 1986–2001. The upturn in anticipated demand during this period is apparent throughout the South East: by 8.3% in London (from 2 710 000 to 2 930 000 households), and by 17.7% in the rest of the region (from 2 940 000 to 4 640 000 households). However, there is considerable conflict about the level and location of new housing in the region to match the increased demand. Certain interest groups (such as the House Builders Federation) and to some extent central government, intent on not hampering economic growth by lack of housing, have supported development on green field sites outside London or on the peripheries of existing settlements. However, there is considerable resistance on environmental grounds among local authorities and residents' groups to such new building: labelled the 'NIMBY' (not in my back yard) syndrome by the current Secretary of State for the Environment.

Planning constraints on new building in the private sector, the shift to net migration into the region, and the cutback in public-sector building all underlie the house price inflation which has disproportionately affected the region in the mid and late 1980s (see Barlow, this volume). The rate of increase in house prices has indeed been advocated by interest groups such as the House Builders Federation as a true indicator of 'market demand' for housing between different areas. Those taking the 'market demand' approach to housing demand have criticised the reliance on household projections as a demand indicator. For example, in England as a whole, the majority of the projected net increase in households is in numbers of household heads aged over 45, but house purchase is currently dominated by heads under that age (83% in 1987 for the United Kingdom, according to the Nationwide Anglia Building Society) (Adams and King, 1988).

There are more specific indications of housing market mismatch. For example, there is a growing problem of homelessness in the region (up by 43% in the period 1980/81 – 1985/86 to a total of 40000 households officially accepted as homeless), especially in London (up 60% in the same period to a total of 30000). There are also considerable numbers of unofficial homeless, especially of young single people. This growth in homelessness is associated with the considerable reductions in public-sector housebuilding for renting to low-income households, and the continued contraction of the private rented sector. Thus public-sector provision accounted for only 17% of the regional total of new housing in 1986 (26% in London), whereas in 1976 the respective proportions were 55% and 80%. The reduction in new building in the public sector reflects recent government policy which shifts the emphasis to private-sector provision of housing for sale in response to market demand. The increasing reliance on the private sector to satisfy housing demand means that low-income groups in greatest need of housing are increasingly unprovided for. The present government intends to shift the emphasis in the supply of low-income housing towards housing associations, and they account for an increasing share of new low-cost housing. However, their output remains a small part of total housebuilding activity (SERPLAN, 1988a).

There is also differentiation within the demand for private-sector housing, with implications both for the spatial variation in the rate of growth of property prices and for the supply of a range of housing, to cover the demands of all potential labour migrants or newly forming households. Segmentation of housing demand by income has consequences for the distribution of private-sector housing by price and for the differential location patterns of new or migrant owner-occupiers (Barlow, this volume). Such housing market differentials are not necessarily optimal in terms of labour supply; for example, there are difficulties in meeting the housing needs of middle-income skilled workers in growth areas with high house prices (Palmer, this volume). Several studies have pointed to the contrast in house prices within the region, with the highest-priced areas in a crescent to the west and south of London, whereas the eastern parts of the region, especially the Lower Thames Corridor, have considerably lower prices (SERPLAN, 1988b). It has been argued that the growth of house prices in relation to incomes in London has encouraged an upturn in migration from the capital among middle-income households in search of cheaper housing to buy (Barlow, this volume).

Housing demand is segmented not only by income or social group but by age and household type (though the 'market demand' approach emphasises income, especially in the supply of new private housing). For example, a high proportion of regional household growth in the most recent set of government household projections consists of small households, with a particular concentration among elderly households. Given the nature of housing demand by household type, and the restrictions governing additions to stock through new building, other forms of gain to stock increase in importance. In London especially, conversions of existing dwellings, either through subdivision or merger, are a major component of net additions to dwellings. In London converted dwellings for owner-occupation are the typical entry point to house ownership for middle-income and higher-income households, usually either one-person households or married couples without children (Hamnett, this volume). However, again the evidence is that over time the increased demand for housing has led to this type of housing being increasingly restricted to the better-off purchaser (Barlow, this volume).

2.2.1 Housing and demographic change

Assessment of future housing demand and of the underlying demographic changes, especially through migration shifts, is crucially bound up with differential economic growth in the subregions of the South East. There is considerable debate about how far job growth and differentials in spatial labour demand within the South East underlie variation in rates of population growth through net in-migration. There would seem to be an association between economic growth and net in-migration during the 1980s. For example, in 1981 to 1986 the fastest growth through net migration has taken place in the western crescent counties of Buckinghamshire, Berkshire and Oxfordshire, and in East and West Sussex, with growth foci such as Gatwick and Crawley.

In their paper, Congdon and Champion consider these associations more formally, using labour market accounts calculated at county level over the intercensal period 1971–81. They find a positive association between net in-migration by the economically active, and the rate of employment surplus—that is, growth in job opportunities in excess to that which can be met by indigenous increases in the labour force through natural change and changed rates of activity. The association between employment increase and net migration is of course modified by local planning strategies and by housing availability. Nevertheless, economic shifts—for example, decentralisation of 'producer-service' office jobs or differential location of high-tech jobs—may be seen as a source both of continued net migration gain to the South East outside London and of differentials between counties in net migration gains. Analysis of the relation between population and employment shifts in local labour markets in the South East tends to confirm this.

There has also been discussion about how far reduced net migration losses from London are associated with the employment revival in the capital. Congdon and Champion argue that factors such as the expansion of financial services would seem to be a potential explanation for the increases in net migration gain to the capital from Britain outside the South East and from abroad, as much of this migration is job related. Out-migration from London to the ROSE was also at low levels in the early 1980s (in comparison with the heavy decentralisation of the 1960s and 1970s), though the last couple of years have seen an upturn in this flow. Again, employment stability and the diminution of planned decentralisation may be seen as potential explanatory factors together with levels of housing prices and new housebuilding—though some studies ascribe primacy to the housing market (Gordon, 1987).

2.2.2 Housing prices and land

House price changes and their causes and consequences (such as on migration, discussed above) have become a major topic of conversation in Britain in the 1980s. Nowhere has this been more so than in the South East. With rising levels of owner-occupation, many households have a direct interest in house price changes. The reason for the intense interest at this time is the large and rapid rise in prices during the 1987–88 period, beginning in London, but spreading wave-like across the rest of the South East and, belatedly, to the rest of the country. House prices in Britain are the subject of popular and political debate. To individual owner-occupier households, the equity held in their houses will be far and away the largest source of their wealth. To politicians, this enormous and increasing commitment to private housing is both a problem, as it absorbs a large proportion of national investment, and a vote winner because of its direct importance to so many voters.

Periodic explosions in house prices occur in Britain at regular intervals: 1972 and 1979 saw the two most dramatic changes prior to 1987. But why do these occur? Evans addresses this question in his paper, focusing on house price changes in the South East during the 1980s. His major conclusion is that house price increases have followed land price increases, which in turn appear to be due to restrictions on land availability for housing. This is a controversial conclusion because other researchers argue that it is the demand for houses that is the sole determinant of house prices. To counter these views, Evans builds up his case from first principles, looking at the operation of the housing market from supply and demand perspectives in turn.

Evans also considers the reasons for the differential growth in house prices between the South East, where rises have been most rapid, and the rest of the country. He attributes this differential to a higher rate of demand in the region, resulting from three factors: a reduction in migration from the country has produced unexpected growth in population and hence in housing demand, a weakening of regional policy has allowed more industrial development in the South East, and local changes in housing policy have increased the potential mobility of the population.

Because of the pressures which Evans describes, the problem of finding land available for housing has been the biggest single planning issue in the South East in the last decade or more. Hooper, Pinch, and Rogers address this whole question of the availability of land for housebuilding. The issue arises because of the antagonism between the major national housebuilding companies, who are anxious to satisfy what they see as enormous demand pressures, particularly in the outer South East, and the local authorities in those areas, who operate policies of development restraint. Under pressure from the volume house builders, who have become increasingly well organised under their representative body, the House Builders Federation, central government has since the early 1970s required local authorities to have identified sufficient land for housing development for a continuation of the building rate of the previous five years.

This, in turn, has raised heated debates about what constitutes 'available land', the relative merits of land with planning permission and land allocated in plans, the spatial units to which the regulations apply, and so on. All of these issues are discussed in general in the paper and then illustrated with two case studies, of Essex and Kent.

Hooper and colleagues point out the significance of these issues at two levels. First, they demonstrate the technical complexity that arises from the apparently simple notion of making available five years' supply of land. Alternative methods of calculation are available, each with different consequences and each generating heated exchanges. Second, the whole question of the effect of the land availability regulations on planning policy is considered. Generally, the effect is to perpetuate past policy, as future land allocations have to reflect building rates of the immediate past. Also, planning policy tends increasingly to reflect market demands rather than guiding those demands. The overall effect is to produce planning policies that always give more of the same. In many cases, it is just this effect that is resented. In Berkshire, for example, which has

been a growth area for some time, the system means that Berkshire has
to continue to take more than its fair share of the South East's growth.
The result has been bitter local resentment.

2.2.3 Demand and supply in the owner-occupied sector
The location of new housing—as determined by planning policy, partly
in response to market demand—is a major influence on intraregional
migration. So also are the costs of housing in relation to the income
group of purchasers. In his paper, Barlow considers differentials in
migration patterns within the South East according to income group,
with particular concern for explaining the decentralisation of lower-
income and middle-income households from London. House price
inflation in London has been adduced by some studies as a reason for
the recent upturn in migration from London to the ROSE, and for other
trends such as a rise in long-distance commuting to the capital from
lower-priced housing areas. Barlow addresses the question of whether
the housing market for London's work force is becoming regionalised,
that is, spreading throughout the entire region. This question is considered
within the wider framework of access to London's owner-occupied housing
by lower-income and middle-income groups, and of house price variations
in the region and their relation to differential migration. Thus, outside
London first-time and/or skilled-manual buyers are a greater proportion
of the owner-occupier market in counties such as Bedfordshire, Kent,
and Essex.

Within London, the concentration of first-time buyers in the market
for converted flats is noted: such buyers are on relatively high incomes
(as compared with the average for all households if not that for all buyers).
There is evidence that this restriction of the first-time buyer market to
higher-income workers is increasing over time, and this is linked by
Barlow to signs of increased occupational segmentation in the labour
market of London. The exclusion of lower-income buyers from London's
owner-occupied housing market is proposed by Barlow as a major reason
for out-migration by such purchasers to areas of lower house prices in
the rest of the region or beyond (for example, in East Anglia), and as a
source of the current boom in private housebuilding in the region.

Hamnett also focuses on access to the owner-occupied market but on
a particular facet of that market in London: the conversion of existing
dwellings into flats for sale. This form of addition to the housing supply
is particularly common in inner London, and generally entails subdivision
of existing single dwellings or transformation of formerly rented 'bedsitter'
accommodation. In central London, household spaces in flat conversions
accounted for over 28% of all owner-occupied spaces in 1981, compared
with only 2.4% in outer London. They are a growing share of owner-
occupancy in London, and a major share of net additions to inner
London's housing stock in recent years—given the virtual cessation of

public-sector building there. Thus flat conversions accounted for 16% of all new mortgages in London in 1986 (using the data of a particular building society), and for over 50% of new mortgages in some inner London boroughs.

Hamnett relates the development of the flat-conversion market in London in the 1980s to the wider process of sociotenurial trans-formation in inner London. This process is characterised by the decline of private renting, and the emergence of owner-occupancy and municipal renting as the dominant tenures. In the 1980s, the owner-occupied sector has continued to grow, with flat conversions a major share of this growth, whereas the municipal sector, which increased considerably in the 1970s, has remained static as public-sector building has dwindled. The 1980s are also distinctive in the emergence of large-scale additions to owner-occupancy through sales of council houses to their tenants or through the privatisation of council dwelling stock. These losses to public-sector renting have only been partially offset by an expansion in housing association activity.

The growth of owner-occupancy in inner London has been associated with displacement of young single people in private rented housing, especially those in lower-pay 'junior' nonmanual or service jobs. The typical buyer of a converted flat is a single person or couple without children in the higher-income groups, and for this group flat conversions are often the first step on the owner-occupied-housing ladder.

2.3 Part 3 Strategic planning

It is very clear, then, that a lot is happening in the South East of England as we approach the end of the twentieth century. The region seems to have strengthened its dominant role in the United Kingdom and continues to perform the function of a 'core' economic region within Europe and within the global economy. That role is subject to constant change, but the advent of closer ties with continental Europe in the early 1990s suggests a more profound, but as yet unclear, set of changes. Arguably, with these major events ahead of us, coupled with the evidence discussed above of stresses in the labour and housing markets and major new developments, such as Stansted and the Channel Tunnel, the South East is faced with *strategic* issues of an unprecedented scale and speed.

But these issues arise at the very time that the strategic planning system is being dismantled. Regional strategic plans disappeared in the mid-1970s. Metropolitan authorities were abolished in 1986. The abolition of structure plans—the last remaining vestige of a once comprehensive strategic planning system—announced by the government in 1986, has now been formalised in the "Future of Development Plans" White Paper (Cmnd 569) of January 1989. All of these changes reflect, of course, the principled objection of the Conservative government to a strong planning system. Their belief is that shadowed by a minimalist planning system, the private sector will resolve all of these development issues.

Breheny and Hart address this coincidence of the rise of strategic issues and the demise of strategic planning; a coincidence that is most obvious in the South East. They suggest that the rise of strategic issues in the region occurs at just the point when the strategic planning system has never been weaker. They put the case for a resurrection of strategic planning, arguing that, contrary to government assumptions, this would be in the interests of business as well as providing more obvious community benefits. They contend, however, that an understanding of the reasons for the recent demise of strategic planning in the United Kingdom is necessary for any attempt at resurrection, or, more likely, recreation.

This attempted explanation is approached by way of an inquest into the death of strategic planning; an attempt to determine the means of death, and, if necessary, motive, opportunity, and culprit. A number of possible causes of death is examined. The evidence for death by natural causes is considered. Although the health of strategic planning in Britain may never have been robust, such a death seems very unlikely. Thus, the evidence for murder, suicide, and euthanasia are considered. The actions and motives of the Conservative government and the planning profession are given particularly close scrutiny in each case. In the end, the most reasonable verdict seems to be death by manslaughter: a rather sickly strategic planning system having been set upon by a government opposed to it in principle and by a planning profession increasingly dominated by localised interests.

There are few mourners for the death of the strategic planning system as devised in the 1960s. However, this does not mean that the demise of strategic planning in principle is not mourned. Indeed, there is evidence in the late 1980s of some renewed sympathy for the idea. This sympathy comes not only from certain elements of the planning profession, but also, less explicitly, from some of the government's own supporters. Many Tory voters in the outer parts of the South East have suddenly realised that the planning system is the only tool they have in attempting to fend off unwelcome development, and that localised development pressures are manifestations of much broader patterns of change that need to be understood and controlled.

If a strategic planning system is to be recreated in the United Kingdom, the lessons from this inquest into the demise of its previous incarnation are very valuable. But we might also look elsewhere for guidance. It is for this reason that an otherwise incongruous paper appears in this collection. A paper on the Dutch strategic planning system in a volume dealing with South East England may seem strange. However, for the Brighton conference a paper was specifically commissioned from van der Knaap and van Delft in order that the British and Dutch experiences with strategic planning could be compared. The significant feature of the Dutch system is that it has survived; during a forty-year period when the UK equivalent has waxed and waned, the Dutch system has been maintained. An understanding of the reason for this may be instructive for the UK case.

Van der Knaap and van Delft begin their paper with a brief historical review of the development of the Dutch strategic planning system and a simple description of the relationships between state, provincial, and municipal governmental levels. The latest strategic planning statement—carefully not called a plan—is the Fourth Report. The nature of this report is explained, along with an assessment of the changing context within which it has been produced: a context of uncertainty and—familiar in Britain—the retreat of central government from previous public interventions. In the report specific themes are addressed: inter-nationalisation of the Dutch economy, the question of continued economic prosperity, and technological innovation. The contrast between the Dutch and British experiences is very illuminating; from broad, contextual differences such as the popular, cultural preference for consensus in the Netherlands, to interesting technical differences such as the relative absence of numbers (houses, jobs, etc) in Dutch planning compared with their dominance of British strategic planning.

Hall concludes our collection with some thoughts on London 2001. He returns to the broad canvas on which in 1963 he painted a picture of London 2000. He starts his paper, however, with an account of some of the problems and trends currently being witnessed in the South East. He focuses on two polarising trends, one social, the other spatial; and both of which we do not fully understand. The 1980s have seen a widening of the social divide between an increasingly affluent, largely service class—conveniently labelled as the 'yuppie' syndrome—and an 'underclass' that becomes increasingly marginalised by the 'job twist' that removes unskilled work and escalates the qualifications required for almost any job. This social divide is also paralleled by a spatial divide, with continued decline of population in London itself—albeit now at substantially reduced rates—and rapid decentralisation of growth to the outer parts of the South East. Indeed, the areas of the most rapid growth are now beyond the official boundaries of the region; in the adjacent counties, at the edge of what Hall now calls the "Greater South East".

The paper goes on to consider both existing and possible future planning responses to all of the problems of the South East. The pressures for large-scale housing growth in the region are contrasted to the lack of any serious strategic planning response. Comparing the proposals of the 1970 *Strategic Plan for the South East*, which tried to focus growth, with the current SERPLAN proposals to spread growth evenly, Hall concludes that the "strategic planners have completely

rejected the strategic planning orthodoxy of eighteen years ago". A
return to genuinely strategic thinking is proposed, and a number of
possible foci for development are suggested. These proposals are
related directly to an issue that suddenly looms very large in the South
East: transportation. After years of 'starvation funding', the public
transport system is woefully inadequate for the task. New road and rail
investments, some obvious, some more imaginative, are needed desperately.
This emphasis on transportation is probably the biggest single difference
between London 2000 and London 2001.

3 Concluding comments
A thorough understanding of the causes and consequences of growth in
a 'core' region is a big undertaking. The papers presented here were not
commissioned with such a grand objective in mind. The aim was to
make a modest contribution by bringing together some of the early
fruits of the renewed research interest in the South East.
   On the question of the role of a core region in the wider national
and international economy, these papers offer little by way of a direct
answer. Indirectly, by providing insights into various features of the
internal workings of such a region—from different economic, social, and
policy perspectives—they may go partway to such an answer. On the
question of the internal workings of the region, the contributors do offer
more. The specific insights provided in individual papers are valuable
in their own right, but read together they do begin to give some idea of
how the region ticks, of how it is responding to—and indeed influencing—
the rapidly changing political and economic context of the United
Kingdom as we approach the end of the century.
   The region warrants much more research. However, one thing seems
clear, even at this stage: the 'success' of the South East has its price.
Part of this price remains relatively hidden. As Hall points out in this
volume, the rise of the service economy and the decline of the production
sector, coupled with the government's 'rolling back' of welfare provision,
has exacerbated social divides. Although the large majority of the
population are experiencing increased standards of living, with some
enjoying the enormous fruits of the 'yuppie' economy, a residual 'underclass' has been created. Another part of the price, far from being hidden,
has now become very obvious. The government's own supporters in the
outer shires of the region are now making their anguish felt as they
come under increasing pressures for more and more growth—either from
local housing proposals or from major developments such as the Channel
Tunnel rail route or Stansted airport. The NIMBY attitude gets stronger
as they feel the consequences—of congestion, environmental degradation,
and rising costs—that such growth can bring. There is a sudden
realisation that such consequences are felt most sharply when they are
not controlled by the planning system. So, just at the time when the

government is reducing the power of that system, its own traditional supporters are rediscovering its merits. This particular debate will run for some time yet.

References

Adams M, King D, 1988, "Demographic issues in housing developments", paper presented to the annual conference of the British Society for Population Studies, Nottingham University, September; copy available from House Builders Federation, 82 New Cavendish Street, London W1M 8AD

Amin A, 1989, "Flexible specialisation and small firms in Italy: myths and reality" forthcoming in *Antipode* (April) **21**

Beresford P, Craig J, 1988, "Where they have run out of workers" *The Sunday Times* 11 December, page A4

Breheny M, 1987, "The state of the region—economic developments in the South East of England", paper presented to Town and Country Planning Association conference on The Future of the South East, in London, April; copy available from Department of Geography, University of Reading

Breheny M (Ed.), 1988 *Defence Expenditure and Regional Development* (Mansell, London)

Champion A, Congdon P, 1987, "An analysis of London's population change rate" *Built Environment* **13**(4) 193–211

Champion A, Green A, 1988, "Local prosperity and the North–South divide: winners and losers in 1980s Britain", authors at the Universities of Newcastle and Warwick, copy available from Institute for Employment Research, University of Warwick

CSO, 1988 *Economic Trends* number 421, Central Statistical Office (HMSO, London)

DoE, 1988, "1985 based estimates of numbers of households in England, the regions, counties, metropolitan districts and London boroughs", Department of the Environment (Government Statistical Service, London)

Egginton D, 1988, "Regional labour markets in Great Britain" *Bank of England Quarterly Bulletin* **28** 367–375

Forrest R, 1987, "Spatial mobility, tenure mobility, and emerging social divisions in the UK housing market" *Environment and Planning A* **19** 1611–1630

Gillespie A, Green A, 1987, "The changing geography of producer services employment in Britain" *Regional Studies* **21** 397–412

Gordon I, 1987, "Resurrecting counterurbanisation: housing market influences on migration fluctuations from London" *Built Environment* **13**(4) 212–222

Green A, 1988, "The North–South divide in Great Britain: an examination of the evidence" *Transactions of the Institute of British Geographers* **13** 179–198

Hall P, Breheny M, McQuaid R, Hart D, 1987 *Western Sunrise: The Genesis of Britain's Major High Tech Corridor* (Allen and Unwin, Hemel Hempstead, Herts)

Harvey D, 1987, "Flexible accumulation through urbanisation: reflections on 'Post-modernism' in the American City" *Antipode* **19** 260–286

Hughes G, McCormick B, 1981, "Do council housing policies reduce migration between regions?" *Economic Journal* **91** 919–937

Jones Lang Wootton, 1988, "Decentralisation report, 1988", research report, Jones Lang Wootton, 22 Hanover Square, London W1R

Marshall N (Ed.), 1988 *Uneven Development in the Service Economy* (Oxford University Press, London)

Martin R, 1988, "The political economy of Britain's North–South divide" *Transactions of the Institute of British Geographers* **13** 389–418

NEDO, 1988, "Young people and the labour market: a challenge for the 1980s", National Economic Development Office, London

Robert S, Randolph W, 1983, "Beyond decentralisation: the evolution of population distribution in England and Wales, 1961–81" *Geoforum* **14** 75–102

Schoenberger E, 1988, "From Fordism to flexible accumulation: technology, competitive strategies, and international location" *Environment and Planning D: Society and Space* **6** 245–262

Scott A, Cooke P, 1988, "Guest editorial: the new geography and sociology of production" *Environment and Planning D: Society and Space* **6** 241–244

SERPLAN, 1988a, "Regional trends in the South East: the South East regional monitor, 1987–88", RPC-1060, SERPLAN (London and South East Regional Planning Conference), 50–64 Broadway, London SW1H 0DB

SERPLAN, 1988b, "House price differentials in the South East, 1981–86: South East regional monitor 1987–88 technical appendix", RPC-1062, SERPLAN (London and South East Regional Planning Conference), 50–64 Broadway, London SW1H 0DB

Thrift N, Leyshon A, Daniels P, 1988, "'Sexy Greed': The new international financial system, the City of London and the South East of England", Working Papers on Producer Services Number 8, St David's University College, Lampeter, and University of Liverpool

The Changing Geography of the South East: Housing and Labour Market Constraints

D J PALMER
Confederation of British Industry

1 Introduction

Companies located in the South East are currently faced with a particular problem of skill shortages and difficulties in recruitment. These are already serious and are likely to worsen significantly. Labour mobility is constrained by shortages of housing and land for development in the South East thereby discouraging inward migration. Furthermore, demographic trends, continued economic growth, the completion of the Single European Market, and the opening of the Channel Tunnel will all place further pressure on companies in the South East.

In this paper I analyse the problems facing firms operating within the South East over the next few years and highlight some options open to companies helping to overcome them. Three issues are covered: a diagnosis of the current operating constraints on business; a prognosis of future trends, especially the worsening situation in the South East; and potential remedies open to firms. A view is given of how the labour market has moved from a 'buyer's' to a 'seller's' market, presenting employers with even greater recruitment problems at a time of continued economic growth.

2 Current skill shortages and recruitment difficulties

The CBI Industrial Trends Survey (CBI, 1988a) monitors the problem of skill shortages in manufacturing industry. Currently (third quarter, 1988) 28% of firms are citing skill shortages as likely to restrict output over the following four months (see figure 1). This shortage has grown

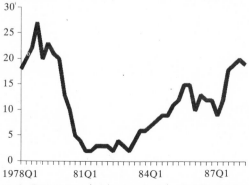

Figure 1. Percentage (of respondents) of skilled labour that is likely to limit output over the four months following each CBI survey. Source: CBI, 1988a.

steadily since the end of the recession in 1982/83, when fewer than 5% of manufacturing companies were experiencing the problem, and is at the highest level recorded since 1974. Furthermore, for the first time for a decade about 5% of manufacturing firms are suffering from general (that is, unskilled as well as skilled) labour shortages.

However, this problem is not confined to the South East. The latest CBI/MSC Special Skills Survey (CBI/MSC, 1987) shows that nationally 37% of manufacturing companies were suffering from skill shortages—a dramatic rise from the 15% recorded in 1985. In the South East the problem was even greater, with 42% of firms having difficulties. Although small, this difference is important, reflecting not only the industrial structure of the region but also the relative severity of the problem.

In an economy-wide survey undertaken by the CBI (CBI, 1986) almost two-thirds of companies claimed to be suffering from skill shortages. Thus the problem is not confined to the manufacturing industry alone. For example, the public sector is experiencing very high labour turnover especially in London.

Over the last year, recruitment difficulties have worsened significantly. The pressure of demand for labour is indicated by the ratio of registered unemployment to notified vacancies (the $u:v$ ratio). Nationwide, this has fallen by 16% over the last year to 9.4:1 in September 1988, but the tightening up of the labour market in the South East has been even more rapid (DE, 1988b). Over the last twelve months the $u:v$ ratio fell by 19% to 5.5:1 in the South East, but in the South East excluding Greater London (the rest of the South East) the fall was even greater—a 39% decline to a $u:v$ ratio of 3.3:1. Even allowing for the effect of changes in the method of calculation of unemployment, this represents a significant tightening up of the labour market. It is estimated that notified vacancies underrecord job opportunities and that only one-third are recorded in official statistics. If so, then the $u:v$ ratio in the rest of the South East could be as low as 1:1.

Almost all occupations are affected, but the problems of recruitment and skill shortages worsen at higher levels of skill. Evidence for the wide range of skill shortages is also given by the Training Commission's Skills Monitoring Report (TC, 1988). In July 1988 the Commission pointed out that reports of shortages of skilled labour and recruitment difficulties appeared to have increased significantly during 1987 in line with the "exceptional" growth in output during the year, although the latest evidence, the Commission argued, suggested that recruitment difficulties in manufacturing industry may have eased slightly in early 1988. Recruitment difficulties were much worse at higher skill levels, particularly in microelectronic technology, and most employers were seeking experienced staff, rather than qualified people who had recently completed training. The higher rates of growth in the South have led to a concentration of recruitment difficulties in those regions.

One cause of current recruitment difficulties may have been a reduction in investment in training during the recession of the early 1980s. Government policy now encourages companies to pay greater attention to training employees but such training is not always undertaken. For example, smaller companies (those employing fewer than 200 staff) face worse skill shortages than others—34%, according to the CBI (1988a). This is due to a variety of factors, including the lack of training skills for working in new markets and products, the lack of formalised training policies, and the inability of small firms to change operating schedules to permit training.

This combination of evidence from a variety of sources illustrates the current severity of the problem of recruitment facing many employers. That such serious labour shortages, particularly in skilled occupations, should exist after five years of steady economic growth alongside high unemployment in some areas should not be surprising. Mismatch (when job opportunities exist but the jobless either lack the relevant skills or are in different locations) in the labour market was identified many years ago (Gleave and Palmer, 1980), and more recently it has been acknowledged that progress in lowering regional unemployment is likely to be slow (Gordon, 1987). But in the future, difficulties from mismatch are expected to worsen, especially in the South East, as illustrated in section 4.

3 Recruitment difficulties will worsen

Demographic trends show that the overall supply of labour through natural increase will not grow as fast as in the past and will virtually stabilise at a low level in the early 1990s. Whereas in 1987/88 a rise of 380000 in the UK labour force occurred, in 1992/93 this will have fallen to 30000, albeit with a slight increase thereafter (DoE, 1988a). As a share of the total labour force the male component will fall.

Of particular importance is the effect of the numbers of younger people entering the labour market. Whereas in 1982 there were 3.7 million 16–19 year olds in the United Kingdom, by 1994 this will have fallen to below 2.6 million, a drop of 30% (NEDO, 1988). In the decade to 1985 there were over 3 million more school-leavers than there will be in the next ten years. This has been described as a "demographic time bomb".

Within England, the 16–24 age cohort is projected to fall by a fifth between June 1987 and June 1995 (NEDO, 1988). In the South East the fall is projected to be slightly below average (18.7%) but still represents a substantial decline in labour availability. Above average falls in those aged 16–24 are projected to occur in Essex, Hampshire, and Oxfordshire but London faces the greatest decline—27.4%. The number of 16–19 year olds in the capital is projected to fall by over 100000 in eight years.

Furthermore, the structure of employment will continue to change. Already one in nine of the labour force is self-employed. Part-time work and female employment are continuing to grow in importance. Almost a quarter of all employees work part-time, and for women the proportion is 44% (DE, 1988b). Female employment is projected to grow and by 1995 women will comprise 43% of those of working age. In addition, the trend towards earlier retirement could also change the nature of the labour market, further reducing the possible options to employers when recruiting.

The activity rate effect for men is anticipated to further reduce the numbers aged 55 and over who will participate in the labour force (DE, 1988a). Such trends will reduce the freedom for recruitment that employers experienced during the recession and will possibly encourage them to consider new patterns of work organisation.

Likewise the continuing development of new technology will further change the nature of the skills demanded by employers. In certain skills the United Kingdom is already seriously deficient. Skill shortages are particularly acute in the electrical, instrument, and engineering industries with 38% of manufacturing firms currently (third quarter, 1988) facing the problem. Despite the increase in the numbers employed, the supply of engineers with microelectronic experience has been unable to catch up with demand. The Policy Studies Institute (PSI, 1988) has estimated that the shortfall in the United Kingdom has been around 40% in recent years. Perhaps surprisingly the problem is almost as serious in textiles, where a quarter of companies face skill shortages. Recruitment difficulties in such sectors are largely due to the introduction of new technology.

Meanwhile, economic growth is projected to continue, generating further demands for labour. Indeed, for every 3% rise in GDP, job opportunities may grow by 1%. Thus the demand for labour could grow by almost 250 000 a year, depending on the rate of economic growth.

4 Companies in the South East will suffer most
4.1 Economic development pressures
The South East is the largest single region within the United Kingdom, containing almost one in three of the population. It is therefore the largest individual market within the United Kingdom and compared with other regions is heavily developed. It is also closest to the UK's major overseas market, the European Community. Additional pressure for companies to be sited in the South East follows from the location of Government and the City institutions in the capital. Although manufactured goods can be efficiently transported to their markets, most services must still be physically close to their customers. The exceptions are those services which can be provided at a distance from the customer, such as financial and information services, or for which the customer will travel,

tourism, for example. The South East is already well endowed with such opportunities.

Thus despite the diseconomies of agglomeration, caused by the costs of congestion and competition for skilled recruits, economies of scale will continue to encourage firms to retain sites within or near to London. Yet as we have seen, for those that will remain in the South East the demographic trends will impede recruitment. Furthermore, some development within the region will exacerbate labour shortages. In addition to the Channel Tunnel and Stansted Airport, new building in London Docklands and Sizewell will further increase pressure on the labour market. These four large projects have generated a considerable demand for construction workers in addition to that from elsewhere.

4.2 Housing market pressures
One alternative to the recruitment problem is relocation. But this is already difficult and expensive, both for firms and employees, owing to the large gap in house prices between the South East and elsewhere. Average house prices in the South East, excluding London, are 42% above the national average (third quarter, 1988), and are 2.5 times more expensive than those in the lowest cost regions, Northern Ireland and the North (Halifax, 1988a). House prices on average in London are now less than 10% more expensive than the rest of the South East (ROSE) as a result of the 'ripple effect', with house prices in the areas adjacent to London rising faster than in the capital. Increases in house prices in the capital appear to be slowing down and in the year to the third quarter of 1988 increased by 27% compared with rises of 36% in the ROSE. However, the greatest growth occurred in East Anglia where a 55% rise in average prices was recorded. Meanwhile in Northern Ireland house prices over the same period grew by less than 7%, marginally below those in Scotland. Such widening disparities between the North and South, which have been forecast to quadruple within five years, have led to a claim that an "unbridgeable chasm" has opened up (Homequity, 1987). House prices in the East Midlands, for example, must double if they are to match those in Greater London (alternatively, those in London must halve).

The current boom in house prices is the third since 1970 and average house prices in the United Kingdom are approaching four times the average male earnings (Black Horse Relocation, 1988). The gap between the South (the South East, East Anglia, and South West) where prices have increased by over 50% in two years, and the other regions where prices rose by 10%–25%, is greater than in previous booms. Although the gap should reduce, it will not close the widening experienced since 1984. Thus a greater inequality in house prices is expected and the gap will continue for some time. Although dampening down the demand for housing, even a substantial rise in mortgage interest rates (such as occurred in late 1988) is unlikely to lead to a major reduction in regional price variations.

It is also worthwhile noting that the eleven most expensive counties for housing are all based in the South East (Halifax, 1988b). The Isle of Wight has the lowest prices in the region, owing to its relative inaccessibility. Yet within the South East a wide range in prices can be found. Excluding London and the Isle of Wight, house prices in the most expensive area, Elmbridge in Surrey, are twice as expensive as in the cheapest, Gosport in Hampshire (NBS, 1988). If the capital and Isle of Wight are included, the range extends from the lowest, South Wight, to the highest, Haringey, where house prices are 170% higher.

A recent CBI survey (1988b) showed that in the southeast corner of the region (East and West Sussex, Surrey, and Kent), 61% of firms found housing was a major problem, particularly for skilled employees. For almost half of firms it was affecting their expansion plans, and for 28% the housing market was having a significant effect. But not only do companies face problems in moving employees from low-cost to high-cost housing areas, moves in the other direction are becoming increasingly difficult. Staff are reluctant to move from the South East for fear of being unable to afford to return. Rather than selling up, many are now leasing their original property and renting or purchasing a new house in the area into which they have been relocated.

Two other trends have been generated by the growth in the house price differential. Improved communications has led to some employees accepting longer commuting. Thus Grantham and even Manchester are becoming, to a limited extent, 'dormitory towns' for people with jobs in London. A related trend has been the growth of the weekly commuter who spends from Monday to Friday away from home. Rigidities in the housing market, leading to high differentials in prices, are again a major cause (Hogarth and Daniel, 1987). Many such employees work in and around London but reside in the North.

Tight controls on land for housing development generate further pressures on companies operating within the South East. For example, strong opposition remains from the London and South East Regional Planning Conference (SERPLAN, 1988) to options involving the general easing of Green Belt policy, including the development rather than the restoration of damaged or derelict Green Belt land[1]. In addition, tight controls on development have been maintained on other land in the South East not designated as Green Belt or as Areas of Outstanding Natural Beauty. Not only do such controls prevent companies already located in the region from expanding, either owing to physical constraints on sites or an inability to provide affordable housing for new recruits, but inward investment may also be deterred.

[1] The Green Belt is a cordon of land around London, confined to agricultural and leisure uses and where development is restricted.

4.3 Infrastructure constraints

A further constraint on firms in the South East is the high cost of traffic congestion. In London alone the cost of traffic congestion amounts to £1.45 billion, almost half of the total cost of congestion in all of England's conurbations (BRF, 1988). With the steady growth of car ownership and usage, plus the extra traffic likely to be generated by the completion of the Channel Tunnel the problem will worsen. Furthermore, the rail system is inadequate in providing opportunities for travel into the centre of London (for example, for commuters), and is even less able to satisfy the demand for other types of journey.

Indeed, the opening of the Channel Tunnel planned for 1993, following the completion of the Single European Market the previous year, will further increase the competitive pressures on British companies. Yet at this time of greater competition, firms in the South East may well be facing more serious recruitment and operating difficulties. If the pressures on companies based in the South East become too great, inward investment may be discouraged from locating there. However, it is not certain that they would move to the North and West. Some may choose to locate in the Pas-de-Calais region of Northern France, that has the benefits of cheaper land, high unemployment, and easy access to the rest of the Continent.

5 Options for employers

In order to cope with this changing environment the evidence suggests that companies are considering several options.

5.1 Improving manpower planning and human resource development

Employers are tending to integrate their manpower plans with their business and financial plans. A more sophisticated approach to manpower planning is being introduced in many companies and greater emphasis is now being placed on training programmes, particularly on-the-job training. Other companies are reconsidering their recruitment approach and are looking at different groups for employment. Alternative forms of working patterns are being introduced with variations in working time arrangements, such as the introduction of shift working and flexitime or annual hours systems (CBI, 1985). Similarly, many firms are investigating subcontracting work as a means of overcoming skill shortages and other output constraints.

However, this merely passes the recruitment problem to another firm. The most common approach is to reorganise pay structures and benefits to give greater emphasis to the skill content of jobs.

5.2 Relocating employees

Large differentials in house prices deter labour mobility. Yet the benefits of moving individuals from low-cost to high-cost areas may far outweigh the costs involved. These have been estimated to exceed £10000 in mid-1988 (ERC, 1988) excluding the cost of assistance with alternative housing. Many firms are providing financial assistance to employees to help with moving expenses, but this can be very costly. Alternative approaches to merely funding moves are being investigated by several firms, including linking up with housing associations (CBI, 1988c).

5.3 Introducing new technology
Some companies are overcoming skill shortages by investing in new technology and expert systems to raise productivity. Although eliminating some skill requirements, this approach may also generate others. Improved telecommunications can, however, eliminate, in some industries, the need for relocating employees or activities.

5.4 Relocating activities
The growing pressures of cost on companies operating within the South East are forcing them to reconsider their location. For example, a recent survey in Hertfordshire found that high operating costs were forcing firms to move from the area. For many this means moving their activities away from London to another site within the South East. Indeed, relatively few companies move activities further than 60 miles away from London when relocating. This may be because wage and land cost gradients flatten out or because of the need to be relatively close to London. Many advantageous sites can still be found within the region but these tend to be in the periphery of the South East. For example, development pressures tend to be stronger in the Western crescent than in the Lower Thames corridor where opportunities for new building exist.

In advance of 1992 and the completion of the Single European Market, followed by the planned opening of the Channel Tunnel in 1993, some companies are already looking at sites in the north of France, especially the Pas-de-Calais, and Flanders in Belgium, where the benefits of a location on the Continent with close proximity to the Channel Tunnel will be advantageous. Such locations have other advantages relative to the South East: lower prices of land, a plentiful supply of labour, good transport links to the rest of the Continent, and eligibility for grants from the European Commission. Rationalisation of company organisation on a European-wide basis in order to benefit from economies of scale, combined with the constraints on expansion in the South East of England as well as the peripheral location of other areas of the United Kingdom, could encourage more firms to locate in Northern France. Indeed, not only would such companies benefit from a mainland European location, but there is spare capacity in the form of land and labour as well as a government eager to encourage new investment.

6 Conclusions
Constraints on companies operating within the South East already exist and are likely to worsen at a time of increased international competition

resulting from the completion of the Single European Market and the opening of the Channel Tunnel. Skill shortages and lack of housing are two major problem areas already affecting employers and which are likely to worsen. Although employers are introducing measures to ameliorate the problems, these could be inadequate. Government action could be required in the future. Not only does this involve ensuring the greater release of land for new building in some areas, but pressure in the South East could be reduced by the relocation of some of its functions elsewhere. Furthermore, it may need to reconsider the provision of greater assistance to firms to encourage them to move their head offices and other activities to the North and West of Britain, as has been recommended by others (TCPA, 1987).

The opening of the Channel Tunnel could well worsen the economic divisions between the South East and other areas. With the United Kingdom on the geographic periphery of the European Community, there is a need to change the economic geography of the nation. Much of the nation's infrastructure reflects economic history, providing good access to the west coast ports of the United Kingdom that were so important for trade with North America and the Commonwealth. If British business is to be able to compete with Europe, much better infrastructure links to the east coast ports and the Channel Tunnel will be needed. Otherwise, the danger remains of the South East alone benefitting in terms of economic growth.

References

Black Horse Relocation, 1988, "Beyond the North/South divide: the facts behind the headlines", CES Ltd, 5 Tavistock Place, London, WC1

BRF, 1988, "The way ahead—the cost of congestion", British Road Federation, 6 Portugal Street, London WC2A 2HG

CBI, 1985, "Managing change: the organisation of work", Confederation of British Industry, June; available from CBI, Centre Point, 103 New Oxford Street, London WC1A 1DU

CBI, 1986, "Attitudes to employment", a survey by Gallup for the Confederation of British Industry, October; available from CBI, Centre Point, 103 New Oxford Street, London WC1A 1DU

CBI, 1988a, "Industrial trends survey", Confederation of British Industry, quarterly report, October; available from CBI, Centre Point, 103 New Oxford Street, London WC1A 1DU

CBI, 1988b, "Survey of housing in the South East", Confederation of British Industry, August; available from CBI, Centre Point, 103 New Oxford Street, London WC1A 1DU

CBI, 1988c, "Companies and the housing market", Confederation of British Industry, March; available from CBI, Centre Point, 103 New Oxford Street, London WC1A 1DU

CBI/MSC, 1987, "Special skill survey", Confederation of British Industry/ Manpower Services Commission, October; available from CBI, Centre Point, 103 New Oxford Street, London WC1A 1DU

DE, 1988a, "Labour force outlook to 1995", Department of Employment
   Employment Gazette March, pp 117-129

DE, 1988b, "Labour Market Data" *Employment Gazette* Department of Employment,
   November, pp 51-564

ERC, 1988, Internal estimates, Employee Relocation Council, Confederation of
   British Industry, Centre Point, 103 New Oxford Street, London WC1A 1DU

Gleave D, Palmer D, 1980, "Spatial variations in unemployment problems: a
   typology" *Papers of the Regional Science Association* **4** 57-71

Gordon I R, 1987, "The structural element in regional unemployment", in
   *London Papers in Regional Science 17: Unemployment, the Regions and Labour
   Markets: Reactions to Recession* Ed. I R Gordon (Pion, London) pp 67-88

Halifax, 1988a *House Price Index Regional Bulletin* number 19, third quarter,
   Halifax Building Society, Trinity Road, Halifax

Halifax, 1988b *Home Price County Supplement* number 3, second quarter, Halifax
   Building Society, Trinity Road, Halifax

Hogarth T, Daniel W, 1987, "The long distance commuters" *New Society* 29 May,
   pages 11-13

Homequity, 1987, "Survey forecasts north/south 'Chasm'", press release, November,
   PHH Homequity, PHH Centre, Windmill Hill, Whitehill Way, Swindon SN5 97T

NEDO, 1988, "Young people and the labour market: a challenge for the 1990s",
   National Economic Development Office, 21 Millbank, London SW1

NBS, 1988, "House prices, a local view", June, Nationwide Anglia Building
   Society, Chesterfield House, Bloomsbury Way, London WC1V 6PW

PSI, 1988 *The Impact of Microelectronics* Policy Studies Institute, 100 Park Village East,
   London NW1 3SR

SERPLAN, 1988, Newsletter, March, South East Regional Planning Conference,
   50-64 Broadway, London SW1H 0DP

TCPA, 1987, "The north-south divide, a new deal for Britain's regions", Town
   and Country Planning Association, 17 Carlton House Terrace, London
   SW17 5AS

TC, 1988, "Skills monitoring report", July, Training Commission, Moorfoot,
   Sheffield S1 4PQ

Unbalanced Growth? Public Services and Labour Shortages in a European Core Region

J MOHAN, R LEE
Queen Mary College, London

1 Introduction

Researchers on uneven regional development have tended to focus on the dynamics of growth or decline (for example, the expansion of industrial regions based on high technology, or restructuring and labour shedding in old industrial regions) and the social consequences of underdevelopment. Relatively little attention has been paid to the consequences of growth and the possibilities of 'overdevelopment' (but see Barlow and Savage, 1986). Furthermore, analyses of 'regional problems' are conventionally concerned with geographically uneven conditions of production, or with distributive inequalities, to the neglect of a concern for the influence of unevenness itself on development. For example, some patterns of territorial development can give rise to problems such as inflation, arising out of 'overheating' in economic 'core' regions.

Rapid growth in 'core' regions, such as South East England, drives national and global economies (see Scott and Storper, 1986). However, a frequent consequence of such growth is that regional social structures become polarised between high-earners and low-earners (to say nothing of disparities in other forms of wealth). Housing and labour markets may also be increasingly out of kilter as the ability of labour to accept employment is constrained by the unavailability of affordable housing. Shortages of staff may then result as employers are unable to raise the levels of wages sufficiently to compete for scarce personnel.

Our concern is with this aspect of the regional problem and its impact on the provision of public services in core regions. Public-service provision in the United Kingdom has been headline news for some time now. Key areas of concern have been the extent of cuts in resources and services, and the problems of labour shortages. We focus on the latter. This paper is a preliminary analysis of the extent, causes, and implications of inadequacies in the supply of labour to public services in South East England.

Our underlying premise is that the rapid growth currently being experienced in the South East is beginning to pose serious problems for those agencies charged with providing public services. These problems are due to the extent and pace of demographic change, the rapidly increasing cost of land and residential accommodation, and the reliance upon large numbers of staff who are relatively poorly paid. They are compounded by central government public expenditure policies, and by the government's apparent determination to impose new methods of working on the public sector. The dynamics of change are therefore very complex, but it is apparent that real problems of labour supply do now exist which potentially threaten the ability of statutory authorities to provide services.

The paper comprises three major parts: an initial comparative section deals with public services and public-service workers in core regions of the EEC and is followed by a case study of the pressures on public services within South East England. The actual and possible policy responses by statutory agencies are discussed. In the concluding section a theoretical context in which the implications and meaning of the empirical sections may be pursued is set out.

2 Public services and regional development
2.1 Public services in core regions
Many writers in geography and urban and regional studies have noted the neglect of the study of services. Although recent workers have begun to rectify this, they have focused largely on the actual and potential role of these in supporting both national and regional economic growth (NEDO, 1983); consumer services, as distinct from producer services, have been neglected (Damesick, 1986). Allen (1988) has attempted to develop analyses of the service sector, questioning the simplistic distinction between producer and consumer services, and implying that the study of services and their production should be tied more closely into the circuit of capital and processes of accumulation. This would suggest that public services should be analysed as a component of regional development, and that the precise relationships between public-service provision and regional development require elaboration. This has not been achieved to date. The state has received increasingly sophisticated treatment, but little attention has been paid to what the provision of the "general conditions of the wage-earning class" (Dunford, 1988, page 56) means on a daily basis, or to the circumstances—for example, the "adequacy of labour-power reproduction"—which may define the limits of the provision of these conditions. Harvey (1982, pages 398–405) has offered speculations about the "territoriality of social infrastructures". These infrastructures are financed out of the production of surplus value and can be regarded as having 'salutary' effects on this production: improvements in the quantity or quality of labour power, through, for example, health care and education, can "enhance the social conditions for surplus value production" (page 401).

At the level of abstraction at which Harvey is writing, such arguments are difficult to refute. So, likewise, is his contention that social infra-structures—patterns of service provision and the like—must be adjusted to the needs of capital. But this adjustment can be accomplished only with difficulty. The huge cumulative investments in such infrastructures mean that they are relatively fixed while, all around them, housing and labour markets are fluid, dynamic entities. South East England offers a particularly striking example of the problems of adjusting the distribution of public services to the distribution of the population.

In this paper we retreat from such general discussions, into a more empirical analysis of problems of labour supply within labour-intensive public services. We are especially interested in whether this problem is of particular concern within an expanding, dynamic region linked into a competitive world economy. We argue that services concerned with the reproduction of labour, principally education and health care, are in fact crucial to the continued economic health of a region like South East England.

We can demonstrate this by reference to data for four economic 'core' regions of the European Community (EC). These regions were defined using the EC's 'level 2' regions, and were chosen on the basis of levels of economic activity as indicated by output measures. They are 'core' regions in the sense of being substantially above the EC average on measures such as output per head or the ratio of output in market services to industrial output [1]. Despite their economic primacy, nonmarket services play an important role in these regions (see table 1).

Table 1. Nonmarket services (NMS) in four core regions of the EEC. Source: EUROSTAT, 1987.

Region	Regional share[a]			NMS GVA		Employment in NMS	
	pop.	GVA	NMS GVA	% reg. GVA	per capita	number	% reg.
West Germany							
Nordrhein–Westfalen	27.5	23.7	26.1	14.4	1523	1.2×10^6	18.5
France							
Île de France/ le bassin parisien	36.8	47.0	41.0	14.1	1609	1.6×10^6	18.6
Italy							
Nord Ovest/ Lombardia	26.8	33.6	23.2	10.5	902	9.0×10^5	14.3
United Kingdom							
South East	30.1	32.5	33.7	17.3	1589	1.7×10^6	21.5
Total[b]				14.2	1435	5.4×10^6	18.4

[a] Expressed as a percentage of the country's total.
[b] The sum of the share of all four regions taken together in all four countries taken together.
Note: GVA gross value added at market prices, pop. population, % reg. percentage of the regional value (or number).

[1] Market/nonmarket services: the definition of these services is that used in the European System of Integrated Economic Accounts, which distinguishes, as two of its six categories, 'market' and 'nonmarket' services. In this context, 'nonmarket' services are defined to include 'government services' and 'other nonmarket services' (EUROSTAT, 1979).

Although it is conventional to suggest that "education, health, welfare and personal services fall neatly under the category of consumer services" (Allen, 1988, page 18), the distribution of output in these services is far from simply related to the distribution of population. Furthermore, this unevenness varies from country to country, as does the value of output per head of such services. Nonmarket services account for a significant level of output within each of these core regions—and this despite the overall economic significance of such regions within the market economy. In South East England—having a regional economy with the highest level of specialisation in market services in the EEC—the output of nonmarket services accounts for a greater proportion of output than in the United Kingdom as a whole. Finally, and perhaps more to the point, nonmarket services account for a higher proportion of regional labour than of regional output in each of the four regions under consideration. Only in the north of Italy does the proportion of regional labour employed in nonmarket services fall below 18%. In South East England, where the proportion of labour in nonmarket services is over 21%, and in the Île de France/le bassin parisien—the two regions with the most pronounced development of a market-service economy—the proportion of labour employed in nonmarket services exceeds that for their respective nations.

What this suggests is that nonmarket services are indeed important to the economies of such core regions, and that they are labour-intensive services which have a high demand for labour and which may, therefore, run into problems of labour supply, especially in periods of high overall economic growth.

2.2 Public-service workers and public-service incomes: housing and labour market constraints

If there is a general microeconomic problem of labour supply resulting from the macroeconomics of geographically uneven development, that problem is particularly intense for those agencies charged with the supply of social services within two sorts of locality: municipalities with limited taxable resources and high levels of demand for services (the exemplar is the 'inner city') and regions of rapid economic growth, in which house prices and wages tend to be set by a concentration of high-income earners. In the latter type of region, the difficulty is less the shortage of fiscal resources than the need to sustain an adequate labour supply in the face of two countervailing tendencies. Alternative labour market opportunities and rapidly escalating house prices both combine (for example, see Bover et al, 1988) to squeeze those on low incomes (see Green, 1988; Martin, 1988).

The problems posed by regionally differentiated *housing* markets are well known. They include rising house price to income ratios *nationally* and especially in South East England; widening gaps in house prices between the South East and the rest of the country; shortfalls in housing supply; lack of housing to rent, especially with the decline of the private rented sector; and the 'residualisation' of the public rented sector (see Champion et al, 1987; Hamnett, 1989a; 1989b). These housing issues pose a particular problem for statutory authorities in the South East because public-sector wage levels are simply inadequate to enable incoming staff to purchase property. Clear evidence of this 'mobility trap' (Bover et al, 1988) is provided, for the education service, by the often substantial package of incentive schemes designed to assist personnel, notably teachers, with the costs of housing and removal.

These arguments about the housing market assume, implicitly, that wage levels in the public sector do not match those in the rest of the regional economy. That assumption may not necessarily be correct. Table 2 provides data on the relative levels of remuneration in nonmarket services. They do appear higher, in some cases substantially so, than wage levels in the rest of the economy, but several caveats should inform interpretation of these data. They include *all* workers in nonmarket services and consequently they incorporate large numbers of high-grade civil servants, and do not compare, or allow for, relative levels of skills and training. In all cases, however, the ratio of remuneration in public services to that in the rest of the country is lower within each of the regions considered than it is in the countries in which they are located.

Thus it is demonstrable that nonmarket service workers are, on average, not especially disadvantaged. However, table 3 indicates that, despite substantial interregional differences in living costs, regional differences in earnings by professional public-service workers are lower than for any other group in the labour market. One reason for this is that almost all the 5 250 000 public-service workers in Britain (including 634 212 local authority nonmanual workers, 501 124 teachers, 490 900 nurses

Table 2. The remuneration per employee in nonmarket services (NMS) in 1983 for the core regions of the EEC, expressed as a ratio ($\times 100$) of the total remuneration per employee throughout the regional economies. Source: see table 1.

Region	Remuneration
West Germany	
Nordrhein – Westfalen	119.7
France	
Île de France/le bassin parisien	nd
Italy	
Nord Ovest/Lombardia	122.0
United Kingdom	
South East	111.9
nd no data.	

and midwives, 130 900 administrative and clerical workers, 171 800 ancillaries, and 97 930 doctors and dentists in the NHS) are covered by national paty rates which, apart from 'London weighting' payments, provide for uniform national pay scales. In the South East outside London the earnings of public-service workers are lower than for Britain as a whole (NEDO, 1986).

In this section we have argued that public services are a significant component of the economy of core regions and that the problem of labour supply is central to the provision of public services within such regions. Within South East England in particular, this problem looks likely to intensify given the relatively low wages offered in the public services, the downward pressure on levels of remuneration consequent upon new work practices associated with subcontracting and competitive tendering, and the declining numbers of potential entrants to the labour market (see TC, 1988). Some of the wider implications for regional and national economic growth of this problem of labour supply will be considered in the concluding section. But before embarking on such a discussion, we look in more detail at aggregate trends in employment in public services (especially health care) within South East England, and, using data from health authorities, we outline some of the immediate effects of, and policy responses towards, shortages of labour within the region.

Table 3. Index of average gross weekly earnings by occupational groups: South East England, 1985. (The average for Great Britain is taken as 100.) Source: NEDC, 1986.

Occupation	Males[a]		Females[a]	
	London	ROSE	London	ROSE
All	121.2	102.0	122.2	100.5
Professional and related in education, welfare, and health	110.5	99.1	110.8	99.8

[a] Full-time on adult rates.
Note: ROSE South East excluding London, that is, 'rest of South East'.

3 Public-sector employment in South East England

There is substantial evidence of labour shortages in public services in South East England. Many strategic planning documents by health authorities refer to local recruitment difficulties; several government committee reports have noted this problem; health authorities are now spending substantial sums of money on agency staff (personnel engaged through a private-sector organisation to cover for temporary shortages), and many local education authorities (LEAs) now offer substantial inducements to teachers to move into South East England (*Times*

Educational Supplement, 1988). Research from the Oxford Headships Monitoring Project also shows that 20% of all headships are not filled when first advertised, and that half of all readvertisements are for jobs in South East England.

On the other hand, monitoring of staffing levels in public services—notably health and education—is at best at a rudimentary stage. For example, the Department of Education and Science does not know how many teachers are required in England and Wales, how many teachers are currently in post as a consequence of salary or grade/incentive allowances, the size of the current salary bill, what the target numbers for 1990 and beyond should be, or the current scale of use of supply teachers. Likewise, a persistent criticism of NHS management has been the absence of reliable estimates of the numbers of nursing staff required by health authorities. Even if they existed, global figures are of limited relevance to individual local education and health authorities or schools and hospitals. One objective of our research is to establish the extent of local variations in shortages, despite such gaps in the evidence available. We concentrate here on health care employment as we have yet to extend our work to the detailed documentation and analysis of staff shortages in education and other services.

3.1 Health care employment in the South East: aggregate trends
For some thirty-five years continuous expansion in the NHS meant that health care absorbed steadily rising numbers of the work force. In the United Kingdom as a whole, employment rose from 654 000 in 1952 to 1 280 000 in 1978. All regions had benefitted, but differential resource allocation, reflecting perceived needs for health care in different areas, meant more rapid growth in areas such as Northern Ireland, the East Midlands, and East Anglia (Fothergill and Gudgin, 1975; Mohan, 1988a). Subsequently, this growth has been checked by central government's insistence on tight controls on NHS staffing levels. Health care employment grew by only 6000 between 1981 and 1984, and this growth conceals some sharp reductions—of 21 800 in Greater London and 8600 in South West England.

These aggregate trends are the result of at least three separate influences. First, there is the growing technical sophistication of health care, so that increasing numbers of paramedical staff—radiographers, pathologists, and so on—have been recruited. This trend will continue as diagnostic and treatment methods continue to improve.

Another factor is the demand of central government that the NHS be run in a more efficient manner, with an emphasis on increasing the proportions of staff devoted directly to patient care. Government policy makes an explicit distinction between 'front-line' and 'support' staff, and argues that health authorities must maximise the proportions of the former at the expense of the latter. This mirrors the distinction between 'core' and 'peripheral' workers advanced in notions of the 'flexible firm' (Atkinson and Meager, 1986), although in the opinion of some commentators (Pollert, 1988) government policies have done at least as much to promote this dualism in the labour force as any developments within the private sector (also, see Pinch, 1989). Clearly the 'support' staff—especially ancillaries, but also administrative personnel—are regarded as 'unproductive', an attitude which is consistent with what has been interpreted as a deliberate politics of inequality: a 'two nations' strategy pursued by the Conservative government (Gamble, 1988; Jessop et al, 1984).

Third, policies of spatial resource allocation in the NHS have meant almost no growth in resources to the Thames Regional Health Authorities (RHAs) (the four RHAs covering London and most of South East England) since 1983, as funds have been transferred (in net terms) from these RHAs to the rest of England. Within the Thames RHAs, resources are being transferred from central London to District Health Authorities (DHAs) in the rest of the region (DHSS, 1976; LHE, 1987; Mohan, 1988b).

These developments ought, in principle, to release staff through greater efficiency. This has been explicit NHS policy for some years, the aim being to improve productivity via the more efficient use of finance and staff (DHSS, 1984). One notable development has been the process of competitive tendering for 'ancillary' services. This has exerted downward pressure on wages and has progressed further in South East England than elsewhere (Ascher, 1987; NAO, 1987). If so, ancillary workers resident in the region could be doubly disadvantaged: by working in jobs affected by competitive tendering, and by living in a region where the cost of living is rising while their wages are declining.

Although all these developments ought to release labour for the NHS, there is no guarantee that those staff released by such developments are able to move as resources are transferred from central London. Further, low pay in the NHS limits its attractiveness to potential employees in localities in the outer South East, where unemployment is very low and there are numerous employment opportunities competing with each other. Hence there are specific shortages of particular staff in particular places.

3.2 NHS staff shortages
Although the NHS in London employed 3790 fewer nursing staff in 1986 than in 1982, there is evidence of substantial turnover of staff, and of important recruitment difficulties. Some of this evidence is anecdotal, in numerous press reports indicating interruptions to services owing to staff shortages, but several health authorities, in London itself and in the rest of the South East, have produced a substantial amount of evidence, and their reports are drawn on in what follows.

At the most general level, an indication of shortages in the NHS is given by expenditure on agency staff. These are personnel supplied by commercial organisations to cover temporary shortages in NHS facilities. Nursing agencies must pay identical wage rates to those of the NHS; agencies supplying other staff (such as secretaries) are not bound in this way. All health authorities in London and in much of South East England now spend substantial sums on agency staff. Expenditure more than doubled between the 1983/84 and 1986/87 financial years, rising from £67.3 million to £140 million at 1986/87 prices. Most of this money is spent within the Thames RHAs: £104.4 million in 1986/87. Several DHAs in London (Paddington and North Kensington, Newham, Bloomsbury, Riverside) spent over 5% of their revenue budget (figure 1) on agency staff. Nine other DHAs spent over 4% of their budgets in this way. This is an uneconomic way to obtain staff, because of the agency fees (around 10%) which are charged. It is also regarded as a less than ideal way to operate services, because staff rarely stay on wards long enough to build up working relationships and this is not conducive to quality and continuity of care.

Aggregate data on expenditure on agency staff provide only a partial picture. For more details it is necessary to look at the experience of individual health authorities. Various DHAs have produced reports about their staffing and recruitment situation. To give just one detailed

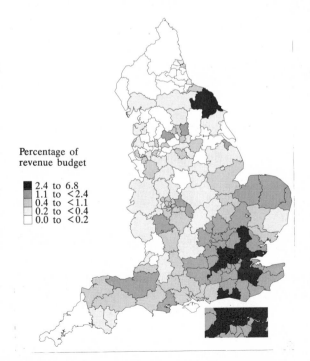

Percentage of
revenue budget

2.4 to 6.8
1.1 to <2.4
0.4 to <1.1
0.2 to <0.4
0.0 to <0.2

Figure 1. English district health authorities: expenditure on agency staff, 1986/87.

example of the extent of problems with staff recruitment, the Riverside DHA (covering Westminster, Hammersmith, and Fulham in central London) reported in January 1987 that it had 657 unfilled nursing vacancies whereas its funded establishment (that is, the number of staff thought to be necessary to run the hospital) of nurses was 2896, which represented 22.6% of its total establishment of nurses. This was an overall figure which, when disaggregated, revealed an even worse situation, because in individual units within the hospital service, vacancy levels were as high as 86%. Community services suffered rather more tolerable vacancy levels, at around 10%–15%, but even these could have a severe impact because the services were organised on a 'patch' basis, so that small numbers of nurses had sole responsibility for particular local areas. The findings of this report were echoed by the Royal College of Nursing (RCN), which interviewed directors of nursing services in eight inner London DHAs and found that vacancy levels for trained staff were between 20% and 25%. Turnover of staff was also very high: for instance City and Hackney DHA reported turnover rates of 22% for ancillary staff, 42% for nursing staff, and 25% for administrative and clerical staff.

What effects do these staff shortages have on service delivery? The most dramatic effects are the newsworthy ones, such as closures of hospital wards. However, the less easily quantifiable impacts, such as those on staff morale and quality of service, may be more important in the long term. For instance, a report produced jointly by the Special Health Authorities for the London Postgraduate Teaching Hospitals suggested that these hospitals were "now able to function in many cases only by using expensive agency staff and/or by expecting staff in post to cover vacancies for considerable periods". The same report went on, "it is not unusual for the services involved to be provided incompletely or not to the required standard". Another inner London DHA considered that the quality of patient care "could not be maintained" when a high percentage of agency staff were being employed. The overall effect of recruitment difficulties was felt by one DHA to produce a vicious circle: staff shortages led to higher work load, reduced job satisfaction, and lower morale, thus prompting more staff to leave the NHS. We return to the issue of the impact on service delivery in our conclusions.

What accounts for these problems? Here one has to distinguish between difficulties in sectors where the NHS is virtually the sole employer of labour and in areas where the NHS faces competition from other employers. In occupations where the NHS is a de facto monopsony employer, the problem is genuinely one of labour supply. Nursing is no longer recruiting the proportion of new female entrants to the labour force that it previously did, and retention of staff is proving more difficult. Low pay is the primary cause (NUPE, 1987) but there is also survey evidence of increased frustration and disillusionment among NHS nurses throughout the country. This has been explained in terms of poor working conditions and increased throughput of patients (and hence increased work load) (Waite and Hutt, 1987). Low pay among nurses is especially serious in the South East because of housing market constraints. In addition, the demands for nurses in the private health sector are rising steadily. Private hospitals and nursing homes in England employed 62000 nurses in 1986, compared with 30000 in 1982, and the bulk of this increase was in the South East (DHSS, 1987). Little evidence is available on the movement of nurses between the NHS and the private health sector, apart from estimates of a net loss from the NHS of 1100 nurses per annum. This loss tends to be concentrated disproportionately in the more skilled areas of nursing (intensive care and theatre nurses) (Thomas et al, 1988).

Where the NHS is not a monopsonistic employer its problems are much more severe. The differentials in London allowances alone are enormous. Many banks now pay a London Weighting of £3000 per annum to all staff employed at banks inside the M25; this is nearly three times the NHS London Weighting allowance (IDS, 1988). Nor is this problem confined to London: it is entirely feasible for private-sector secretarial staff to commute from, say, Brighton to London, especially if they receive assistance with the cost of travelling. Recruitment problems are also occurring in respect of financial and computing staff and this is of considerable importance, given the growing stress in the NHS upon information technology as a means towards more cost-effective use of health care resources. The recruitment difficulties and turnover of ancillary staff have been exacerbated by the downward pressure on wages implicit in competitive tendering, by demands for high levels of work load, and by competition from other services. The uncertain future of many hospitals in inner London, which are threatened by rationalisation proposals, is not conducive to stability in the work force, and one could argue plausibly that this is owing to the scale and pace of resource transfers out of London under the Resource Allocation Working Party (Mohan, 1988c).

3.3 Responses by statutory authorities
The actual and potential options open to health authorities are somewhat limited. They are at present constrained by national pay agreements which mean they cannot always respond flexibly to competition for staff. They have limited accommodation to offer their work force, other than that available in nurses' homes. Here we briefly discuss the scope for health authorities to intervene in the housing market before considering their attempts either to restructure work organisation or to draw on hitherto untapped reserves of labour.

3.3.1 Intervention in the housing market
So far the options introduced essentially involve either offering incentives to enable employees to compete in the owner-occupied market or ensuring

that at least some low-cost rented accommodation is on offer to incoming staff.

Of the former option, the NHS shared-equity mortgage scheme is the best known. Several health authorities have negotiated packages under which NHS staff become eligible for mortgages of up to $4\frac{1}{2}$ times their salaries, on the understanding that the building societies involved receive a share of any capital gain in the property. These mortgages depend on propeprty values continuing to rise, since without a capital gain there is no benefit from the point of view of the financial institutions. It is too early to evaluate their impact, but a pessimistic scenario is that they could exacerbate the very problem they are designed to solve, because they could expand the numbers of potential buyers competing for a limited number of properties. In addition, they could pose difficulties for DHAs on the margins of areas in which such incentives are available, because their staff could seek jobs in adjacent districts. Last, it is already clear that house prices in the South East will not continue to rise at the rates experienced in the mid-1980s, and so joint-equity mortgages may eventually prove unattractive to financing organisations.

Another option has not yet been widely employed in the NHS, although it is common practice for LEAs. This involves offering incentives to new appointees to assist with relocation and accommodation costs. In 1988 at least twenty-eight LEAs were offering some such incentives (*Times Educational Supplement*, 1988; see figure 2). These are flexible, short-term responses but they implicitly pit authority against authority in offering the best deal. The packages available are nowhere near as generous as those in the private sector (see Forrest and Murie, 1987) so it is debatable whether they are likely to enable relatively low-paid staff to compete.

As for the second option, that of ensuring that low-cost rented accommodation is available, health authorities are beginning to investigate options such as joint-equity housing developments with housing associations. Such developments would aim to exploit land held by DHAs to produce housing for which DHAs would hold nomination rights.

3.3.2 *Labour market responses*
Several reports have highlighted the exceptionally difficult task facing the NHS, notably with respect to nurse recruitment (Conroy and Stidston, 1988). As the number of entrants to the labour force declines, the NHS will have to increase substantially the proportions of school-leavers that it attracts. In the case of nursing, the NHS nationally now recruits around 30% of all female school-leavers with five O-levels and two A-levels. This proportion will have to rise to 50% if staffing levels are to be maintained; alternatively, the NHS will have to attract substantially more male recruits than has hitherto been the case. Conroy and Stidston (1988) have characterised the situation facing the NHS as a 'black hole', on the

grounds that a combination of factors (technological change, increased competition for staff, service-sector growth, reduced female unemployment, increased part-time working) will make it virtually impossible for the NHS to retain the requisite number of staff. Indeed they envisage the NHS *underspending* on its staff budget. Their analysis does not take account of the specific additional problems likely to be faced by individual RHAs, notably those in South East England.

What they do point to is the difficulty the NHS will face in making the kind of adjustments necessary to cope with increased competition in the labour market. The possibilities for substitution of capital for labour are very restricted in health care. Technological change increases the requirements of the NHS for *skilled* labour (for example, radiographers, technical staff), which is already in very short supply in the South East. Greater throughput of patients could be one answer but is widely held to be associated with greater pressure and low morale within the nursing

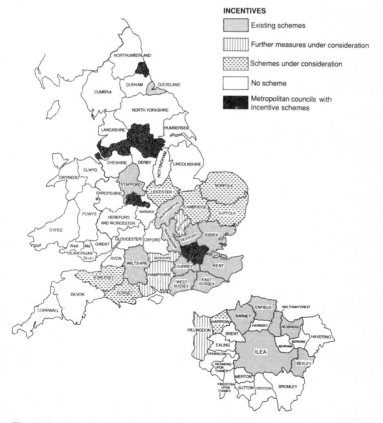

Figure 2. Local education authorities offering recruitment/relocation incentive packages, 1988. Inset: London education authorities.

profession (Waite and Hutt, 1987). In these circumstances there appear to be two main options: to draw on untapped sources of labour and to increase flexibility in work organisation.

Several DHAs in the South East have made strenuous efforts to recruit nursing staff from outside the region, most notably by recruiting from Northern Ireland and Eire. What is not known is how successful these steps have been. Furthermore, they are unlikely to be successful without the NHS being able to *guarantee* the availability of accommodation for such staff. This is one area where the limits on the capacity of the public sector to *plan* its services are thrown into sharp relief. Public-sector agencies in the South East cannot ensure that accommodation will be made available. They depend on the operation of housing markets, and on decisions taken by other agencies to ensure that their staff can find accommodation. Furthermore, NHS-trained nurses are in demand internationally. Regular recruitment fairs take place in London with a view to attracting staff to hospitals in Canada, Australia, and the USA. It is not known whether this has a disproportionate effect on NHS hospitals in the South East, but it certainly adds to the competition for staff in the region.

Increased *flexibility* in staff recruitment and deployment is clearly in accord with the Government's wider policies towards the labour market which stress the need to eliminate inflexibilities and rigidities. Many DHAs are consequently attempting to cope with staff shortages by introducing more flexible working hours, to attract part-time staff, and also by setting up 'bank' systems. These work by establishing a register of qualified nurses who are no longer employed by the NHS but who have indicated their willingness and availability to undertake occasional work (as such, they are similar to the labour market in 'supply' teachers). Participants are paid per shift worked and do not receive the protection to which employees (whether full-time or part-time) are entitled. These are obvious drawbacks to potential members of 'banks'. The NHS will need to invest in its (potential) work force in other ways, notably through the provision of childcare facilities, if it is to overcome some of its recruitment difficulties.

An alternative suggestion, which has also been widely canvassed as a way to remove 'inflexibilities' in the NHS, is that the national system of wage determination should be replaced by decentralised pay bargaining. There have been indications that the Government wish to see local market forces dictate the wages paid to NHS staff, and the recent White Paper on the NHS (Secretary of State for Health, 1989) endorses these, arguing that one advantage of 'self-government' for hospitals would be freedom from national pay bargaining. This is surely debatable: it is difficult to see how, in the tight labour markets of the South East, freedom from such national systems would enable hospitals to save money. Instead they would, presumably, have to pay above-average rates of pay to attract staff, which would be inconsistent with the present system of cash-limiting NHS finance. Such proposals would also make it harder for the remaining NHS hospitals to attract staff, for personnel would be attracted to the 'prestige' hospitals run by NHS Hospital Trusts.

4 An interpretative conclusion and a research agenda

In our introductory remarks we argued that the more 'developed' a regional economy in terms of market services (an indicator which may be taken as a proxy for the 'core' status of the region) the more important are nonmarket services, both as producers of output and consumers of labour. We then demonstrated not only that shortages of labour exist but that they have disruptive effects and are eliciting numerous short-term responses within the public sector. These problems are not unique to the health service: similar evidence can be produced for education, social work, transport, and the postal service. In this concluding section we briefly outline directions for future research and then raise some wider theoretical implications of this discussion.

First, there is the question of the impact of recruitment difficulties on service quality. The *general* problems of recruitment and retention in the NHS are, and will continue to be, especially severe in South East England. This would, a priori, be expected to reduce the *quantity* of service delivered. Increases in productivity could alleviate this, but may themselves be inimical to recruitment and retention. Service *quality* might therefore be expected to decline. This is notoriously difficult to measure (Flynn, 1986; Pollitt, 1986). The available measures do not indicate outcomes, for example the connection (if any) between inputs (resources) and health status. Still less do they suggest in what way standards of service provision are linked to or have an impact upon regional development. The recent discussions about 'rating places' in Britain have barely touched upon service provision as an issue, focusing instead on easily quantifiable indices of consumer spending (RRS, 1987), economic prosperity (Champion and Green, 1987), or the cost of living (Mintel, 1988). One exception to this (Morris et al, 1987) has been an analysis of some broad and subjective indicators of quality of life. One aim of future research will be to determine, for a range of public services, what effect recruitment difficulties have on quantity and quality of provision.

A related point is the extent to which recruitment difficulties are a general problem for all statutory authorities, as opposed to there being specific problems in recruiting particular staff in certain places. There are obvious grounds for suggesting that a disaggregated analysis, looking at particular occupational categories and relating demand for and supply of labour to local needs for and provision of services, is essential. There are a number of recruitment problems and their causes are very diverse. This diversity must be recognised.

Third, there is the question of the actual and potential effectiveness of the various measures designed to cope with labour shortages. Will subsidised mortgages and recruitment incentives make it possible for the NHS and LEAs to attract the number and quality of staff they require, or will such schemes add a further twist to inflation in house prices? Will new methods of working be adopted, involving subcontracting or competitive tendering? What will be the effect of policies designed to draw on untapped pools of labour in the region? If these measures are not enough, is it likely that the scenario is one in which the ability of the NHS to maintain services is threatened, leading to a heightened contrast between private affluence and public squalor? These questions are likely to be crucial both to the future provision of public services in the South East and to the maintenance of regional growth rates.

It is for reasons such as these that our interest in public services is defined less in terms of particular sectors of the economy or branches of polity than in the question of the relationship between uneven development and what Baumol (1967) terms 'unbalanced growth'. In those activities (such as health care or education) which have an intensive labour input, involving face-to-face interaction with consumers, the scope for restructuring the labour process (for instance, by substituting capital for labour) is limited. This led Baumol to divide the economy into its 'progressive' and 'nonprogressive' sectors, according to the ability of each to cope with competitive cost pressures by increases in productivity. If wages in both sectors rise at the same rate as increases in productivity in the progressive sector then, Baumol (1967, pages 419–420, emphasis in original) argues,

"... relative costs in the non progressive sectors must inevitably rise, *and these costs will rise cumulatively and without limit* ... [and] the output of these sectors may in some cases tend to be driven from the market. If relative outputs are maintained, an ever increasing proportion of the labor force must be channeled into these activities and the rate of growth of the economy may be slowed correspondingly."

With unregulated capitalist competition, the low-productivity sector would be unable to compete in the market place and would decline to a point at which the demand for its output was so great that the price was bid up to a level at which even low-productivity production techniques could produce at a profit. But this resolution may be inefficient from the point of view of the profitability and expanded reproduction of the economy as a whole and so public provision of low-productivity, but essential goods and services may be induced. Following O'Connor (1973) we may argue that a fiscal crisis might then result as growth generates further demands for services whilst profits from capitalist production remain in private hands and conflicts over taxation and the allocation of resources generate a tendency towards a structural gap between spending requirements and the ability to pay for them. This gap is widened by rising expectations (in some public services like health care, demand is partly a function of supply) and by the dual role of the state in both facilitating and legitimating capital accumulation.

By recognising the positive relationships between public-service provision and capital accumulation, such analyses undermine the simplistic notion (Bacon and Eltis, 1978) that public services are merely parasitic on the surplus produced within the private sector and so 'crowd out' the productive economy by absorbing resources. (For a concise critique of the severe limitations of the Bacon and Eltis thesis as applied to local public expenditure, see Newton and Karan, 1985, chapters 2 and 3.) But, by the same token, analyses of the fiscal relations between capitalist state and capitalist economy point up the real problem of unbalanced growth. And, as we argued in section 2 of this paper, there are clear grounds for believing that problems of unbalanced growth are particularly severe in core regions experiencing rapid economic growth. Furthermore, such problems are the more significant when such regions act also as the engine of growth for national and international economies.

What solutions are available to the state which could help solve such problems? There seem to be three: the raising of productivity within the limits of 'nonprogressive' sectors; the disengagement of the state from service provision; and the exposure of the public sector work force to the dictates of competition via the abolition of national collective bargaining and the lowering of entry requirements.

Increased productivity might overcome short-term problems of labour supply at the expense of more serious longer-term difficulties of low morale, staff retention, and a decline in the quality of service. It is also possible that higher levels of throughput are inimical to the maintenance of service quality. To give a genuine evaluation of the issue of service quality, in health care for example, one would have to look at changes in lengths of stay and waiting lists as well as less-easily-measurable characteristics of service such as the amount of time spent by staff with individual patients.

Greater privatisation of services seems to be a preferred option for the present government. Here we distinguish between privatisation in the sense of greater private-service provision, and privatisation in the sense of exposing the public-sector work force to greater competition, with a view to introducing greater flexibility into the labour process.

Increased private-service provision has been encouraged by successive Conservative governments as a way of reducing pressure on the over-stretched public services. Indeed, it might be argued that the Thatcher government is attempting to break the contradictory link, in O'Connor's (1973) analysis, between the state's involvement in accumulation and legitimation. They are doing this by the simultaneous but selective withdrawal of state involvement and the promotion of an ideology of individualism and, more recently, the notion of 'active citizenship'.

And it may be that it is in regions like South East England that such a strategy may be most efficacious. Relatively high levels of per capita income facilitate consumer expenditure on the private provision of expensive services like education and health care, and decisions to purchase such services are, at least in part, informed by perceptions of declining public services. However, the extent to which the private sector will relieve the burden on the public sector is debatable.

First, commercial considerations dictate that the private sector concentrates on a limited range of people. Private hospitals typically deal with middle-class families and individuals in the professional and managerial socioeconomic groups. There are large proportions of such people in the South East but the range of treatments carried out on them is limited (Mohan, 1985; Nicholl et al, 1989a; 1989b). Hence it is debatable whether privatisation will remove much of the greatest burdens on the NHS—the elderly and the chronically sick. Second, to the extent that private nursing homes for the elderly are relieving pressures on the NHS, they are doing so by being subsidised, at great expense, from the public purse. Around £400 million *per annum* is now spent in the Thames RHAs on private nursing care for the elderly. This gives a further twist to problems of labour supply within those RHAs. Third, there is evidence of a net loss of staff from the public to the private sector. The reasons are complex but essentially revolve around conditions of work. The private sector of health care is able to plan a specialised division of labour, in which nurses are free to employ their particular skills in a working environment that can be tailored to the circumstances of individual staff. This is in contrast to what are generally perceived as the inflexible shift systems available to staff in the NHS. Private education has the advantages of far lower staff–student ratios, longer holidays, and higher pay compared with publicly-funded education.

So, there are clear interdependencies in the simultaneous provision of 'public' and private services. Not the least of these is a further twist to the increase in labour costs within the public sector which is forced to compete not only with wage levels in the rest of the regional economy but with the higher wages payable to professionals in the private health service. And yet there is only a limited amount of manoeuvre available to the suppliers of public services in restructuring a labour process which embodies high levels of skill and training and is designed to provide services to whoever requires them.

Furthermore, a new international division of labour in the provision of education and health care may result from the development of private services. Such a development might further enhance the attractions of core regions for high-level economic and state functions. But it would also exclude a large proportion of the labour force within such regions from adequate service provision and this in turn would reduce the attractiveness of core regions for investment. And if there is a connection between the adequate provision of "the general conditions of reproduction of the wage earning class" and accumulation, the underprovision within core regions will, given their importance to national and international economic development, be particularly problematic.

For these various reasons it seems unlikely that private-service provision will solve the problems of labour supply in the public services; it may exacerbate them. Alternative responses might then involve removing 'inflexibilities' in the labour market so that labour supply and demand are matched through the free play of market forces. This might entail remodelling the public-sector work force along the lines of the 'flexible firm' (Atkinson and Meager, 1986; see also Pollert, 1988), in which the labour force are segmented into 'core' and 'peripheral' workers. Competitive tendering for 'ancillary' services in the NHS and within LEAs is one example, but the downward pressure that this typically exerts on wage levels leads to high vacancy and turnover levels for staff. The contracting out of services merely passes the problems of labour supply from one employer to another. Nationally agreed wage rates in the public services are often cited as an inflexibility, but a consequence of their removal could be that statutory authorities in the South East would have to pay more to recruit staff, which seems incompatible with their legal obligations to keep expenditure within centrally imposed limits.

Neither greater privatisation nor increased flexibility in the labour market seem likely to alleviate these problems of labour supply. Baumol (1967, page 422) envisaged that one alternative solution to unbalanced growth could involve voluntary public support of the 'nonprogressive' sectors. This has been espoused by the present government via their promulgation of an ideology of 'active citizenship' and voluntary support for services. However, there are obvious limitations on the extent to which this kind of 'amateurisation' can help: "amateur activity offers a highly imperfect substitute for the highly polished product that can be offered by the professional" (Baumol, 1967, page 422).

What this suggests is that the problems of unbalanced growth will not simply disappear. Here we refer not merely to the problem of labour supply in public services but to the maintenance of growth in core regions. There seems little to be gained by making 'public' services private. Underlying difficulties remain and the burden of cost is simply transferred to consumers from taxpayers. Even if we ignore issues of justice and fairness, there must be some mechanism to enable the adequate flow of resources for the provision of public services. Of course, the policy discussion could hinge around the definition of 'adequate', and here the lowering of expectations performs a crucial material role. But such a debate should be informed by direct indicators of the efficacy of health care or education (international comparisons of infant and perinatal mortality rates or life expectancy or of measures of value added in terms of educational achievement in schools, for example, rather than indirect indicators like throughput).

By such indicators the British systems of public health and of education, although economically efficient by international standards, may have begun to underperform over the past decade or so. Insofar as this is a question of the *allocation* of resources to, as well as the *use* of resources *within* public services, two broad sets of responses seem feasible. At the macroeconomic level, a means must be found to link the gains in productivity within the 'progressive' parts of the economy to the 'nonprogressive' sectors. Taxation and public expenditure is one such mechanism which, if administered in certain ways, has the advantage of the possibility of fairness and justice. Another mechanism is the promotion of charitable effort, through an ideology of active citizenship, but such a mechanism has severe disadvantages as a basis for resource provision in that charitable effort is the more easily organised for certain projects than for others. There is, therefore, no escape from statutory provision at a level which enables continuous improvements in levels of health care or educational achievement.

But this is not a ploy to enable the state to tell us all what we should receive. Rather it is a mechanism for ensuring the efficient transfer of resources from the loci of productivity gains in the economy to those equally vital areas of reproductive activity capable of only limited productivity improvements. Against such a background, the first type of response to unbalanced growth—that of conscious efforts to improve the use of resources within public services (see page 49)—takes on a qualitatively different objective. The concern is not with managing externally imposed cuts but with designing policies to meet genuine productivity improvements (that is, more effective health care and education) at least cost.

Acknowledgements. John Mohan would like to acknowledge the support of an ESRC Postdoctoral Research Fellowship (grant number A23320036) and the assistance of numerous health and education authorities in supplying material drawn on in this paper.

References
Allen J, 1988, "Service industries: uneven development and uneven knowledge" *Area* **20**(1) 15–22
Ascher K, 1987 *The Politics of Privatization: Contracting-out Public Services* (Macmillan, London)
Atkinson J, Meager N, 1986 *New Forms of Work Organisation* IMS report number 121, Institute of Manpower Studies, University of Sussex, Brighton
Bacon R, Eltis W, 1978 *Britain's Economic Problem: Too Few Producers* (Macmillan, London)
Barlow J, Savage M, 1986, "The politics of growth: cleavage and conflict in a Tory heartland" *Capital and Class* **30** 156–182
Baumol W J, 1967, "Macro-economics of unbalanced growth: the anatomy of urban crisis" *American Economic Review* **LVII** 415–426

Bover O, Muellbauer J, Murphy A, 1988 *Housing, Wages and UK Labour Markets* DP-268, Centre for Economic Policy Research, 6 Duke of York Street, London SW1

Champion A, Green A, 1987 *The Booming Towns of Britain* DP-72, CURDS, University of Newcastle upon Tyne, Newcastle upon Tyne

Champion A, Green A, Owen D, 1987, "Housing, labour mobility and unemployment" *The Planner* **73**(4) 11-17

Conroy M, Stidston M, 1988 *The Black Hole* South West Thames Regional Health Authority, Eastbourne Terrace, London W2

Damesick P, 1986, "Service industries, employment and regional development in Britain: a review of recent trends and issues" *Transactions, Institute of British Geographers* **11** 212-226

DHSS, 1976 *Sharing Resources for Health in England* Department of Health and Social Security, Alexander Fleming House, Elephant and Castle, London SE1 6BY

DHSS, 1984 *Health Services Development: Resource Distribution for 1984-5, Service Priorities, Manpower and Planning* circular HC(84)2, Department of Health and Social Security, Alexander Fleming House, Elephant and Castle, London SE1 6BY

DHSS, 1987 *Independent Sector Hospitals, Nursing Homes and Clinics in England* Department of Health and Social Security, Alexander Fleming House, Elephant and Castle, London SE1 6BY

Dunford M F, 1988 *Capital, the State, and Regional Development* (Pion, London)

EUROSTAT, 1979 *European System of Integrated Economic Accounts* (Office des publications officielles des Communautés éuropéens, Brussels, Luxembourg)

EUROSTAT, 1987 *Regions: Statistical Year Book 1987* (Office des publications officielles des Communautés éuropéenes, Brussels, Luxembourg)

Flynn N, 1986, "Performance measurement in public sector services" *Policy and Politics* **14** 389-404

Forrest R, Murie A, 1987, "The affluent home owner: labour market position and the shaping of housing histories" *The Sociological Review* **35** 370-403

Fothergill S, Gudgin G, 1975 *Regional Employment Statistics 1952-75* available from CES Ltd, 5 Tavistock Place, London WC1

Gamble A, 1988 *The Free Economy and the Strong State* (Macmillan, London)

Green A, 1988, "The North-South divide in Great Britain: an examination of the evidence" *Transactions, Institute of British Geographers* **13** 179-198

Hamnett C, 1989a, "The owner-occupied market in housing: a North-South divide?", in *The North-South Divide: Regional Change in Britain in the 1980s* Eds J R Lewis, A R Townsend (Paul Chapman, London) pp 97-113

Hamnett C, 1989b, "The political geography of housing in contemporary Britain", in *The Political Geography of Contemporary Britain* Ed. J Mohan (Macmillan, London) pp 208-223

Harvey D, 1982 *The Limits to Capital* (Basil Blackwell, Oxford)

IDS, 1988 *London Allowances (IDS Study 400)* Incomes Data Services Ltd, 193 St John Street, London EC1

Jessop B, Bonnett K, Bromley S, Ling T, 1984, "Authoritarian populism, two nations, and Thatcherism" *New Left Review* **147** 32-60

LHE, 1987 *Patients or Profits?* London Health Emergency, 335 Grays Inn Road, London WC1

Martin R, 1988, "The political economy of Britain's North-South divide" *Transactions, Institute of British Geographers* **13** 389-418

Mintel, 1988 *Regional Lifestyles* (Mintel Publications, 7 Arundel Street, London WC2

Mohan J, 1985, "Independent acute medical care in Britain: its organisation, location and prospects" *International Journal of Urban and Regional Research* **9** 467–484

Mohan J, 1988a, "Spatial aspects of health-care employment in Britain: 1. Aggregate trends" *Environment and Planning A* **20** 7–23

Mohan J, 1988b, "Spatial aspects of health-care employment in Britain: 2. Current policy initiatives" *Environment and Planning A* **20** 203–217

Mohan J, 1988c, "Restructuring, privatization and the geography of health care provision in England, 1983–87" *Transactions, Institute of British Geographers* **13** 449–465

Morris A S, Findlay A M, Rogerson R C, 1987 *The Geography of Quality of Life* OP-22, Geography Department, Glasgow University, Glasgow, Scotland

NAO, 1987 *Competitive Tendering for Support Services in the National Health Service*, National Audit Office, House of Commons Paper HC-318 (HMSO, London)

NEDC, 1986, "Regional pay variations—note by the Chancellor of the Exchequer and the Secretary of State for Employment", leaflet, available from National Economic Development Council, 21 Millbank, London SW1

NEDO, 1983, "Changing employment patterns: where will the new jobs be?", leaflet, available from National Economic Development Office, 21 Millbank, London SW1

Newton K, Karan T J, 1985 *The Politics of Local Expenditure* (Macmillan, London)

Nicholl J P, Beeby N R, Williams B T, 1989a, "Comparison of the activity of short-stay independent hospitals in England and Wales, 1981 and 1986" *British Medical Journal* **298** 239–242

Nicholl J P, Beeby N R, Williams B T, 1989b, "Role of the private sector in elective surgery in England and Wales, 1986" *British Medical Journal* **298** 243–246

NUPE, 1987 *Nursing a Grievance: Low Pay in Nursing* National Union of Public Employees, Civic House, 20 Grand Depot Road, London SE18 6SF

O'Connor J, 1973 *The Fiscal Crisis of the State* (St Martin's Press, New York)

Pinch S, 1989, "The restructuring thesis and the study of public services" *Environment and Planning A* **21** 905–926

Pollert A, 1988, "The flexible firm: fixation or fact?" *Work, Employment and Society* **2** 281–316

Pollitt C, 1986, "Performance measurement in the public services: some political implications" *Parliamentary Affairs* **39** 315–329

RRS, 1987 *UK Regional Cost of Living Report* Reward Regional Surveys, Reward Consultants, 9 Savoy Street, London WC2

Scott A J, Storper M (Eds), 1986 *Production, Work, Territory: The Geographical Anatomy of Industrial Capitalism* (Allen and Unwin, Hemel Hempstead, Herts)

Secretary of State for Health, 1989 *Working for Patients* Cmnd 555 (HMSO, London)

TC, 1988 *Labour Market Quarterly Report* July, Training Commission, Moorfoot, Sheffield S1 4PQ

Thomas K, Nicholl J P, Williams B, 1988, "A study of the movement of nurses and nursing skills between the NHS and the private sector in England and Wales" *International Journal of Nursing Studies* **25**(1) 1–10

Times Educational Supplement 1988, "The respectable face of bribery", 22 July, page 9

Waite R, Hutt R, 1987 *Attitudes, Jobs and Mobility of Qualified Nurses* IMS report 130, Institute of Manpower Studies, University of Sussex, Falmer, Brighton BN1 9RH

Inside the 'Sunbelt': Industrial Change in Southampton

C MASON, S PINCH, S WITT
University of Southampton

1 Introduction

Much of the debate about the North–South divide in Great Britain has focused upon inequalities as manifest at the broad regional scale. The resurgence of locality studies in recent years (Cooke, 1986a) has drawn attention to the considerable variations in economic circumstances and social conditions that exist *within* regions which are inevitably obscured by regional-level analyses. However, there have been relatively few locality studies within 'Sunbelt' Britain; moreover, the geographical focus of these studies has been confined to the 'M4 Corridor', and in at least some cases they have had an undue emphasis on high-technology industry. Consequently, explanations for the economic buoyancy of southern England and for the recent widening of the North–South divide tend to overemphasise the role of high-technology industries, generalise on the basis of evidence from the 'M4 Corridor' (or even Berkshire) and under-play the diversity of economic processes that have contributed to the economic buoyancy of different localities within the area.

In this paper we seek to complement and extend the limited range of locality studies within 'Sunbelt' Britain by providing an account of recent economic and social change in the economy of the Southampton city-region, a part of southern England which has not previously been the subject of intensive research. We have two main objectives. First, the detailed analysis of industrial change in Southampton highlights some key processes that have contributed to the expansion of the local economy which have not been identified in previous studies of 'Sunbelt' Britain. Second, by comparing the findings with those of other localities within southern England (notably Bristol and Reading) we emphasise both the differences in economic structures within the 'Sunbelt' and the diversity of economic processes which are contributing to its economic growth. However, before presenting the detailed evidence for Southampton it is appropriate to put the study into context with a brief review of the reasons proposed by previous studies for the growth of the UK 'Sunbelt' and the limitations of such accounts.

2 The growth of the UK 'Sunbelt': an overview

The post-1979 economic recession resulted in a substantial decline in industrial output and employment throughout all parts of Britain, although in proportionate terms the regional impact has been distinctly uneven.

Industrial decline has been most acute in those regions dependent on a specialised or long-established industrial base, including the 'traditionally depressed' industrial regions of Scotland, Wales, and the North as well as the major conurbations, including London, and the 'industrial heartland' regions of the North West, Yorkshire and Humberside, and the West Midlands. By contrast, industrial decline in the South East (excluding London), East Anglia, and most of the South West has been less severe on account of their smaller manufacturing base, greater economic diversification, and concentration of service industries, including higher-level corporate functions (Martin, 1986; 1988). For many of the same reasons, this North–South divergence in industrial decline is now being replicated and reinforced in the economic recovery of the second half of the 1980s. For example, between December 1986 and December 1987 the number of people in employment including self-employed increased at a faster rate in the South East and East Anglia (2.9% and 5.5%, respectively) than in any other region. Moreover, the absolute increase in employment in these two regions (241000 and 49600, respectively) represented 57% of the total increase in Great Britain (TA, 1988), compared with their 38% share of total employment. Thus, southern Britain has not only been less vulnerable to industrial decline but has also been the main beneficiary of economic recovery (Martin, 1988). Hence, by the mid-1980s "regional differentials [in unemployment] had reached their widest since the 1930s" (Martin, 1988, page 397).

However, the examination of the UK space-economy through the lens of standard regions inevitably gives a highly generalised perspective. Economic and employment growth in the late 1970s and 1980s has been concentrated in a broad swathe of southern England—now widely referred to as 'Sunbelt' Britain—which straddles regional boundaries. Its geographical extent has been variously described as "stretching from Cambridge through Berkshire to Bristol" (Martin, 1988, page 399), "the crescent of country stretching from Bristol through the Home Counties and into East Anglia" (Massey, 1984, page 287), and "stretching between the Severn estuary and the Solent north and east to Cambridgeshire" (Damesick, 1987, page 26). This belt of growth and prosperity is well exemplified by the index of local economic performance developed by Champion and Green. Their 'Mark One' index, largely based on measures of change from 1971 to 1981, highlights "the overwhelming concentration of the most successful places in southern England, particularly within a 100 km arc to the west and north of London ... . This zone focusses on the ... 'M4 Corridor', but also embraces the M3 belt of western Surrey and northern Hampshire" (Champion et al, 1987, pages 111 and 105). In their 'Mark Two' index, based on the period since 1981, "all of the ... highest scoring places ... lie on or south of a line between the Severn estuary and Lincolnshire and ... form a continuous crescent around London from

Crawley, Chichester and Winchester in the south to Cambridge, Newmarket and Thetford in the north" (Champion and Green, 1988, page 38). Explanations for the rapid rate of economic and employment growth in 'Sunbelt' Britain emphasise its specialisation in four areas of economic activity: high-technology industries; corporate and government R&D activities; producer services; and high-level corporate functions. On the first of these characteristics, the South East, South West, and East Anglia contained 59% of the employment in UK high-technology manufacturing in 1981 (Keeble, 1987): "the core of [this] high technology activity, and particularly electronics, ... is at the London end of the 'M4 Corridor', in a belt running from Hertfordshire to the north-west of London, through Berkshire and into Hampshire and Surrey" (Hall et al, 1987, page 47). In similar vein, Kelly and Keeble (1988, page 8) report that employment growth in computer manufacturing between 1978 and 1984 is concentrated in a "crescent around London from Cambridge to Southampton, centred on Berkshire". Military markets account for a considerable proportion of the output of these industries (Hall et al, 1987; Law, 1983; Lovering and Boddy, 1988), thus limiting their exposure to international competition (Kaldor et al, 1986). Second, the 'Sunbelt' contains the majority of both corporate and government R&D establishments (Gillespie and Green, 1987; Howells, 1984). Keeble (1987) notes that the South East, South West, and East Anglia contained two-thirds of UK employment in R&D services in 1981, much of it concentrated in the South East of England outside Greater London: this area contained 45% of total employment in R&D services (Damesick, 1987). This, in turn, has contributed to high levels of product innovation by manufacturing establishments in the 'Sunbelt': Thwaites (1982) and Oakey et al (1980) have noted that it is common for the initial manufacture of new products to occur either on the same site as the R&D function or at a nearby location. Third, the 'Sunbelt' is a major concentration of producer services activity and has been the focus for a considerable amount of employment growth in producer services since the early 1970s, largely as a result of the decentralisation of activity from central London to freestanding towns and cities within a radius of about 150 km of the metropolitan area (Champion et al, 1987; Daniels, 1986; Gillespie and Green, 1987; Leyshon and Thrift, 1989). Last, the 'Sunbelt' contains a significant concentration of high-level corporate planning and control functions (Crum and Gudgin, 1977). The presence of corporate head offices and divisional offices is, in turn, one of the major factors in the concentration and growth of producer services and R&D activity in the south of England (Goddard, 1979; Marshall, 1985). The resultant concentration of high-earning professional and managerial workers in corporate offices and producer services industries (notably financial services) has also stimulated the expansion of consumer service industries in the 'Sunbelt' (Thrift et al, 1987).

A number of commentators have also emphasised the importance of social factors in accounting for the economic dynamism of the 'Sunbelt'. First, on account of its urban structure, which comprises smaller, non-industrialised settlements in extensive and open countryside, and the recreational opportunities provided by its countryside and coast, the 'Sunbelt' is widely regarded as a highly desirable location in which to live and work. Managerial, professional, and technical staff—whose skills are in short supply—have been able to exercise this residential preference, thus forcing firms and sectors that are dependent upon recruiting such staff to locate where these key workers wish to live and work (Damesick, 1987; Keeble, 1987). This, in turn, creates a cumulative and self-reinforcing process advantageous to employers and employees alike: employers are able to recruit skilled manpower from other firms and employees are able to advance their careers by moving to other firms without the need for residential movement (Damesick, 1987). Second, because of the absence of highly-unionised heavy industries the industrial relations climate is neither antagonistic nor burdened by inflexible working practices (Martin, 1988), making it particularly attractive to the new regime of flexible accumulation (Scott, 1988).

However, our understanding of the reasons for the growth of the UK 'Sunbelt' is deficient in several key respects. First, because they are derived largely from nationally-focused studies of the evolving UK space-economy, explanations for its growth are inevitably somewhat overgeneralised. Such studies tend to view the 'Sunbelt' as a homogeneous area in terms of its economic and social characteristics: consequently, there is little or no recognition of the variety of possible economic processes operating in different localities within the 'Sunbelt'. Yet, as Boddy and Lovering (1986, page 218) emphasise, there are a "variety of economic structure and generative processes" along the 'M4 Corridor'. Similarly, 'high-tech' development in Berkshire is significantly different from that in Cambridge (Hall et al, 1987; SQP, 1985; also, see Massey, 1988, pages 265–266). Major urban centres of southern England also exhibit differences in the processes of expansion in financial services (Leyshon and Thrift, 1989). Second, a disproportionate amount of attention has been devoted to the role of high-technology industries in the 'Sunbelt', despite the evidence that other sectors—notably services—have been responsible for most of its employment growth (Breheny et al, 1985; Boddy et al, 1986). Third, detailed studies of the economic expansion of localities within the 'Sunbelt' have been largely confined to the 'M4 Corridor'—notably, studies by Hall et al (1987) and Savage et al (1988) on Berkshire and by Boddy et al (1986) on Bristol—but also include studies of Newbury (MacGregor et al, 1986) and Slough (Dickens and Savage, 1988). Consequently, there is a tendency to equate the 'Sunbelt' to the 'M4 Corridor'. However, the 'M4 Corridor' is only one of a number of motorway growth-axes which form the 'Sunbelt'—albeit the largest and with the strongest image and identity. Others include the M11 from Hertfordshire to Cambridge, the southern stretches of the M25 and the M3/M27 corridor in Hampshire. The consequence of these shortcomings has been a tendency to provide an "overstylized description" (Townsend, 1986, page 530) of the growth of the UK 'Sunbelt'.

In this paper we seek to address all three of these shortcomings. First, by focusing on the Southampton city-region (figure 1) we provide an account of recent economic change in a previously unresearched part of the 'Sunbelt'. Second, we seek to compare industrial change in Southampton with other parts of southern England (notably Bristol and Reading) in order to highlight the diversity of economic processes operating in different localities within the 'Sunbelt'. Third, attention is not confined to the high-technology sector: we consider the role of both the manufacturing and the producer service sectors in the recent economic growth of the Southampton city-region.

In the following section we provide a brief overview of the economic and employment structure of the Southampton city-region and highlight the rapid growth of employment in the area during the 1970s and the continuing employment increase during the recession of the early 1980s. In subsequent sections, which are based largely on material derived from structured interviews with employers in the city-region, we examine recent employment trends in the major manufacturing and service sectors of

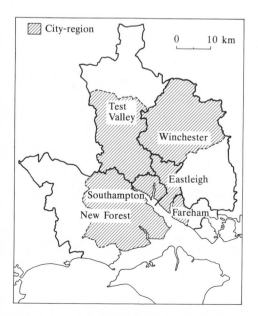

Figure 1. The Southampton city-region (post-1974 local authority boundaries).

the local economy in order to highlight some of the reasons for the extremely favourable economic performance of the Southampton city-region in the 1980s. In the concluding section we consider the extent to which the economic expansion of the Southampton city-region conforms to the conventional explanations for the growth of the UK 'Sunbelt' that have been outlined in this section of the paper.

3 The Southampton city-region: an economic and employment profile
3.1 Spatial definitions
The Southampton city-region (figure 1) is defined on the basis of journey-to-work flows as comprising the City of Southampton, the surrounding local authority districts of Eastleigh and Winchester and parts of New Forest (Totton and the Waterside parishes), Test Valley (Romsey), and Fareham (western wards) districts. Although the case for including some of the more peripheral areas as part of the city-region (for example, Fareham western wards) may be questionable on the basis of 1981 census journey-to-work flows, impressionistic evidence strongly suggests that the completion of the M27 motorway in 1984 and development of major new private-sector housing projects in a number of suburban locations within the city-region has significantly altered commuting patterns within this part of south Hampshire during the 1980s. Our definition of the city-region closely corresponds to the pre-1984 Southampton travel-to-work area (TTWA). However, with the change in the definition of TTWAs the city-region now approximates to the Southampton and Winchester TTWAs. In terms of the CURDS functional regions framework the city-region is broadly equivalent to the Southampton and Winchester local labour market areas (LLMAs) (Champion et al, 1987).

A strong case can be made for regarding the Southampton city-region as part of the 'Sunbelt'. First, as indicated by the earlier discussion, it is widely perceived to be part of the 'Sunbelt'. Second, at the county scale the large employment in high-technology industries and R&D services in Hampshire (Keeble, 1987) puts it unambiguously in the 'Sunbelt'. According to Hall et al (1987) Hampshire had the fourth largest number of high-technology jobs in 1981 (behind Greater London, West Midlands, and Hertfordshire), the eighth highest relative concentration of high-technology jobs (location quotient of 2.0), and the fourth highest absolute growth of high-technology employment between 1975 and 1981. Kelly (1987) further notes that Hampshire had the fourth largest number of computer manufacture jobs and the second largest number of computer software jobs (behind Greater London) in 1981. Third, Southampton and Winchester were both amongst the top ten LLMAs in terms of absolute employment growth between 1971 and 1981 (and Winchester was second in terms of its percentage increase). Moreover, Winchester had the lowest unemployment rate of any LLMA in 1981 (and was the only LLMA to record a *decrease* in unemployment between 1971 and 1981). Winchester was also top of the 'Mark One' index of local economic prosperity and in the top octile in the 'Mark Two' version (Champion and Green, 1988; Champion et al, 1987). Last, as a result of the escalating interest of property developers, institutional investors and high-technology firms in the M3/M27 corridor, this area is now attracting the volume of journalistic and academic interest that a few years previously was directed to the 'M4 Corridor' (Cooke, 1986b; *Financial Times*, 1985; 1986; 1988b; HCC, 1984; *Sunday Times*, 1986). Indeed, Hampshire has been described in recent estate-agent hyperbole as "the California of the UK" and the M27 corridor as "its Silicon Valley" (*Sunday Times*, 1986).

3.2 Data sources
This analysis is based primarily on material derived from structured interviews (using a combination of closed and open-ended questions) with senior managers at the Southampton establishments of approximately 100, mainly medium-sized or large, companies in the city-region, supplemented where available by financial and press analysis, annual reports, and other company literature. The sample of companies comprised independent businesses and subsidiaries of public companies, covered all of the major sectors of the local economy (manufacturing; port/transport/ shipping; retailing; financial services; leisure; public utilities) and included both private-sector and public-sector organisations. We also utilised two sources of aggregate statistics as background material: the Department of Employment's annual census of employment (the latest data available is for 1984) and the South Hampshire Establishment Databank which provides a comprehensive coverage of the manufacturing sector in 1979 and 1985.

3.3 Economic and social characteristics: an overview
Total employment in the Southampton city-region in 1984 was 235 712, 70% of which was in the service sector, compared with a national proportion of 65%. By comparison, the Bristol city-region had approximately 300 000 employees, of which 65% were in services (Boddy and Lovering, 1986). Five SIC 1980 divisions each accounted for over 5% of total employment (table 1): other services (predominantly public administration, defence, education, and health); distribution, hotels, and catering; metal goods, engineering, and vehicle industries; transport and communications; and banking, finance, insurance, business services, and leasing. However, only three of these industries—other services; transport and communications; and metal goods, engineering, and vehicle industries —are disproportionately concentrated in the Southampton city-region with location quotients greater than 1.0 (table 1).

Total employment in the city-region increased by over 35 000 between 1971 and 1981, an 18% increase, and by a further 3500 jobs between 1981

and 1984, whereas, nationally, employment declined in both periods
(figure 2). Southampton's employment growth during the 1970s compares
particularly well with Bristol—widely regarded as the archetypal 'Sunbelt
City'—which experienced a modest decline in employment between 1971
and 1981 (all of which occurred between 1978 and 1981) (Boddy and
Lovering, 1986; Boddy et al, 1986). The main source of employment
growth in Southampton has been the service sector which increased by

Table 1. Employment in the Southampton city-region, 1984. Source: DE, 1984.

Division	Employment		GB (%)	Location quotient
	no.	percent		
0 Agriculture, forestry, fishing	3579	1.5	1.7	0.88
1 Energy and water supply	5442	2.3	2.9	0.79
2 Extraction of minerals; manufacture of metals, mineral products, and chemicals	4418	1.9	3.8	0.50
3 Metal goods, engineering, and vehicle industries	35779	15.2	11.7	1.30
4 Other manufacturing industries	10818	4.6	10.1	0.46
5 Construction	10568	4.5	4.9	0.92
6 Distribution; hotels and catering	45731	19.4	20.1	0.97
7 Transport and communications	21059	8.9	6.4	1.39
8 Banking, finance, insurance, business services, and leasing	20974	8.9	9.5	0.94
9 Other services	77346	32.8	28.9	1.13

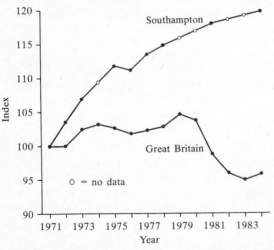

Figure 2. Index of employment change, 1971–84, for the Southampton city-region
and Great Britain. Source: Department of Employment "Census of Employment"
(Southampton data); *Employment Gazette*, various issues (national data).

over 48 000 jobs between 1971 and 1984, well over twice the national rate of increase (41% compared with 16%). There was an increase of 2500 manufacturing jobs in the city-region between 1971 and 1978 (4%)—a remarkable trend when set against the 10% decline in manufacturing employment nationally over the same period—but a loss of 11 500 manufacturing jobs between 1978 and 1984: nevertheless, this represented a considerably slower rate of decline than nationally (− 18.5% compared with − 25.2%). Moreover, the effects of the recession were felt much later in Southampton than in many other parts of the country: the rate of job loss in manufacturing was half the national rate between 1978 and 1981 (− 8.0% compared with − 14.9%) whereas between 1981 and 1984 the two rates were almost identical (− 11.4% in the Southampton city-region compared with 12.1% nationally). Manufacturing has therefore declined as a proportion of total city-region employment from 31% in 1971 to 28% in 1978 and to 22% by 1984, whereas services have expanded from 59% to 70% between 1971 and 1984.

These divergent sectoral trends have had a significant effect on the gender distribution of employment. There was an increase of 5500 males in employment between 1971 and 1984, a 4.3% increase, whereas female employment expanded by 33 500, a 48.5% increase. Thus, by 1984 females accounted for 43.5% of employees in the Southampton city-region compared with 35.1% in 1971. Almost half of all females in employment in 1984 were in the other services division.

In terms of socioeconomic structure (table 2) the city-region has above average proportions of professional workers, clerical and administrative workers, and unskilled and semi-skilled workers, whereas skilled manual workers are underrepresented. The socioeconomic structure of the Southampton city-region is similar to that of Avon, but dissimilar to that of Berkshire which has a higher proportion of nonmanual workers— especially in the higher-status managerial and professional occupations.

Table 2. Socioeconomic structures (expressed as a percentage of economically active people) of the Southampton city-region, Berkshire, and Avon. Sources: Boddy et al, 1986; 1981 Census of Population).

Profession (SEG)	Southampton city-region	Berkshire	Avon	England and Wales
Employers and managers (1, 2)	11.6	14.5	11.5	11.4
Professional workers (3, 4)	4.3	5.9	4.8	3.7
Clerical and administrative (5, 6)	32.7	34.5	33.5	30.5
Skilled manual (8, 9, 12)	22.8	20.4	23.5	24.2
Unskilled manual (7, 19, 11)	22.8	19.9	21.2	19.9
Armed forces and inadequately described	5.8	4.8	5.5	10.3

The size and structure of Southampton's 'service class' also differs from other localities within the 'Sunbelt' (table 3). The proportion of the economically active population in Southampton in the service class is above the national average but smaller than in Berkshire and Avon. The composition of the service class is similar in Southampton and Avon, but differs from Berkshire. The distinctiveness of Berkshire lies in the predominance of professional rather than managerial workers, especially those working in management, government, and scientific occupations. Berkshire is, however, close to the national average for managerial groups and professionals in the service sector (Savage et al, 1988). In contrast, the largest element of the service class in the Southampton city-region is professional occupations in services. The proportion of professionals in management, government, and scientific occupations in Southampton is less than in Berkshire but nevertheless above the national average, whereas its proportion of workers in managerial occupations is similar to Berkshire.

Unemployment in the city-region is well below the national average. In July 1988 the unemployment rate was 6.6% in the Southampton TTWA and 2.6% in the Winchester and Eastleigh TTWA, compared with a national figure of 8.0%. However, as this contrast in unemployment rates in the two travel-to-work areas which comprise the city-region indicates, all parts of the city-region have not shared equally in the growth in employment—and, indeed, the general economic prosperity—of the area. There is a marked divergence between the City of Southampton and the rest of the city-region both in job losses and in new employment growth (tables 4 and 5). Moreover, the unemployment rate (April 1988) in the three inner-city wards of Southampton ranged from 15% to 21%, two to three times above the city-region average. Southampton City Council (SCC, 1986) has recently documented the existence of significant pockets of poverty in the City of Southampton.

Table 3. The 'service class' (given as a percentage of economically active people) in the Southampton city-region, Berkshire, and Avon. Sources: 1981 Census of Population 10% tables; Savage et al, 1988.

Profession	Southampton city-region	Berkshire	Avon	England and Wales
Professionals in management, government	4.1	6.1	4.4	3.1
Professionals in services	8.2	7.6	8.9	7.6
Literary, artistic	0.9	1.1	1.0	1.0
Professionals in science	5.4	6.7	5.6	4.0
Managerial	9.4	9.9	9.7	9.2
Total service class	28.0	31.4	29.6	24.9

Note: figures relate to place of work.

Table 4. Redundancies and new jobs: April 1986 to June 1988. Source: Southampton City Council Press Monitoring Service.

Region	Redundancies	New jobs
City of Southampton	3608	1841
Rest of city-region	2311	3273
Total	5919	5114

Table 5. Employment change in manufacturing in the Southampton city-region, 1979–85. Source: South Hampshire Establishment Databank.

Region	Employment		Change, 1979–85	
	1979	1985	number	percent
City of Southampton				
inner Southampton	11 522	6 744	−4 778	−41.5
rest of City	14 699	10 161	−4 538	−30.9
total	26 221	16 905	−9 316	−35.5
Rest of city-region	31 795	26 696	−5 099	−16.0
Total in city-region	58 016	43 601	−14 415	−24.8

4 Trends in manufacturing

4.1 Aggregate employment trends, 1979–85

The best perspective on the characteristics of the manufacturing sector in the Southampton city-region and the nature of manufacturing employment decline since the late 1970s is provided by the South Hampshire Establishment Databank which contains information on the location, industry (1968 SIC), employment, and ownership of all manufacturing establishments in the city-region in either 1979 or 1985. In addition, each establishment has been classified according to whether it was an opening, a closure, or a survivor over this period: this allowed the components of change (Lloyd and Mason, 1978) to be identified. The data is derived from the records of the Health and Safety Executive, supplemented by ownership information from business directories, and although the records have been subjected to extensive verification and 'cleaning' it nevertheless suffers from the generic disadvantages of this source (see Thompson, 1983).

The Southampton city-region (see figure 1) lost 14 415 manufacturing jobs between 1979 and 1985, a decline of almost one-quarter of its work force. However, the steepness of this decline in employment was not matched by the decline in the number of establishments, which fell by 18.5%, from 800 to 652. Manufacturing decline has been concentrated in the City of Southampton, and particularly in the inner area of the City (table 5). Inner Southampton, defined as the edge of the continuously built-up area in 1914, lost over 40% of its manufacturing jobs between

1979 and 1985 compared with 30% in the rest of the City of Southampton and 16% in the remainder of the city-region.

Employment in manufacturing in the Southampton city-region is concentrated in three sectors—electrical engineering (including electronics), vehicles (including aerospace, hovercraft, and railway engineering), and shipbuilding and marine engineering—with two further industries (the food, drink, and tobacco industry and the mechanical engineering industry) also providing significant sources of employment (figure 3). These five industries accounted for 72% of total manufacturing employment in 1979. The electrical engineering industry lost 17% of its employment between 1979 and 1985; each of the other dominant sectors contracted by at

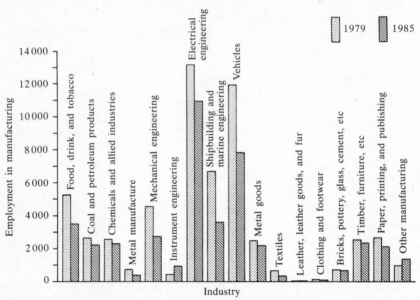

Figure 3. Employment change in manufacturing in the Southampton city-region, 1979–85, by industry. Source: South Hampshire Establishment Databank.

Table 6. Employment change in manufacturing in the Southampton city-region by industry, 1979–85. Source: South Hampshire Establishment Databank.

1968 SIC	Industry	Employment		Change, 1979–85	
		1979	1985	number	percent
IX	Electrical engineering	13124	10936	−2188	−17
XI	Vehicles	11907	7801	−4106	−34
X	Shipbuilding	6668	3591	−3077	−46
III	Food, drink, tobacco	5283	3507	−1776	−34
VII	Mechanical engineering	4535	2717	−1818	−40
	Other manufacturing	16499	15049	−1302	−8
	All manufacturing	58016	43601	−14415	−25

least one-third (table 6). By 1985 these five leading sectors together
accounted for only 65% of total manufacturing employment.
'High-technology' industry is an integral part of the image and
reputation of the 'Sunbelt'. As noted above, the 'Sunbelt' is the major
locational focus for such industries in the United Kingdom, although they
are neither a major source of jobs nor do they account for a significant
proportion of the employment growth in the area. Boddy and Lovering
(1986) have defined high-technology industries as comprising:
  pharmaceutical chemicals and preparations (MLH 272),
  scientific and industrial instruments and systems (354),
  telegraph and telephone apparatus (363),
  radio and electronic components (364),
  broadcasting equipment (365),
  electronic computers (366),
  radio, radar, and electronic capital goods (367),
  aerospace equipment (383).
On this basis, high-technology industries have become relatively *more*
significant to the Southampton economy over time, their share of total
manufacturing employment increasing from 18% to 21% between 1979
and 1985. In addition, there has been a slight increase in the number
of high-technology establishments (table 7). Nevertheless, employment in
high-technology industries has *declined* by over 1000 jobs during this
period, although this represented an 11% loss compared with a contraction

Table 7. High-technology employment in the Southampton city-region. Source:
South Hampshire Establishment Databank.

1968 SIC	Industry	Employment		Change, 1979–85	
		1979	1985	number	percent
272	Pharmaceutical chemicals and preparations	796	851	55	6.9
354	Scientific and industrial instruments and systems	229	398	169	73.8
363	Telegraph and telephone apparatus and equipment	0	0	0	0.0
364	Radio and electronic equipment	3698	3765	67	1.8
365	Broadcast receiving and sound reproducing equipment	450	370	−80	−17.8
366	Electronic computers	23	122	99	430.4
367	Radio, radar, and electronic capital goods	2895	2296	−599	−20.7
383	Aerospace equipment manufacturing and repairing	2196	1361	−835	−38.0
Total in high-technology industries		10287	9163	−1124	−10.9

of 28% in the rest of the manufacturing sector. The bulk of the job losses in the high-technology sector have occurred in just two industries—aerospace (which also includes the manufacture of hovercraft), and radio, radar, and electronic capital goods. The remaining high-technology industries *increased* their employment by around 400 jobs (8%) (table 7).

It is not possible to make a detailed comparison of the high-technology sectors in Southampton and Bristol on account of the different data sources used. Nevertheless, two contrasts are clear from even a broad-brush comparison. First, high-technology employment is relatively more significant in Bristol: Boddy et al (1986, pages 30–31) report that high-technology industry accounted for around 29% of Bristol's manufacturing jobs in 1981. Second, Southampton has a more diversified high-technology sector: aerospace accounted for 88% of all high-technology jobs in Bristol in 1981 (Boddy et al, 1986).

The most significant feature of manufacturing decline in Southampton in the period 1979–85 is that it has occurred without large-scale plant closures. The components of change employment accounts for the city-region (figure 4) show that by far the main source of job loss has been in

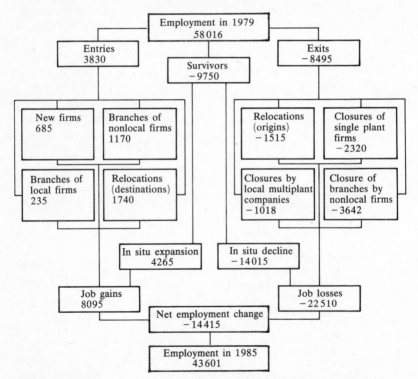

Figure 4. The components of employment change in manufacturing in the Southampton city-region, 1979–85. Source: South Hampshire Establishment Databank.

been in situ decline: labour shedding by establishments that were in existence in both 1979 and 1985 resulted in the loss of over 14 000 jobs, twice the number of jobs that were lost through plant closures. It is also apparent from the employment accounts that sources of new jobs in manufacturing have been extremely limited: the surviving establishments which expanded their employment between 1979 and 1985 only created a little over 4000 jobs, branch plant openings (predominantly by non-locally-owned companies which were present in the city-region in 1979) added a further 1400 jobs, and new manufacturing firms contributed just 685 jobs.

Southampton's manufacturing sector is characterised by an extremely top-heavy plant size structure (figure 5). Small establishments dominate in numerical terms although their contribution to employment is modest: in 1985, 81% of establishments had fewer than 50 employees but accounted for only 17% of all manufacturing jobs. Conversely, just 2% of establishments, each with 500 or more employees, provided 47% of manufacturing jobs in the city-region in 1985. It is these "prime movers" (Lloyd and Reeve, 1982) which have been responsible for the bulk of the manufacturing job losses. The fifteen largest employers in 1979 provided over 31 000 jobs (figure 6), 54% of the city-region total (the top five accounted for 29% of total manufacturing employment). All of these establishments survived to 1985, in each case with a reduced labour force, although there have been considerable variations in both the absolute and the relative rate of job loss (figure 6). The combined work force of these establishments in 1985 was 11 000 less than in 1979 (− 35%), equivalent to over three-quarters of the net job loss in manufacturing in the city-region between 1979 and 1985.

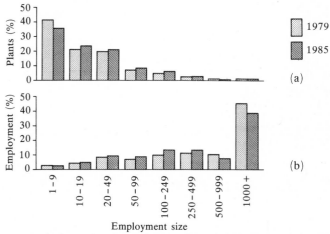

Figure 5. Plant-size distribution in manufacturing in the Southampton city-region, 1979 and 1985, for (a) establishments, and (b) employment. Source: South Hampshire Establishment Databank.

The large job losses which have resulted from in situ decline in the city-region is confirmed by our interview survey. The forty manufacturing organisations covered by the survey (two of which were freestanding R&D establishments), which included twenty-seven of the thirty largest manufacturing establishments in the city-region in 1985, shed approximately 7000 jobs between 1981 and 1987, a 21% decline.

The nature of manufacturing decline in the Southampton city-region, involving widespread labour shedding by almost all of the large establishments but no large plant closures, has mitigated the adverse impacts on the labour market of the large decline in employment in four key respects. First, the majority of companies have shed jobs gradually and in small batches, often extending over one or more years. For example, Pirelli General shed 1500 jobs between 1981 and 1987, but only involving a maximum of 200 redundancies at any one time, and the loss of over 2000 jobs at Ford's transit van plant has involved a steady trickle of job losses with a maximum of 100 at any one time. Second, a substantial proportion of the job losses have been achieved through voluntary redundancies; Ford achieved all of the job losses at its transit van plant without resorting to compulsory redundancies, and the warship builders Vosper Thornycroft, whose work force has declined from 3900

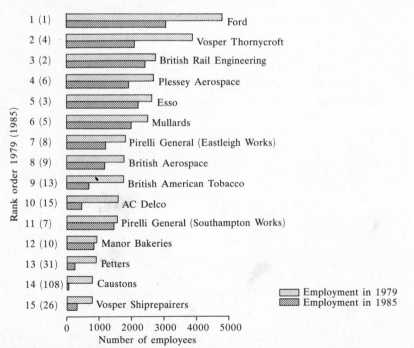

Figure 6. Employment change in the largest manufacturing establishments in the Southampton city-region, 1979 and 1985. Source: South Hampshire Establishment Databank.

to 1200 by means of over a dozen separate redundancy exercises, has only had to resort to declaring any compulsory redundancies in its two most recent labour shedding rounds. Many other companies also reported no shortage of workers willing to take voluntary redundancy. This implies that many of the workers made redundant from the manufacturing sector have been 'self-selecting', possibly either because they had another job lined up or else they planned to take early retirement. Certainly, many firms structured their redundancy packages to favour older (+ 50 years old) workers, and anecdotal evidence suggests that many younger workers who volunteered for redundancy did so in order to become self-employed. A case study of redundancies at BAT Industries' Southampton factory noted that 42% of the workers who left the company under a voluntary redundancy scheme had subsequently withdrawn from the labour market, primarily through retirement (Mason and Pinch, 1988). Third, because of the often protracted time-scale over which job losses have occurred many firms have been able to achieve part of their desired employment cutbacks through alternative means, notably nonreplacement, early retirements, and, to a lesser extent, redeployment (usually after retraining) and transfer. Last, in a few cases firms have taken back some workers which they had previously made redundant following an upturn in the level of their business activity. The nature of manufacturing decline in the Southampton city-region has therefore enabled the local labour market to adjust more easily to the scale of job losses than in areas where industrial decline has been dominated by plant closures.

4.2 Product changes in manufacturing
A second important aspect of the change in manufacturing in the Southampton city-region has been changes in the product base of many companies. Over three-quarters of companies in the survey (thirty-one out of forty) reported that they had made "significant" additions to their product range since 1981. Moreover, in only three cases were these product changes limited *exclusively* to a modification of their existing products: these included Ford's restyled transit van, a meat producer's diversification of its meat products, and a carpet manufacturer's introduction of new designs and colours of carpets. Thus, about 70% of firms had made genuine additions to their product base, just over half of which involved moves into new markets.

These products have been introduced from one of three sources. First, thirty of the manufacturing firms in the survey undertake at least some on-site research, development, and design, although with a strong emphasis on development, and in a number of cases this has been the source of the new product. Second, in at least four cases, new products have been transferred from other plants within the company (in each case located elsewhere within the South East region). These findings therefore fully support CURDS studies which show first that there is a strong relationship between product innovation and on-site R&D activity (Thwaites, 1982), and second that transfers of new products within multiplant companies occur predominantly within the South East (Oakey et al, 1980). However, seven companies in our survey (five of them in electronics) obtained at least some of their new products through acquisition—a source not identified in the CURDS studies (although this is likely to reflect their focus on innovative products): this included the acquisition of specific products from other companies, acquisition of the rights to products of companies in receivership, and the transfer of products from newly acquired companies to Southampton. Many of these product acquisitions were local; almost all of the nonlocal acquisitions involved products which were previously manufactured by companies located in the Midlands and northern regions of England.

Many of the product additions of Southampton-based manufacturing firms were unremarkable. For example, a domestic furniture manufacturer included the production of bedding and office furniture, Solent Flour Mills added brown flour to its product range, British Bakeries added a range of new "morning goods" (rolls and scones) plus a new branded white bread, Dimplex added a range of metal fan-heaters to its range of storage heaters and oil-filled radiators, and Dreamland diversified from the manufacture of electric blankets to include the production of electric duvets and physio-pads. However, there were a number of examples, particularly in the electronics and chemicals industries, of much more significant product changes involving major increases in the technological sophistication of the firm's product base and, as a result, a move into higher-value products. In some cases this was accompanied by the dropping of mature, standardised products.

The electronics industry provides three examples of this process. Mullard (part of Philips) has increased its production of electro-optic detectors—now its primary product area—and has introduced new types of application-specific integrated circuits (for example, for compact discs and teletext). At the same time, production of metal transistors and other basic electronic components, which had previously been the plant's main products, were transferred to the Philippines and Hong Kong. The plant has therefore shifted to higher-value products and its technological profile has been enhanced. Pirelli General, with three plants in the city-region, has invested in a sophisticated new factory to manufacture fibre-optic cables for the telecommunications industry (under licence from a Japanese company) and introduced fire-resistant cables and a range of other special cable products that were developed by its R&D unit which is based in the city-region. It has also transferred the manufacture of plastic cables—a standard product with no scope for technological enhancement and thus competing on price—from Southampton to a new, highly automated plant in South Wales. This plant also has a very high-level of flexible working practices (Leadbeater, 1988).

The development of digital fibre-optic systems in the telecommunications industry has also resulted in a dramatic change in manufacturing activity at Standard Telephones and Cables plant in Southampton, involving a shift out of analogue cable manufacture and into fibre-optic cable manufacture. All of these changes have had significant impacts on the numbers employed, working practices, the skill composition, and, in the case of Mullard, the gender composition of the work force of the companies involved (see Witt et al, 1988).

The chemical industry also provides examples of this process. Three major chemical plants in the city-region have each undergone a significant transformation of their product base. Hythe Chemicals, part of BP, has switched during the 1980s from a bulk chemicals producer to a manufacturer of speciality chemicals following the establishment of a separate Specialities Directorate within BP Chemicals in response to the global overcapacity in commodity chemicals in the early 1980s. Consequently, the plant is now manufacturing products which are nearer to the end-user rather than at an intermediate or early stage in the production process and are sold in growing niche markets rather than mass markets whose growth has reached a plateau. Exxon Chemicals has similarly shifted the emphasis of its Fawley plant away from basic chemicals and towards specialised chemical products which are more profitable and face less competition. Its only other UK plant, at Mossmorran in Scotland, is largely a producer of basic chemicals. Third, Borden Chemicals has introduced new speciality chemicals products through its own on-site R&D efforts. Indeed, most of the products manufactured at its Southampton plant are now speciality chemicals whereas its plant at Peterlee in North East England—which is much more capital intensive—is a bulk chemicals producer. Although each company has reduced the size of its Southampton work force during the 1980s, both the scale of the job losses and the changes in work force composition which have resulted from these product changes have been much less dramatic than those resulting from similar product changes in the electronics industry.

4.3 Defence-oriented manufacturing

It is widely argued that defence expenditure—notably the procurement of defence equipment—has played a major role in the relative economic prosperity of the 'Sunbelt' (Hall et al, 1987; Lovering, 1985). Lovering and Boddy (1988) estimate that defence procurement accounts for one in nine manufacturing jobs in both the South East and the South West, and they go on to argue that "the areas which are economically buoyant, the 'M4 Corridor', the 'Outer South East arc' and the emergent 'M11 Corridor', are those which have benefitted disproportionately from military spending" (page 48). Hall et al (1987) provide survey evidence which shows that 40% of high-technology firms in Berkshire sell more than 20% of their output to the Ministry of Defence.

However, this association between defence procurement and local economic prosperity is not found in the Southampton city-region (table 8). Although 40% of manufacturing organisations in the survey make sales to the Ministry of Defence—in both 'high-tech' and 'low-tech' sectors (for example, cigarettes, bedding, vehicles)—the level of dependence upon military sales is very low. Only four of the forty manufacturing organisations surveyed (10%) derive over 20% of their sales from the Ministry of Defence (electronics, aerospace, antennas, warships, and minehunters) and only one organisation makes over half of its sales to the Ministry. Even in high-technology sectors, only 19% of firms derive over 20% of their sales from the Ministry of Defence—well below the proportion reported by Hall et al (1987) for Berkshire. The dependence of Southampton's manufacturing sector on the Ministry of Defence is also much lower than in Bristol: Lovering (1985) describes the Bristol region as "the most defence-dependent area in the United Kingdom" (page 95).

Table 8. Sales by manufacturing establishments in the Southampton city-region to the Ministry of Defence (MoD). Source: interview survey.

Industry	Sales to MoD (percentage of total output by value)				
	0	not significant	5-20	21-50	>50
Electronics (n = 19)	11	4	2	1	1
Other industries (n = 21)	13	5	1	2	0
All industries (n = 40)	24	9	3	3	1

5 Trends in the service sector
5.1 Introduction
As noted earlier in this paper, employment growth in the Southampton city-region in the late 1970s and 1980s has been primarily a result of the expansion of the service sector. In this respect, the Southampton city-region is no different from other parts of the 'Sunbelt' such as Bristol (Boddy et al, 1986) and Berkshire (Breheny et al, 1985). However, again in line with other areas, by no means all parts of the service sector have expanded during the 1980s. In particular, the Port of Southampton has shed 1400 jobs between 1981 and 1987 as a result of loss of trade (container traffic and passenger ferries), the introduction of new cargo handling technologies, the changing nature of port traffic, and changing working practices. The decline of the port has also had knock-on effects on various port-serving activities such as tugs, road haulage, the freightliner operation, and customs: moreover, even new port-related

activities such as motor vehicle imports have shed labour. The public sector has also shed about 3500 jobs (-7%) between 1981 and 1987 (Mason et al, 1988).

The size of the service sector, its establishment size-structure, and its heterogeneity made it impossible for us to replicate in the survey the coverage that was achieved for the manufacturing sector (which included companies employing over 60% of the 1985 work force in manufacturing). The survey therefore includes companies that are significant employers and broadly representative of the major service-sector industries in the city-region; however, it is important to emphasise that no attempt was made to interview all firms over a certain size, as this would not have provided sufficient coverage of all of the major service-sector industries. (In any case, we could not identify any comprehensive listing which ranked service-sector companies by size of employment.) This approach gave us a sample of fifty-nine firms/organisations, comprising ten companies in the port/transport/shipping sector, fourteen retailers, thirteen financial-services firms, eight firms in the leisure sector, and fourteen public-utilities/public-sector establishments. Local government, the local health authority, and some miscellaneous companies (for example, private hospitals, cleaning, catering, and security firms) were also interviewed either as part of a related project (Mason et al, 1988) or for contextual purposes.

Much of the expansion of service-sector employment in Southampton is simply a function of the rapid growth and relative affluence of the area. Rapid population growth as a result of major new housing developments in the city-region has led directly, although not proportionately, to employment growth in various population serving services such as gas, electricity, telephones, and post: for example, one additional postman is needed for every five-hundred new homes. However, in many cases these increases in employment have simply offset job losses resulting from technological changes and productivity gains. Of greater significance has been the wealth effect: anecdotal evidence from public-utilities and financial-service companies all indicate that the volume of business being administered in their Southampton region is significantly higher than in northern regions, which in turn translates into additional staff requirements. Indeed, the manager of one insurance company which sells up-market policies dismissed the company's branch offices in Leeds and Manchester as "nice hobbies".

Nevertheless, growth and wealth effects provide only a partial explanation for the expansion of the service sector in the Southampton city-region. Moreover, these factors are common to all parts of the 'Sunbelt'. Both points are confirmed by Leyshon and Trift (1989) who note that financial and producer-service employment in Southampton—and also in Reading, Bristol, Brighton, and Norwich—is much greater than 'expected' given their prevailing levels of local consumer and business demand. A number of other processes have therefore also contributed to the growth of

service-sector employment in 'Sunbelt' localities. In the following sections
three of these processes which have particular relevance to Southampton
are examined: first, the growth of high-level corporate functions; second,
the establishment and development of regional branch offices; and third,
territorial reorganisation of networks of regional branch offices.

5.2 Growth of high-level corporate functions
Unlike many other parts of the 'Sunbelt', the Southampton city-region
does not have a major concentration of corporate head offices. Only six
of the *Times 1000* companies (1986–87) have their head offices in
Southampton. However, as four of these companies are UK subsidiaries
of foreign companies (three of which are US-owned and one Netherlands-
owned), Southampton is not the location of ultimate ownership and control.
Moreover, two of the three US-owned companies (all of which were
included in the survey) have an international product-division structure
in which their UK plants report to either a worldwide or a European
product group-headquarters. The UK subsidiary head office therefore
has very limited responsibility and status, and is in existence largely for
legal and accounting reasons.

Furthermore, a preoccupation with the location of corporate head
offices gives an extremely partial indicator of the location of corporate
higher-level management functions as it ignores divisional/subsidiary
management functions in manufacturing firms and regional management
functions in service-sector businesses. Given that many companies have
sought to decentralise decisionmaking and responsibility from corporate
head office to operating groups in recent years, it can be argued that
the location of corporate second-tier-management functions is now of
greater economic significance than the headquarters as a source of
employment and local multiplier effects.

In the case of the manufacturing sector, exactly half of the nonlocally-
owned firms (sixteen out of thirty-two) had on-site divisional or subsidiary
management functions, including five companies which were part of
holding company structures with no intermediate tier of management
between the subsidiary and the corporate headquarters. Moreover, five
companies have significantly *increased* the scale of their corporate
functions in the city-region during the 1980s: Plessey Aerospace became
a completely separate division in 1981; Plessey's three research
establishments were grouped into a separate division in 1983, with its
management based at Roke Manor near Romsey; Borden's PVC marketing
function was transferred from Bridgewater; the restructuring of BP
Chemicals (see above) involved the transfer of management, development,
and marketing staff from Geneva to the Hythe Chemicals plant; and
Warner-Lambert (a US-owned pharmaceuticals company) has transferred
its finance, personnel, and marketing functions from Pontypool (South
Wales) to Eastleigh. All of Warner-Lambert's UK headquarters functions—

which previously had been split between Eastleigh and Pontypool—are now concentrated in Eastleigh. The company has subsequently relocated *all* of its manufacturing operations from Eastleigh to Pontypool and the factory has been demolished to make way for an office block to house the company's enlarged UK headquarters.

Accompanying this growth of higher-level corporate functions in Southampton's manufacturing sector during the 1980s has been an increase in management autonomy and greater local discretion in many other local companies as a result of corporate decisions to decentralise responsibilities to subsidiaries and operating divisions. However, this has been offset by the loss of autonomy by local subsidiaries of some US-owned companies—particularly those with their UK headquarters in the city-region—as these companies have reorganised on a European or global basis into international business divisions/groups.

The Southampton city-region is also quite well endowed with higher-level corporate functions of service-sector companies. First, in contrast to the manufacturing sector, a relatively high proportion of service-sector companies are a product of local entrepreneurship and are still locally-owned and managed and thus contain a range of managerial functions. These include companies engaged in shipping, road haulage, retailing, and leisure. By far the largest of these companies is Leading Leisure Plc, a company which is quoted on the over-the-counter market: it was established in 1981 and by 1986/87 had a turnover of £35m, with interests in gaming (casinos, bingo halls, a chain of bookmakers); pubs, discos, and hotels; event catering; security products; and construction. About one-third of its 1500 employees are in the Southampton city-region, including 100 at its head office. TVS Plc (a *Times 1000* company) also has its headquarters in Southampton. It won the independent television franchise for the south of England in 1981 and acquired television studios in Southampton from the previous franchise holder.

Second, eleven service-sector companies in the survey have their head offices in the city-region. However, as in the case of manufacturing, the majority of these companies are subsidiaries of other companies, so the Southampton head office is not the location of ultimate ownership and control. Two insurance companies—Bishopsgate and Skandia—which are subsidiaries of Dutch and Swedish companies, respectively, have their head offices in the city-region. Bishopsgate relocated from London to Southampton in two stages during the 1970s. Skandia was founded in Southampton in the late 1970s, although its marketing and sales functions are based in London; thus, its Southampton office, although regarded as its head office, is in reality performing 'back office' functions. However, the company plans to move all of its London staff to Southampton in 1989. Two port-related companies with their head offices in Southampton are ACT Services Ltd and World Shipping and Freight Ltd; both are owned by consortia of other companies, thus limiting their operational autonomy. The Ordnance Survey also has its head office in Southampton; however, as part of the public sector its management have had to accept government controls on costs, manpower ceilings, and demands for greater value for money. Another company with its head office in Southampton is ARC Marine: however, it is owned by ARC Ltd which, in turn, is a subsidiary of Consolidated Gold Fields. Last, two retail companies—B&Q (a DIY chain) and Sperrings (a chain of convenience stores)—also have their head offices in Southampton. Both companies were started in Southampton by local entrepreneurs and began their initial rapid growth while still owned and managed by their founders. They subsequently sold out to large companies—in the case of B&Q to Woolworths and in the case of Sperrings to Circle K. Since our survey was completed exactly the same process has occurred with Share Drug Stores, which was founded by another innovative Southampton retailing entrepreneur. The company, which was quoted on the Unlisted Securities Market, has also been acquired by Woolworths. The head offices of both B&Q and Sperrings (since renamed Circle K) have been retained in Southampton; indeed, the postacquisition expansion of both companies (in the case of B&Q from 52 stores in 1981 to 201 in early 1987) that was facilitated by the injection of new capital by the parent companies has resulted in a major expansion of head-office functions. Whether a similar process will occur in the case of Share Drug is less certain: Woolworths already owns Superdrug and Tip Top Drug Stores—two other chains of discount drug stores—(both through acquisition) and seem likely to absorb Share Drug into its Superdrug structure, as it did with Tip Top Drug Stores (*Financial Times*, 1988a).

   The acquisition of rapidly-growing independent companies and subsequent expansion of their head offices is also occurring in other parts of the service sector. For example, a firm of estate agents which was started in the Southampton city-region in 1967 has been acquired by Lloyds Bank through its Black Horse Agencies subsidiary and has merged with another south-coast estate agency that it acquired. The firm is now one of a number of operating subsidiaries within Black Horse Agencies but its head office, which as a result of the merger now oversees a substantially larger number of branches, remains in Southampton. Royal Insurance has acquired another, long-established, Southampton-based firm of estate agents and surveyors which operates throughout the south of England. Prior to this acquisition the company had restructured its grouping of autonomous partnerships covering different areas within the south of England into a limited company, and sold a minority stake to Royal Insurance in order to expand through acquiring other independent estate agents in the south of England. This process resulted in both an expansion and a centralisation of management support functions at its head office in Southampton. This office has now become the southern regional head office of Royal Life Estates.

The majority of the financial-services companies and utilities in the survey are regional or area offices. As in the case of manufacturing, these establishments have benefitted from a fairly general trend involving the decentralisation of decisionmaking away from the head office (Marshall, 1985): indeed, Barclays Bank has removed an entire layer of senior head-office management, giving its local area offices—of which Southampton is one—greater administrative and control functions. Insurance companies in our survey, plus the area/district offices of Southern Water and British Telecom have also increased their local autonomy as a result of corporate reorganisation and restructuring.

In summary, although the Southampton city-region contains few corporate head offices, it is nevertheless an important second-tier corporate control-point in the urban hierarchy, with a significant number of head offices of subsidiary companies, including UK subsidiaries of foreign-owned companies, divisional head offices, and regional offices. Moreover, its range of higher-level corporate functions has been enhanced during the 1980s as a result of three subtle and largely invisible processes. First, in manufacturing there has been an inward relocation of management functions as a result of corporate changes in divisional structures. Second, in retailing and, to some extent, financial services there has been a rapid expansion of locally-headquartered subsidiary companies acquired during the 1980s from their entrepreneurial founders. Third, most manufacturing and financial-services companies and public utilities have been given increased local autonomy as a result of a general decentralisation of decisionmaking within large corporate organisations.

5.3 Branch office establishment and growth

In many parts of the 'Sunbelt' the growth of service-sector employment is to a large extent a result of office decentralisation from London. For example, office firms moving out of London have generated considerable numbers of jobs in Reading, Bristol, Brighton, and Bournemouth – Poole (Leyshon and Thrift, 1989) as well as in smaller localities such as Cheltenham (Cowan, 1986), Basingstoke, and Swindon. Such decentralisation —which is largely associated with the relocation of 'back office' activities— has been motivated by the high costs of property and rising costs of labour in London and has been facilitated by advances in communications technology (Dowall, 1987; Nelson, 1986). In marked contrast, the expansion of the service sector in Southampton during the 1970s and 1980s owes very little to the decentralisation of offices from London (also, see Mason, 1981): indeed, our survey included only three service-sector firms—two shipping companies (ACT Services Ltd and P&O Cruises Ltd) and an insurance company (Bishopsgate Insurance)—which had decentralised from London to Southampton, in each case during the 1970s. At the time of the survey their combined office employment was just 500 jobs. Firms decentralising from London along a southwest axis have tended to favour Bournemouth–Poole and Portsmouth, and, more recently, Basingstoke rather than Southampton. Precisely why Southampton has been unattractive to office firms decentralising from London is unclear. However, the lack of office floorspace—reflecting the strict local authority planning policies of the late 1970s and early 1980s (Mason, 1981)—and poor motorway connections are likely to have been significant factors. The image of Southampton as simply a port (and the negative image created by the industrial relations problems of the port in the early 1980s) and the limited efforts (until recently) by the city to promote itself (in marked contrast to Portsmouth: see Riley and Smith, 1981) may have been additional contributory factors.

Whatever the precise reasons, the consequence has been that the recent growth of service-sector employment in Southampton is almost entirely a result of the establishment and growth of regional/area/branch offices of producer-service firms. Many firms have established branch offices in Southampton since the mid-1970s as a result of the expansion of the Solent region as a major area of business activity and, as noted in the previous section, as a centre for high-level corporate functions. For example, work by Leyshon et al (1987) and Morris (1988) on the geographical expansion of large accountancy firms reveals that most Southampton offices were established during the 1970s. These offices have expanded rapidly during the 1980s: for example, Price Waterhouse's Southampton office, which was established in 1975, has been upgraded from a half to a full practice during the 1980s, involving an increase in the number of partners from four to seven, a widening of the range of services offered, and an expansion in the number of staff from 60 to 110 between 1982 and 1987. The recent and planned future expansion in the number of hotels in the city-region is also related to the growing status of the Solent area as a business centre. All of the major hotels derive a very high proportion of their trade from business clients, often involving regular block bookings by major local companies; this include both accommodation and the hire of function rooms for conferences, training sessions, courses, and exhibitions. [For example, one hotel reported that over 90% of its (bed)room bookings were business-related

5.4 Territorial reorganisation

A third factor in the expansion of service employment in Southampton has been the recent practice of many large companies with a network of area or regional offices to consolidate this structure into a smaller number of larger spatial units through the merger of adjoining areas or regions. Where this has occurred, it has generally been to the benefit of Southampton and at the expense of other urban centres in southern England (for example, Portsmouth, Bournemouth). For example, a restructuring of the National Westminster Bank's regional and area office networks has involved a merger of the Southampton, Portsmouth, and Bournemouth areas, each of which had their own area office, with the regional office for this enlarged territory based in Southampton. In similar vein, a rationalisation of areas within the southern division of British Rail's Network South East has involved the Southampton area absorbing the Bournemouth area. However, not all territorial reorganisations have been to the benefit of the Southampton city-region: the restructuring of Southern Electricity's districts, involving a merger of the Lyndhurst and Test districts has involved a transfer of white-collar jobs from the city-region to Basingstoke.

Many companies adopt a two-tier administrative structure, comprising at the lowest level a network of areas, each with their own area office, which report to a second regional tier. Our survey noted a fairly consistent pattern amongst companies with this structure whereby the Southampton area was part of a southwest region controlled from Bristol. Examples include British Telecom, whose Southampton district is part of the South West region; BBC South, which is part of BBC South and South West; and the Southampton area of the National Westminster Bank, which is part of the South West England region; in each case the Southampton office reports to the regional office which is based in Bristol. Boddy et al (1986) have similarly highlighted Bristol's wider 'regional' function.

Thus, much of the recent growth in service-sector employment in the Southampton city-region reflects its expansion and consolidation as the major regional business and service centre in central southern England. However, Southampton differs from Bristol in that it is a second-tier centre in the 'Sunbelt', subservient to Bristol. It is also different from Reading which has less of a distinctive regional function. For example, Southampton contains a higher proportion of the leading accountancy firms than Reading (Leyshon et al, 1987; Morris, 1988), presumably because some companies serve the Reading area from their West London branch offices. Southampton also is in contrast to Bournemouth–Poole which is primarily a 'back office' location and has a very limited regional role.

6 Conclusion

The Southampton city-region has been a major employment growth area during the 1970s and 1980s despite major job losses in manufacturing and in the port and port-related industries. Indeed, the manufacturing sector has lost one-quarter of its employment between 1979 and 1985. The process of job loss in manufacturing has involved in situ decline by major employers rather than large-scale plant closures; this has enabled the local labour market to adjust more easily to the job losses. This shrinkage in Southampton's manufacturing base has been accompanied by quite significant changes in the characteristics of the manufacturing sector during the 1980s. First, 'high-tech' industry has become relatively more significant because of its slower rate of job loss than the rest of the manufacturing sector. Nevertheless, much of the manufacturing sector in the city-region continues to involve relatively basic, medium, and low-technology products which do not conform to the 'Sunbelt' stereotype. Second, a number of the major companies in the city-region have revitalised their operations in Southampton as a result of the introduction of more technologically sophisticated products and the withdrawal, or relocation to peripheral UK regions and Third World countries, of mature products. The consequence has been a substantial alteration in character, techno-logical profile, and operation of some of the major manufacturing establishments in the city-region in recent years. These changes have, in turn, seemingly improved the future prospects of these establishments but have also—perhaps less beneficially—resulted in a decline in the numbers employed and a shift in the composition of the work force in these plants, involving an increase in the proportion of skilled manual, professional, technical, and managerial occupations.

However, by far the main source of employment growth has been the expansion of the service sector. Southampton is not a major corporate headquarters location, nor has it attracted significant numbers of offices decentralising from London. Rather, growth in service-sector employment reflects three main processes: first, an increase in higher-level management functions in many establishments as a result of corporate restructuring; second, the establishment and expansion of branch offices of producer-services firms in response to the growth of the Solent region as a major area of business activity; and third, territorial reorganisation of regional branch networks and consolidation of the enlarged area/regional offices in Southampton at the expense of other cities in central southern England. The growth of service-sector employment in Southampton is therefore largely explained by two factors (following Leyshon and Thrift, 1989). First, it has benefitted from the growth of export-oriented service activities, notably those engaged in intraorganisation trading. Second, Southampton has increased in functional importance within south central England. The city-region therefore exemplifies what Leyshon and Thrift (1989, page 154) have identified as a "process of regional centralization ... which is pushing just one centre in a region to prominence above all others" and which they suggest is most clearly evident in the north of England.

Thus, although the recent expansion of the Southampton economy parallels the growth of other parts of the UK 'Sunbelt' there are never-theless significant features in its expansion which distinguishes it from other 'Sunbelt' localities and which conflict with the 'Sunbelt' stereotype. For example, the manufacturing sector is less orientated towards defence procurement, high-technology industry is less significant than in Bristol and Reading, and the contribution of office decentralisation to the expansion of the service sector has also been much more limited than elsewhere in the 'Sunbelt'. Southampton also has a distinctive position in the urban hierarchy of the south of England as a second-tier corporate control-point, subservient to Bristol, but with a much clearer regional function than many other 'Sunbelt' localities.

This study therefore confirms the operation of various macroscale processes which are contributing to economic growth throughout the UK 'Sunbelt'. However, it has added new detail to the economic processes at work in individual 'Sunbelt' localities and has highlighted the diversity of economic structure and economic growth processes within the 'Sunbelt' which should not be overlooked or downplayed for the sake of easy generalisations.

Acknowledgement. This research was funded by the Economic and Social Research Council (Ref: D00232180).

References
Boddy M, Lovering J, 1986, "High technology industry in the Bristol sub-region: the aerospace/defence nexus" *Regional Studies* **20** 217–231
Boddy M, Lovering J, Bassett K, 1986 *Sunbelt City? A Study of Economic Change in Britain's M4 Corridor* (Clarendon Press, Oxford)
Breheny M, Cheshire P, Langridge R, 1985, "The anatomy of job creation? Industrial change in Britain's M4 Corridor", in *Silicon Landscapes* Eds P Hall, A Markusen (Allen and Unwin, Hemel Hempstead, Herts) pp 118–133
Champion A, Green A, 1988 *Local Prosperity and the North–South Divide* (Institute for Employment Research, University of Warwick, Warwick)
Champion A, Green A E, Owen D W, Ellin D J, Coombes M G, 1987 *Changing Places: Britain's Demographic, Economic and Social Complexion* (Edward Arnold, London)
Cooke P, 1986a, "The changing urban and regional system in the United Kingdom" *Regional Studies* **20** 243–251
Cooke P, 1986b, "The genesis of high technology complexes: theoretical and empirical considerations", paper presented to the Anglo–American Workshop on The Growth and Location of High Technology Industry, Cambridge; copy available from P Cooke, Department of Town Planning, University of Wales at Cardiff, PO Box 906, Cardiff CF1 3YN
Cowan H, 1986, "Cheltenham: the impact of restructuring on a 'Sunbelt' town", paper presented to the Annual Conference of the Institute of British Geographers, University of Reading; copy available from School of Environmental and Planning Studies, Gloucestershire College of Arts and Technology, Oxstalls Lane, Gloucester GL2 9HW
Crum R E, Gudgin G, 1977 *Non-Production Activities in UK Manufacturing Industry* (Commission of the European Communities, Brussels)
Damesick P, 1987, "Regional economic change since the 1960s", in *Regional Problems, Problem Regions and Public Policy in the United Kingdom* Eds P Damesick, P Wood (Clarendon Press, Oxford) pp 19–41
Daniels P, 1986, "Producer services and the post-industrial space economy", in *The Geography of De-Industrialization* Eds R Martin, B Rowthorn (Macmillan, London) pp 291–321
DE, 1984 *1984 Census of Employment*, Department of Employment, unpublished data

Dickens P, Savage M, 1988, "The Japanization of British industry? Instances from a high-tech growth area" *Industrial Relations Journal* **19** 60–68

Dowall D E, 1987, "Back offices and San Francisco's office development growth cap" *Cities* **4** 119–127

Financial Times 1985, "Property along the M3", 14 June, pages 13–16

Financial Times 1986, "Property along the M3/M27", 25 July, pages 11–13

Financial Times 1988a, "Fashion fades for drugstore chains", 16 February, page 6

Financial Times 1988b, "Hampshire", 15 March, pages 18–22

Gillespie A E, Green A E, 1987, "The changing geography of producer services employment in Britain" *Regional Studies* **21** 397–411

Goddard J B, 1979, "Office development and urban and regional development in Britain", in *Spatial Patterns of Office Growth and Location* Ed. P Daniels (John Wiley, Chichester, Sussex) pp 29–60

Hall P, Breheny M, McQuaid R, Hart D, 1987 *Western Sunrise: The Genesis and Growth of Britain's Major High Tech Corridor* (Allen and Unwin, Hemel Hempstead, Herts)

HCC, 1984 *High Technology Industry in Hampshire* (Hampshire County Council, County Planning Department, The Castle, Winchester, Hants SO23 8UE)

Howells J R L, 1984, "The location of research and development: some observations and evidence from Britain" *Regional Studies* **18** 13–29

Kaldor M, Sharp M, Walker W, 1986, "Industrial competitiveness and Britain's defence" *Lloyds Bank Review* number 162, 31–49

Keeble D, 1987, "Industrial change in the United Kingdom", in *Industrial Change in the United Kingdom* Ed. W F Lever (Longman, Harlow, Essex) pp 1–20

Kelly T J C, 1987 *The British Computer Industry: Crisis and Development* (Croom Helm, Andover, Hants)

Kelly T, Keeble D, 1988, "Locational change and corporate organizations in high technology industry: computer electronics in Great Britain" *Tijdschrift voor Economische en Sociale Geografie* **79** 2–15

Law C M, 1983, "The defence sector in British regional development" *Geoforum* **14** 169–184

Leadbeater C, 1988, "High quality staff is crucial in plant where computers rule" *Financial Times* 12 November

Leyshon A, Daniels P W, Thrift N J, 1987, "Large accountancy firms in the UK: operational adaptation and spatial development", Working Papers on Producer Services, number 2, St David's College, Lampeter, and University of Liverpool copy available from N Thrift, Department of Geography, University of Bristol Bristol BS8 1SS

Leyshon A, Thrift N, 1989, "South goes north? The rise of the British provincial financial centre", in *The North–South Divide: Regional Change in Britain in the 1980s* Eds J Lewis, A Townsend (Paul Chapman, London) pp 114–156

Lloyd P E, Mason C M, 1978, "Manufacturing industry in the inner city: a case study of Greater Manchester" *Transactions of the Institute of British Geographers New Series* **3** 66–90

Lloyd P E, Reeve D E, 1982, "North West England 1971–1977: a study in industrial decline and economic restructuring" *Regional Studies* **16** 345–360

Lovering J, 1985, "Regional intervention, defence industries, and the structuring of space in Britain: the case of Bristol and South Wales" *Environment and Planning D: Society and Space* **3** 85–107

Lovering J, Boddy M, 1988, "The geography of military industry in Britain" *Area* **20** 41–51

MacGregor B, Langridge R J, Adley J, Chapman B, 1986, "The development of high technology industry in Newbury district" *Regional Studies* **20** 433–448

Marshall J N, 1985, "Business services, the regions and regional policy" *Regional Studies* **19** 353–363

Martin R, 1986, "Thatcherism and Britain's industrial landscape", in *The Geography of De-industrialisation* Eds R Martin, B Rowthorn (Macmillan, London) pp 238–290

Martin R, 1988, "The political economy of Britain's north–south divide" *Transactions of the Institute of British Geographers: New Series* **13** 389–418

Mason C M, 1981, "Service sector employment change and office development", in *Dimensions of Change in a Growth Area: Southampton since 1960* Eds C M Mason, M E Witherick (Gower, Aldershot, Hants) pp 75–100

Mason C, Pinch S, 1988, "A study of redundant workers in Southampton", University of Southampton Research Fund: grant completion report, mimeograph; copy available from the authors, Department of Geography, University of Southampton, Southampton SO9 5NH

Mason C, Pinch S, Chandler J, Witt S, 1988 "The public sector and employment creation in the Southampton city-region: a local jobs audit", report by the Economic Development Unit, Southampton City Council, Civic Centre, Southampton SO9 4XR

Massey D, 1984 *Spatial Divisions of Labour* (Macmillan, London)

Massey D, 1988, "Uneven development: social change and spatial divisions of labour", in *Uneven Re-Development: Cities and Regions in Transition* Eds D Massey, J Allen (Hodder and Stoughton, Sevenoaks, Kent) pp 250–276

Morris J L, 1988, "Producer services and the regions: the case of large accountancy firms" *Environment and Planning A* **20** 741–759

Nelson K, 1986, "Labour demand, labour supply and the suburbanization of low-wage office work", in *Production, Work, Territory: The Geographical Anatomy of Industrial Capitalism* Eds A J Scott, M Storper (Allen and Unwin, Hemel Hempstead, Herts) pp 149–171

Oakey R P, Thwaites A T, Nash P A, 1980, "The regional distribution of innovative manufacturing establishments in Britain" *Regional Studies* **14** 235–253

Riley R C, Smith J-L, 1981, "Industrialization in naval ports: the Portsmouth case", in *Cityport Industrialization and Regional Development: Spatial Analysis and Planning Strategies* Eds B S Hoyle, D A Pinder (Pergamon Press, Oxford) pp 133–150

Savage M, Dickens P, Fielding T, 1988, "Some social and political implications of the contemporary fragmentation of the 'service class' in Britain" *International Journal of Urban and Regional Research* **12** 455–476

SCC, 1986 *Poverty in Southampton* Chief Executive's Department, Southampton City Council, Civic Centre, Southampton SO9 4XR

Scott A J, 1988, "Flexible production systems and regional development: the rise of new industrial spaces in North America and western Europe" *International Journal of Urban and Regional Research* **12** 171–186

SQP, 1985 *The Cambridge Phenomenon: The Growth of High Technology Industry in a University Town* Segal Quince and Partners, Mount Pleasant House, Mount Pleasant, Cambridge

Sunday Times 1986, "The Solent fast lane to the future", 25 May, page 58

TA, 1988 *Labour Market Quarterly Report* July; Training Agency, Room W815, Moorfoot, Sheffield S1 4PQ

Thompson A, 1983, "The prospects for establishment-level databanks", in *Urban and Regional Industrial Research: The Changing UK Data Base* Ed. M Healey (Geo Books, Norwich) pp 65–90

Thrift N, Leyshon A, Daniels P, 1987, "'Sexy greedy': the new international financial system, the City of London and the South East of England", Working Papers on Producer Services, number 8, St David's University College, Lampeter, and University of Liverpool; available from Dr N Thrift, Department of Geography, University of Bristol, Bristol BS8 1SS

Thwaites A T, 1982, "Some evidence of regional variations in the introduction and diffusion of industrial products and processes within British manufacturing industry" *Regional Studies* **16** 371–382

Townsend A R, 1986, "The location of employment growth after 1978: the surprising significance of dispersed centres" *Environment and Planning A* **18** 529–545

Witt S, Mason C, Pinch S, 1988, "Industrial change in the Southampton city-region: a study of the electronics and electrical engineering industry", working paper, University of Southampton Urban Policy Research Unit; copy available from Department of Geography, University of Southampton, Southampton SO9 5NH

After 1992—The South East as a Frontier Region

R W VICKERMAN
The University of Kent at Canterbury

1 Introduction

1992 is set as the date by which the European Communities intend to have removed the remaining restrictions on trade between member countries and hence completed a Single European Market. Close examination of evidence on regional output data suggests that the lack of a true Single Market in all goods and services has had a depressing effect on the economies of those regions of member countries which lie alongside internal frontiers (CEC, 1987). This arises from the artificial restriction on the natural economic hinterland of the border region imposed by the frontier. The costs of trading across the frontier increase the effective economic distance between locations on either side of the frontier (Bröcker, 1980). The frontier thus casts what could be termed an 'economic shadow' on the regions either side. For the more peripheral countries such as the United Kingdom or Italy this effect is masked by the fact that the more prosperous regions of those countries are those closer to the economic centre of the Community. The natural shadow effect of the frontier is thus reduced when internal comparisons are made, although it is apparent, especially in the case of the United Kingdom, when cross-frontier comparisons are made.

In this paper I offer some preliminary analysis of the size of the effect of this frontier shadow and how the effects of changing the priorities of the Community policy after completion of the Single Market can be assessed. There is a concentration of internal frontiers at the geographical centre of the Community, covering Belgium, southern Netherlands, northern France, and South East England, which makes this a particularly interesting set of regions. However, the Community is also committed to a concentration of regional and other structural funds away from those more traditional depressed regions towards the poorest, southern regions. This implies that these central regions of the Community will need to look for possible differential benefits from the Single Market as compensation.

A further question is the difficulty of assessing likely future changes in competitiveness arising from improvements in international transport infrastructures, such as the Channel Tunnel. Furthermore, policies designed to promote transfrontier cooperation and programmes between regions in different Community countries will also have an effect on the future performance of frontier regions.

The remainder of this paper is in three sections. In the first of these I establish the nature of the problem facing internal border regions as evidenced by existing data, before outlining an analytical framework for understanding this problem more fully. In section 3 I take the two key factors of the Single Market and the Channel Tunnel to make a preliminary assessment of their likely effects on South East England. In the final section I raise two further issues, the question of fiscal harmonisation and cross-border shopping and the role of transfrontier programmes. I conclude with a brief summary of the likely influences on the South East of England after 1992 and the prospects for the region following on from this time.

2 Internal border regions

2.1 The nature of the problem

The core-periphery model of regional development offers an interesting case for application in the European Community. This model, dating from work by Myrdal (1957) and Hirschmann (1958), suggests that the 'core' of an economy grows faster than the 'periphery' because of a more rapid rate of technical progress and productivity growth. Innovations and productivity growth spread out from the core to the periphery, raising the rate of growth at the periphery. However, instead of producing an ultimate balance, growth at the periphery causes a 'backwash' effect on the core by increasing the demand for goods produced only in the core. This generates a cumulative process of growth. Such a model of development lies behind studies such as that by Keeble et al (1982a) which have emphasised the way that progressive reductions in the economic barriers presented by frontiers within the Community have led to increases in the economic potential of peripheral and more central regions. However, Keeble's work also shows that any notion of a 'golden triangle' in Europe has to be modified to allow for a rather hollow centre in economic terms. Analysis of data either of economic potential or of output per capita shows that there is an area of relatively low values in Belgium and North East France which lies close to the geographical centre of the Community and within a London-Frankfurt-Paris triangle. More detailed analysis of trade flows by Bröcker (1980) and Peschel (1985) and of passenger flows by Evers and Oosterhaven (1988) confirms the suspected importance of national frontiers in reducing flows and income levels. A contrasting view is that of Bröcker (1988) who suggests that, for Scandinavia at least, there is little evidence of such frontier effects having increased the economic divergence between core and periphery.

Figure 1 shows clearly for North West Europe that a combination of frontiers and natural barriers to transport has had a depressing effect on the economic status of frontier regions in Belgium and England. It is also necessary to take into account overall national differences in economic performance. Although the regions of North East France are relatively depressed in a national context, they are rather less depressed in a European context than neighbouring Belgian regions. What figure 1

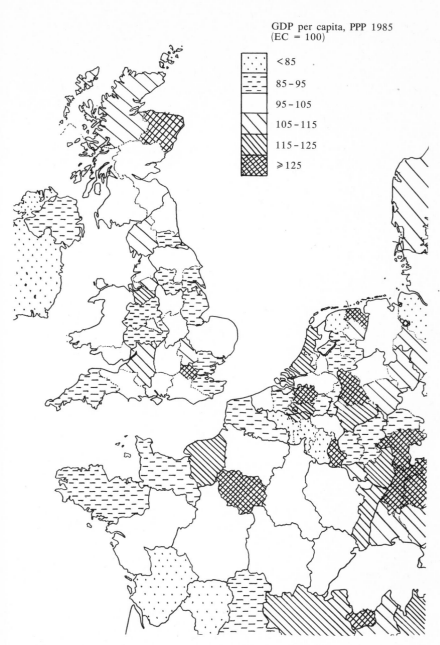

Figure 1. Regions of North West Europe, GDP per capita, 1985 [measured in terms of purchasing power parity (PPP)].

(see also table 1) also demonstrates is that in terms of 'Level Two' Regions, those subregions of South East England to the south and east of London have fared relatively badly in terms of their economic development. Kent and Essex, the two most easterly of these subregions, are not, by national standards, rich regions typical of the popular conception of South East England. County income statistics show that the same is also true of East Sussex. Part of this is an effect of commuting, as output figures are depressed by the large population which produces wealth in London However, the apparent nonuniformity of this in the South East suggests that there is also a problem of London commuters not spending their

Table 1. Details of 'Level Two' regions in proximity to the Channel Tunnel, 1985. Source: CEC, 1987.

Region	GDP[a]	SI[b]	Employment by sector (%)[c]		
			agric.	industry	service
Belgium	105	101	3.6	31.9	64.5
Antwerpen	131	120	2.9	36.6	60.5
Brabant	120	108	2.1	24.3	73.6
Hainaut	81	81	3.2	31.9	64.9
Liège	100	92	3.6	31.6	64.7
Limburg	92	78	2.5	39.6	58.0
Luxembourg	81	99	11.5	24.5	63.9
Namur	82	89	6.7	24.3	69.1
Oost Vlaanderen	94	101	3.1	35.4	61.5
West Vlaanderen	102	106	6.7	35.5	57.7
France	112	116	8.1	32.3	59.2
Île de France	163	152	0.5	29.2	70.0
Haute Normandie	118	104	4.9	39.0	55.8
Picardie	99	104	8.5	35.5	55.7
Champagne – Ardennes	109	112	14.2	35.5	50.2
Nord Pas-de-Calais	94	97	5.3	39.4	55.2
Netherlands	111	108	5.2	28.0	65.9
Zeeland	107	118	8.6	33.2	57.5
Noord Brabant	98	97	5.4	34.8	59.1
United Kingdom	104	100	2.3	34.1	61.9
Beds – Herts	106	114	1.4	39.4	59.2
Berks – Bucks – Oxon	103	110	1.7	31.7	66.6
Sussex – Surrey	96	118	2.2	26.7	71.1
Essex	91	108	2.0	35.6	62.3
Greater London	153	135	0.3	23.7	76.1
Hants – IoW	99	106	1.7	32.1	66.2
Kent	89	97	4.1	29.6	66.3

[a] GDP per capita (EC = 100).
[b] Synthetic index of GDP per capita, GDP per employee, and labour market conditions (EC = 100).
[c] Sectoral employment figures for UK regions are for 1981.
Note: agric. agriculture, Beds Bedfordshire, Herts Hertfordshire, Berks Berkshire Bucks Buckinghamshire, Oxon Oxfordshire, Hants Hampshire, IoW Isle of Wight

incomes in their home regions. Kent and Essex also have a high proportion of lower-income commuters attracted by lower house prices in the less environmentally attractive areas along the Thames Estuary, providing both industrial labour for East London and clerical labour for the City.

Apart from the locational effect and the impact of commuting, Kent is also atypical of the South East in terms of its economic structure, with relatively large primary and traditional manufacturing sectors and relatively underdeveloped new industrial or producer-service sectors (Vickerman, 1987a). Moreover, it has tended to lag behind regional growth rates in all of these sectors and has not shared in the boom in high-technology industries so typical of counties to the west and north of London. The nationally stagnant transport sector has been to some extent the most dynamic locally.

Despite the proximity to continental Europe, there has been little apparent generation of economic activity through membership of the Community, even given the enormous increase in traffic passing through the Kent ports. Less than 20% of Kent firms taking part in a 1987 survey had any sales in Europe and only 12% obtained any supplies from other European countries (for further details, see Henley et al, 1989). These figures are much lower than for the South East as a whole which is itself less oriented towards Europe in terms of trade than the average for the United Kingdom even after allowing for industrial structure (Chisholm, 1985; Hoare, 1985). Local unemployment in parts of Kent increased to levels reminiscent of conventional depressed regions in certain travel-to-work (labour market) areas, and the environment, and hence the attractiveness of the area for new development, has suffered from the increase in through traffic. This suggests the existence of what might be termed a 'corridor' effect, in which any improvements to the transport infrastructure make it less likely for a region to gain economic benefit. Some evidence of this exists for Autoroute developments in France (Bonnafous et al, 1975) and there are fears of a similar effect from high-speed rail developments in Belgium (Durieux, 1988). If we add to these effects the relative isolation from other UK markets and the importance of the domestic market for most firms, we have a region which is a frontier region both in the traditional sense of being peripheral and in the Community sense of being adjacent to an internal frontier.

If we widen the discussion to include the neighbouring continental regions then the importance of considering the interaction between the relative national and international situations of a region is clarified. There is a belt of old industrial regions running along the Franco – Belgian and Franco – German frontiers; Nord Pas-de-Calais, Champagne – Ardenne, and Lorraine in France, Hainault and Namur in Belgium, and Saarland in West Germany. Each of these regions occupies a relatively poor position within its own national context, being both peripheral and having unfavourable economic structures dominated by old, declining industries. Each is also a traditional major target for national regional policy measures, and hence for Community funds from the European Regional Development Fund (ERDF), despite being typically within one-half of one standard deviation of the Community average for most regional output indicators (CEC, 1987). The variations across the frontiers are, however, much more marked, with much lower values for Belgian regions than for the neighbouring French regions. This reflects the smaller size of the Belgian market, the relatively greater frontier effects this imposes, and the tendency for transport corridors in Belgium to be dominated by the needs of transit traffic (for further development of this point, see Vickerman, 1987b).

2.2 An analysis of the effects of existing internal frontiers

The traditional notion of a frontier effect in regional economics is that of the peripheral region, deprived of easy access to the major markets of an economy and suffering from the higher transport costs implicit in its location (for example, Friedmann, 1966; Perroux, 1961; Ullman, 1958). This stems essentially from a view of regional problems within a national economic context. The development of the European Community, in attempting to break down the rigidity of national frontiers, poses problems for this traditional type of regional analysis. The less important the national frontiers become, the more important it is to analyse regional problems in a cross-national framework.

Within a single nation state we do not have to worry about tariff or other, nontariff, barriers to trade—there is a single currency and no formal restrictions on the free movement of factors of production. Some distortions may arise because of deliberate policy interventions either by central or by local governments, but the analytical problem is clear cut: to explain why regional imbalances persist. In the international context, however, these further complications do have to be introduced and may be the major source of the cross-frontier variations between the regional indicators noted above. The question which has to be answered is how far does a removal of these frontier barriers lead to a situation which can be analysed in terms of conventional one-country regional analysis?

At a simple level, frontiers operate rather like transport costs. Conventional analysis either of economic potential or of flows uses the gravity model notion of a deterrence function. Keeble et al (1982b) used this to calibrate the apparent additional deterrence effect of Britain's island status. Bröcker (1980) demonstrated the deterrence effect of internal frontiers by comparing the parameters of the gravity model for internal interregional trade with those for cross-frontier trade to estimate the implied 'width of frontiers' in kilometres.

The Community has concentrated on the economic cost of overcoming these frontier effects in much of the documentation on the so-called 'costs of non-Europe'. It is suggested that around 2% of an average consignment's value may be lost in delays and the costs of administration associated with crossing national frontiers (a total of 8 billion Ecu). The business lost as a result of these costs is at least 4.5 billion Ecu and could be as high as 15 billion Ecu. A direct comparison between an internal haul and one involving frontier crossing suggests that the average costs of the latter may be 50% higher. Which frontiers are involved and which direction trade is going are also important factors. Italy and France present the highest barriers in cost terms, with the United Kingdom and West Germany next. The Benelux countries have traditionally low barriers. The cost to exports leaving Britain is only about 65% of that faced by an average consignment of imports whereas the cost to Italian exports is almost 60% higher than that for Italian imports, so the average cost faced by Italian exporters is over four times that faced by British exporters (for further details, see Cecchini, 1988, and CEC, 1988). These variations occur because of differences in documentation required, the speed with which consignments are cleared, and the pressure of traffic at border crossings. Some of this is purely administrative, but geography plays a part with a restricted number of possible crossings into the United Kingdom or Italy because of the physical barriers of the Channel or the Alps. However, despite this, the more remote regions of Italy do appear to be more integrated into the rest of Europe in terms of the implicit width of frontiers as revealed in Bröcker's (1980) work.

Transport infrastructure itself also contributes to the imposition of costs disproportionate to distance. National frontiers have been reinforced through the operation of national transport policy (Vickerman, 1987b; 1988a). Despite the supposed existence of a common transport policy in the Community, little has been achieved in practical terms over the last thirty years to break down the generally inward looking nature of both infrastructure provision and regulatory policy for the use of that infrastructure. Now, however, the emphasis has been placed more strongly on international infrastructures such as the Channel Tunnel, the creation of a European high-speed rail network, and improving the trans-Alpine crossings. However, as many of these are simply transfrontier links, the Channel Tunnel being the best example, this raises the question of the appropriateness of the national network serving the link. How should the connecting road or rail links be appraised when the national incidences of costs and benefits may not be the same, but to the Community as a whole there is a clear net benefit? This has tended to lead to rather weak links in the communication map, which again reinforce internal frontiers.

2.3 Assessing the effects of frontier liberalisation

It is relatively simple to document the existence of the barriers to trade discussed above and to obtain some estimates of the order of magnitude of the costs associated with them. What is much more difficult is to assess the economic effects of removing these barriers. A static analysis of transport costs can tell us by how much trade would be expected to increase if prices fell by the full amount of the cost savings implied. As these costs actually vary by commodity there would be important differential effects on different industries. Those industries with high transport costs are often also those with typically low price elasticities of demand and low growth potential, that is, traditional older heavy industries. The faster growing industries tend to have much lower transport costs, but they may also face more substantial barriers to trade through technical and other restrictions (Pelkmans and Winters, 1988). By looking at the existing regional distribution of industries we can assess possible regional impacts of policies of liberalisation and harmonisation.

At the macrolevel of the Community as a whole the effects of the Single Market can be identified as arising from three broad areas: economies of scale, increased competitiveness leading to lower prices, and nonprice competition leading to product and process innovation. Sector by sector the likely scope for price reductions has been identified and the effects this may have on consumption of the output of goods or services of that sector, together with the implications of this for consumers' surplus (CEC, 1988). If we take just some of these sectors, in tables 2 and 3, we get a feel for the magnitude of likely effects. The very size of the financial services sector makes the potential gains from liberalisation quite large, although the relative effect on this sector is less pronounced than in those manufacturing sectors where substantial economies of scale are expected to be possible.

One of the major problems of interpreting the regional consequences of these changes for the Community is of understanding the possible effects on the localisation of industries. These arise from the benefits o

Table 2. The financial services sector in the European Community. Source: CEC, 1988, tables 5.1.1 to 5.1.5.

Quantity	UK	EUR8
Gross value added (percent of GDP)	11.8	6.4
Employment (percent of total employment)	3.7	2.9
Income generated (percent of gross remuneration)	8.5	6.2
Indicated price reduction in the Single Market (%)	2 – 12	5 – 15
Gain in value added (percent of GDP)	+ 0.8	+ 0.7
UK gain in GDP (percent of EUR8)	23.8	–

Note: EUR8 Spain, Italy, France, Belgium, Germany, Luxembourg, United Kingdom, and The Netherlands.

being able to reach minimum efficient technical scale in a larger Single Market plus the effects of greater potential competition. On the one hand, these forces may move together towards the achievement of larger units and greater localisation. The regional effects of this will depend on the possibilities for regional specialisation on the basis of comparative advantage. On the other hand, the removal of barriers to the free movement both of goods *and of resources* may have a more pronounced effect on intermediate stages of the production process than on the trade in finished goods. The achievement of minimum efficient scale would occur for each process and it is these processes which could become more localised. Such a result depends critically on the ability of the transport system to deliver components reliably and efficiently to avoid excessive inventories. Hence, in this outcome, production becomes more integrated across the Community as a whole, processes become more localised without the industries necessarily becoming more localised.

Thus improvements in transport enable a more fragmented process of production. In effect, the now cheaper input, transport, is substituted for other factors of production, and processes become more transport intensive. Some of the difficulties associated with the measurement and prediction of these effects have been considered in more detail in a further paper (Vickerman, 1988b). In that paper I highlight very clearly the need to consider transport as an integral part of the production process and not just as a desired demand resulting from the need to move basic materials and finished goods.

3 A preliminary assessment for the South East

The analysis presented in the previous section suggests that there are two basic strands to an assessment of the benefits for a region such as South East England. One is concerned with an essentially static analysis of the way potential sectoral gains affect the region. The second, and potentially the more critical and difficult strand, is the assessment of dynamic effects. Both of these depend on the realisation of two sets of changes. First, we have the effects of the removal of existing frontier barriers liberalising trade flows. Second, we need to consider any additional changes which might result in particular frontiers and regions gaining differentially. The obvious example here is that of the Channel Tunnel which may have an effect independent of the Single Market and is due for completion in 1993, only months after the scheduled date for completion of the Single Market. In practice it is likely to be extremely difficult to isolate Market and Tunnel effects separately and their interaction may be the critical factor for the region. Hence, in this third section I divide the discussion into separate consideration of the static and dynamic effects.

3.1 Static effects of Single Market and Channel Tunnel

The South East as a whole, though not the particular frontier region of Kent, does have a favourable economic structure to benefit potentially from the changes due to the implementation of the Single Market: simply applying the midpoint of the estimated sectoral gains at Community level to the existing economic structure of the South East gives an estimated gain of around 4.1% on 1985 GDP, greater than the average

Table 3. Estimated gains in selected sectors. Source: CEC, 1988, Tables A8 and C2.

Sector	Gross output (percent of GDP)	Estimated gain (billion Ecu)	Gain (percent c gross output)
Motor vehicles	2.87	17.8 – 23.9	18.7 – 25.1
Textiles, clothing, etc	2.05	4.4 – 4.7	6.5 – 6.9
Chemicals	2.42	9.2 – 15.2	11.5 – 18.9
Electrical goods	2.57	15.7 – 19.7	18.3 – 23.1
Food, drink, and tobacco	4.12	8.7 – 18.2	6.3 – 13.3
Wholesale and retail services	11.77	3.5 – 5.3	0.9 – 1.4
Transport services	3.92	3.0 – 3.8	2.3 – 2.9
Credit and insurance institutions	7.98	10.5 – 11.7	4.0 – 4.4
Total	100.00	126.3 – 187.0	3.8 – 5.6

Table 4. Sectoral structure and gains from a Single Market. Sources: CEC, 1988, tables A8 and C2; *Regional Trends* **23** (HMSO, London) table 11.4

Sector	GDP by sector (%)			Estimated growth (percent of GDP, EC)
	EC	UK	South East	
Agriculture etc	2.9	1.7	0.7	2.5
Energy, water	6.8	10.3	3.0	2.7
Minerals, chemicals	4.8	4.4	2.8	10.4
Metal goods, engineering and vehicles	11.0	9.6	9.3	16.8
Other manufacturing	10.2	8.6	7.1	7.9
Construction	5.7	5.7	5.9	3.0
Distribution, hotels, etc	13.8	12.6	13.1	1.4
Transport and communication	5.9	6.7	8.3	2.6
Marketed services	24.3	25.4	34.4	2.4
Nonmarket services	14.5	15.0	15.3	1.5
Aggregate SEM effect[b]	4.7	3.4	4.1	–

[a] Midpoint of range of estimated effect of removal of trade barriers and market integration.
[b] Percentage growth in GDP from applying sectoral Single Market effects to 19 structure of GDP.

gain to the United Kingdom of 3.4%, but less than the Community's gain of 4.7% (table 4). The concentration of financial and producer-services sectors, plus considerable high-technology industry augurs well both for indigenous firms and for the attractiveness of the region to inward investors looking for a base to serve the entire European market. Labour costs too are low by the standards of neighbouring regions, especially compared with France. On average in Kent, where wages are slightly below the regional average for the South East, wage costs are 16% below those in Nord Pas-de-Calais and 23% below the average for France. Land costs, however, are substantially higher, at least 35%–40% higher in Kent than in Nord Pas-de-Calais. Moreover, Kent traditionally has prices well below those in the rest of the South East.

It has already been suggested that the South East is not particularly oriented towards Europe in terms of markets of sources of supplies. Most industries in the South East also tend to have low transport costs relative to total value added. The Channel Tunnel is unlikely to reduce the financial cost of crossing the Channel, except insofar as increased competition promotes a general lowering of fares. The main gain will be a marginal saving of time for road traffic compared with using ferries, and an increase in reliability. Perhaps more important is the opportunity provided by through rail services via the Tunnel, where the potential for both time savings and increased reliability is greater.

The creation of high-speed passenger rail links between London, Paris, and Brussels, with possible later extensions to Amsterdam and Cologne, provides the nucleus of a new transport infrastructure for these most central regions of the Community. City centre to city centre rail lines will be in competition with the airlines, but for the South East outside London the possibility of through international services could be of greater integrational importance. Considerable emphasis has been placed on the need for an international passenger station at Ashford, Kent, in the belief that this could have an attractive power for the high-technology and producer-service sectors similar to that exerted by airports.

On the other hand, through freight services provide more of a problem. A lack of track capacity which would be apparent by the late 1990s according to a conservative estimate by British Rail (1988), and much earlier according to its critics, who include Eurotunnel and SNCF (French Railways), will limit the development of such services. Also the main freight terminal is planned for Willesden, in northwest London, which will accentuate the inaccessibility to this mode for the already poorly served regions to the south and east of London. It could be argued that the major benefits of the Tunnel in this respect will be felt by the more northerly regions of Great Britain and much less by the South East. Hence, despite the Tunnel, locations in the United Kingdom may continue to face a transport cost disadvantage compared with neighbouring continental regions for serving the bulk of the European market.

However, this assessment must be set against the likely competition from neighbouring regions. The great geographical advantage of Nord Pas-de-Calais is the possibility of creating a crossroads close to the economic 'centre of gravity' of Europe, which has itself shifted westwards with the accession of Spain and Portugal. The two major economic axes of the Community are now the axis from Manchester through London, Lille, Basel–Stuttgart, towards Milan and the axis from Hamburg through the Ruhr, the Low Countries, Lille, Paris, towards Spain. These corridors embrace the bulk of economic activity within the Community, although communications along them are generally poor. Here the completion of the North European high-speed rail link and of motorways which do not focus on national capitals are vital links in the international network. Examples of the latter are the French A26 south from Calais via Reims to Dijon or the proposed Rocade Littoral along the Channel coast from the Belgian border near Dunkerque to Rouen and the west of Paris.

On the other hand, the immediately neighbouring regions are mainly old industrial regions which have relied in the past on a considerable injection of financial assistance under regional development programmes and other public-sector programmes for industrial restructuring. The scope and level of this assistance has been substantially reduced over the past two years, especially in France. There is an urgent need for these regions to adjust in terms of their general level of entrepreneurship and to be less reliant on public-sector involvement than in the past. However, the continuing higher level of public infrastructure investment could be seen as an indicator of confidence in the region and which could be important for attracting inward investment. Even if levels of state regional assistance are reduced, the continuing eligibility of the regions for such assistance has an importance in qualifying the region for the European Regional Development Fund and other Community finances which are only available to designated regions.

Thus far there has only been one comprehensive regional assessment in the United Kingdom of the impact of the Channel Tunnel, that for Kent by the Kent Impact Study Team (Department of Transport, 1988). On the basis of the plans of firms in early 1987, this assessment suggested a modest increase in employment in growth industries of some 13 000 to 14 000 jobs in Kent by the mid-1990s as a result of the Tunnel and other improvements to transport infrastructure. Such a figure is only 3%–4% of total employment in Kent in 1986 and is possibly a conservative estimate. However, this research and some further analysis (Henley et al, 1989) does generally confirm the earlier view (Vickerman, 1987a) that the Tunnel will not affect materially the distribution of regional development.

On the basis of these essentially static analyses of the Single Market and of the Channel Tunnel we cannot conclude that there will be a major change in the relative advantages of the South East. Some redistribution within the South East may occur, but that may be more to do with a catching up process by counties such as Kent than with any outside stimulus.

3.2 Dynamic effects in the South East

The question, therefore, is to what extent any initial comparative advantage in certain sectors is sustained or increased by the Single Market and Tunnel. What will be required is continuing progress on the maximising of X-efficiency, that is, the internal efficiency of enterprises in such sectors to maintain the advantage. It may be argued that in those sectors where regulation has been typically much less in the United Kingdom, such as road haulage and, more recently, financial services, UK firms may be better placed than their continental rivals. The latter will need to learn how to operate in a newly liberalised domestic market as well as the international market. As these sectors also have relatively low transport costs, the cost disadvantage of a UK location relative to the rest of Europe may be outweighed by accessibility to destinations outside Europe via the London airports. It is also important not to underestimate the potential advantages of English as a working language.

In addition to these internal effects on the behaviour of firms responding to the challenges of the Single Market or seeking new markets or suppliers because of the perceptions opened up by the Channel Tunnel, there is also the prospect of process innovation and relocation. Traditional multi-process industries are not well represented in the South East, although there are major exceptions in such industries as motor vehicle manufacture. These are the industries which could change most to take advantage of scale economics. Firms in new, high-technology industries usually like to be associated with growing, dynamic areas. The change in perception of a region associated with a new, high-profile form of transport can be very marked as evidenced by the effects of the Train à Grand Vitesse (TGV) on the Rhône–Alpes region of France (Plassard, 1985). This effect can already be detected in parts of Kent with a rapid rise in land prices. However, it is also clear that such dynamic effects may often need to be supported through investment in infrastructure, particularly in transport and in education and training.

Perhaps the major problem facing the South East is the lack of a coordinated strategy toward infrastructure provision. London, and access to London, tend to dominate thinking on the provision of transport infra-structure. The M25 orbital motorway around London and improvements to particular bottlenecks such as the Dartford Tunnel do provide much needed road access to areas beyond London. However, the M25 does serve a confused role as a bypass to London, the link between key centres in the outer South East (particularly access to and between the airports), a major interregional route for parts of the South East to the east and south of London, and an international route for all other regions in the United Kingdom. Rail infrastructure is even more dominated by London, and British Rail's belated plans for high-speed rail links to the Channel Tunnel concentrate on traffic from city centre to city centre. They largely ignore the spatial distribution of demand for international passenger traffic in the South East as well as taking a generally pessimistic view of the likely growth of freight traffic. This ignores the historical tendency in the United Kingdom to underestimate traffic growth resulting from rail improvements. An example of such growth is that associated with the TGV in France. Although this is a passenger-only high-speed service, the main growth in traffic has been of business traffic, and the freeing of capacity on conventional lines has led to a major improvement in the freight service offered. The ability to serve a variety of regional destinations, and the high demand for cross-Paris services on the French TGV also suggest the importance of serving regional railheads to obtain the maximum regional advantage. In the context of South East England, such regional railheads include Stevenage, Watford, and Reading. Easy access to the high-speed network from a variety of points in a region rather than just a single major centre could be critical in determining the balance of regional advantages in the longer term.

The preliminary conclusion of this analysis is, therefore, that although there is a potential benefit to the South East arising from the Single Market, given its existing economic structure, the construction of the Channel Tunnel does not of itself confer any particular advantage on the South East (see also Vickerman, 1987a). Furthermore, the lack of associated infrastructure may be disadvantageous to the South East whilst not conferring any compensating advantage (from a national point of view) on any other UK region. There is, however, considerable dynamic potential which could be realised and this would undoubtedly raise the long-term advantages from both the Single Market and the Channel Tunnel.

4 Further dimensions of integration

4.1 Fiscal harmonisation and cross-border shopping

One issue which features prominently in discussions of the completion of the Single Market is that of the implications of removing frontier controls for the fiscal independence of individual Community members. In the absence of tariffs on trade between member states of the Community most Customs controls relate to controlling the flow of duty-free goods and goods on which there could be financial advantages relating to differential rates of tax or duty. As long as member states have independence in fixing these rates of tax (principally value added tax) and excise duties, they can use the rates to promote or protect domestic industries and hence operate them as a nontariff barrier. This position thus has to be protected against excessive cross-frontier purchases by

final consumers, necessitating limits on the quantities of goods which
can be taken across internal frontiers. In order to remove the need for
frontier controls there has to be some harmonisation of these rates of
tax and duty. Transaction costs imply that full equalisation would not
be necessary (especially in the case of the United Kingdom), hence the
use of the phrase 'fiscal approximation'. Cross-border shopping could
lead to a serious loss of tax revenue for some members (mainly Denmark
and Ireland, although the United Kingdom has significantly higher rates
of excise duty on tobacco and alcohol than neighbouring states). Others
might have a strong incentive to undercut the rates of their neighbours.

The problem with fiscal approximation, however, is that it implies a
redistribution of tax revenues between member states, depending on how
the rates are approximated, and a loss of sovereignty over a particularly
sensitive area of government policy. Ultimately this may not be a very
serious issue for the United Kingdom (for some estimates, see Lee et al,
1988) because its tax rates (except on tobacco and alcohol) are fairly
close to the Community average. It may also be that, given the much
higher than average costs of cross-frontier shopping faced by UK
residents, a lesser degree of fiscal approximation may be acceptable.
Nevertheless, the likely complete abolition of duty-free concessions across
the Channel (one of the very few internal frontiers of the Community
where such concessions exist) could lead to a continuance of substantial
cross-border shopping for tobacco and alcohol products by British
consumers. Sealink British Ferries have already announced the possibility
of developing ferries as "floating department stores", presumably to
exploit variations both in product prices and in residual fiscal variations
between the United Kingdom and France. If this were to persuade a
much larger number of French customers to shop in British shops this
could offset some of the losses on duties goods. This could have
important implications for the coastal areas of the South East or centres
such as Ashford, Kent, in much the same way as hypermarkets in Calais
and Boulogne have been developed on the existing British-based excursion
traffic.

4.2 Transfrontier region policies
At the same time as the Community is trying to reduce fiscal and other
nontariff barriers, it is also attempting to promote cross-border
harmonisation in a more positive way. Much of the emphasis will be on
the poorest regions, particularly in the Community's southern member
states, through an enlargement of the so-called 'structural funds'. However,
one interesting development of relevance to the discussion here is that
of the concept of transfrontier regions.

Article 1 of the revised ERDF regulation of 1984 calls on member
states to "endeavour to pursue, within the framework of their bilateral

relations, transfrontier coordination of regional development ... and ... to support cooperation between the regional and local bodies involved". [1] Particular account of the 'frontier character' of regions is supposed to be taken for projects or programmes supported by the ERDF, although regions do not have to be ERDF designated regions to qualify for financial assistance in drawing up plans. By mid-1987, four transfrontier programmes were under way, all involving the Netherlands and either or both West Germany and Belgium. A further twenty to twenty-five programmes were at various stages of development, split roughly half and half between ERDF-assisted regions and non-ERDF-assisted regions, and covering all the main internal frontiers of the Community including that between Kent and Nord Pas-de-Calais.

Three types of programme have been envisaged: regional development programmes; intervention programmes; and Community programmes. The latter two relate to specific programmes which involve substantial cross-frontier cooperation and which are initiated either by member governments in ERDF-assisted areas or by the Commission either in assisted or in nonassisted areas, respectively. The main programme envisaged is that of 'transfrontier regional development', which would operate rather like any regional development programme in the Community except that it is based on *joint* analysis, diagnosis and policy development, and on a coordinated strategy. The Community can provide funds to assist in the formulation of the regional development programme even where there is no entitlement to the ERDF for implementation. Regional development programmes are simply the outlining of a strategy for a programme of development, based on a thorough diagnosis of a region's current problems. The emphasis is on determining a coordinated strategic programme rather than just giving financial assistance to a set of unrelated projects.

From the Community standpoint, transfrontier regional development programmes have the advantage of working toward a breaking down of national frontiers and the barriers they imply. From the standpoint of the regions involved, they offer the advantage of reducing some of the cross-frontier variations which could pose a problem in the absence of frontier controls. From the standpoint of the member states, however, they could pose a potential threat to regional policy overall where frontier regions are not the main problem regions. This is unlikely to be the case in the more central states of the Community, but could pose problems for the United Kingdom and Italy in particular. It is perhaps not surprising that the Commission has seen the development of such programmes as being essentially a venture of the regions and the Community, with only indirect input from the central governments of the member states.

[1] Taken from Council Regulation (EEC) number 1787/84, in the *Official Journal* number L169, 28 June 1984.

A detailed submission for the Kent–Nord Pas-de-Calais transfrontier region was sent to the Commission in mid-1988. This emerged from a cooperation agreement between the County Council and Conseil Régional signed in April 1987. This has concentrated on a number of areas of common interest to the two regions, including transport infrastructure, education and training, and the development of the tourism sector. In these areas the lack of ERDF-assisted status for Kent would not pose a disadvantage as the Community's infrastructure and social funds can be applied to any region if they enhance integration and the Community's interests. The emphasis has been on identifying complementarities between the regions to ensure consistent planning. More cynically, it may be suggested that the desire to cooperate on such policies is one of reducing uncertainty in the planning process. This could mean that, despite the obvious advantages of breaking down existing barriers between states, frontier controls may be being replaced with agreements in restraint of competition. Put another way, the transfrontier region may replace the national frontier with a much wider frontier zone. How far this is an improvement remains to be seen, but it does add a further dimension to the problem of estimating the nature and size of the changes in train.

5 Some conclusions

In this paper I have taken a preliminary look at some of the possibilities of regional change which could be set in motion in the 1990s as a result of both the completion of the Channel Tunnel, giving Britain a fixed link with the transport system of mainland Europe for the first time, and the Single European Market, which aims to eliminate the remaining frontier controls and nontariff barriers to trade. The purpose has been twofold. One has been the application of some of the European Commission's own estimates on the impact of the Single Market on individual sectors in the South East to get some idea of where the potential for dynamism lies. The other has been to provide a preliminary discussion of the sort of methodology necessary for obtaining better forecasts by understanding the dynamic processes at work.

The analysis suggests that there may be considerable scope for optimism in the South East on the basis of macroforecasts, but that this does not automatically eliminate the difficulties currently faced by the real 'frontier regions' such as Kent. These regions may find that the 'economic shadow' of the frontier is replaced by that of a transport 'corridor effect'. In this context the use by the European Commission of a new designation for policy purposes of the transfrontier region is an interesting means of trying to free nationally peripheral regions from that peripherality. Much of the final outcome for frontier regions may depend on the ultimate answer to the question of fiscal approximation and its implications for cross-border shopping, that is, trade by consumers rather than by producers or distributors.

The distribution of benefits and costs within a region such as South East England is a much more difficult problem. Preliminary work on this suggests that there is a considerable need for a strategy for the South East to distinguish the importance of subregions, by direction as well as by distance from London. In this paper I have provided evidence on the particular problem faced by counties such as Kent and Essex.

At a methodological level, two main issues have been addressed: the distinction of internal frontier effects from the more traditional view of the frontier region as peripheral; and the need to consider dynamic response by firms and industries. The main feature of the internal frontier is that it may well be within the geographical core of the Community economy, but still suffer a relative isolation in national terms. The frontier, because of the costs of trading across it, casts a shadow over the economy of adjacent regions. This effect appears to hold even in cases where a relatively prosperous region is adjacent to the frontier: clear shadow effects are visible on the subregions closest to the frontier. South East England provides a particularly clear example of this as London serves to isolate peripheral counties like Kent from the markets in the rest of the United Kingdom, and a considerable frontier effect is imposed by the Channel.

The dynamic responses to the Single Market and new transport infrastructure, taken together, are judged likely to be in greater localisation of processes rather than of industries. Thus transport is likely to be substituted for other factors of production. The ability of regions to gain from this will depend on the dynamics of local firms, but critically on the provision of supportive infrastructure such as access to new international transport networks, education, and training.

Acknowledgement. The research in this paper was supported by the Economic and Social Research Council (grant YD00250018).

References
Bonnafous A, Plassard F, Soum D, 1975 *Impact of Infrastructural Investment on Industrial Development* Round Table 25, European Conference of Ministers of Transport, 2 Rue André-Pascal, Paris
British Rail, 1988 *Channel Tunnel Train Services: BR Study Report on Long-term Route and Terminal Capacity* (British Railways Board, London)
Bröcker J, 1980 *Measuring Trade-impeding Effects of Distance by Log-Linear Interaction Analysis* DP-16, Institüt für Regionalforschung, Universität Kiel, Kiel, FRG
Bröcker J, 1988, "Interregional trade and economic integration" *Regional Science and Urban Economics* **18** 261-281
CEC, 1987 *The Regions of the Enlarged Community—Third Periodic Report on the Social and Economic Situation and Development of the Regions of the Community* Commission of the European Communities (European Commission, Luxembourg)
CEC, 1988, "The economics of 1992" *European Economy* Commision of the European Communities, number 35, March

Cecchini P, 1988 *The European Challenge 1992—The Benefits of a Single Market* (Wildwood House, Aldershot, Hants)

Chisholm M, 1985, "Accessibility and regional development in Britain: some questions arising from data on freight flows" *Environment and Planning A* **17** 963–980

Department of Transport, 1988 *Kent Impact Study: Overall Assessment* Channel Tunnel Joint Consultative Committee (HMSO, London)

Durieux C, 1988, "Lien fixe transmanche et TGV Nord: quels effets pour la région frontalière du Hainaut?" *Hommes et Terres du Nord* **1-2** 67–69

Evers G H M, Oosterhaven J, 1988, "Transportation, frontier effects and regional development in the Common Market" *Papers and Proceedings, Regional Science Association* **64** 37–51

Friedmann J, 1966 *Regional Development: A Case Study of Venezuela* (MIT Press, Cambridge, MA)

Henley A, Carruth A, Thomas A, Vickerman R W, 1989 "Location choice and labour market perceptions", WP-89/1, Channel Tunnel Research Unit, University of Kent at Canterbury

Hirschmann A O, 1958 *The Strategy of Economic Development* (Yale University Press, New Haven, CT)

Hoare A G, 1985, "Great Britain and her exports: an exploratory regional analysis" *Tijdschrift voor Economische en Sociale Geografie* **76** 9–21

Keeble D, Owens P L, Thompson C, 1982a, "Regional accessibility and economic potential in the European Community" *Regional Studies* **16** 419–432

Keeble D, Owens P L, Thompson C, 1982b, "Economic potential and the Channel Tunnel" *Area* **14** 97–103

Lee C, Pearson M, Smith S, 1988 *IFS Report Series Number 28. Fiscal Harmonization: An Analysis of the European Commission's Proposals* (Institute for Fiscal Studies, 180/182 Tottenham Court Road, London W1P 9LE)

Myrdal G, 1957 *Economic Theory and Underdeveloped Regions* (Gerald Duckworth, London)

Pelkmans J, Winters L A, 1988 *Chatham House Papers 43: Europe's Domestic Market* (Royal Institute of International Affairs/Routledge, Chapman and Hall, Andover, Hants)

Perroux F, 1961 *L'Économie du XXe Siècle* (Presses Universitaires de France, Paris)

Peschel K, 1985, "Spatial structure in international trade" *Papers and Proceedings, Regional Science Association* **58** 97–111

Plassard F, 1985 *Les Effets du TGV sur les Agglomérations du Centre et du Sud-Est* (Laboratoire d'Économie des Transports, Lyon)

Ullman E L, 1958, "Regional development and the geography of concentration" *Papers and Proceedings, Regional Science Association* **4** 179–198

Vickerman R W, 1987a, "The Channel Tunnel: consequences for regional growth and development" *Regional Studies* **21** 187–197

Vickerman R W, 1987b, "Transport and European integration", in *Approaching the Channel Tunnel* UACES OP-3, Ed. C H Church (University Association for Contemporary European Studies, London)

Vickerman R W, 1988a, "Les Transports et l'Intégration du Royaume-Uni dans l'Économie Européene: le cas du Tunnel sous la Manche", paper to Congrès des Économistes de Langue Française, Lille, May; mimeo available from Channel Tunnel Research Unit, University of Kent at Canterbury

Vickerman R W, 1988b, "Measuring changes in regional competitiveness: the effects of international infrastructure investments", WP-88/2, Channel Tunnel Research Unit, University of Kent at Canterbury

Recent Population Shifts in South East England and their Relevance to the Counterurbanisation Debate

P CONGDON
London Research Centre
A CHAMPION
University of Newcastle upon Tyne

1 Introduction

The 1980s saw a cessation or diminution in several countries of population movement to less urbanised regions relatively remote from large metropolitan centres, a phenomenon known as deconcentration or counterurbanisation. It has been argued that the peak of the tendency to counterurbanise, marked by population growth in peripheral rural regions and small towns and by population loss from large metropolitan centres, occurred in the late 1960s and early 1970s (Fielding, 1989; Richter, 1985). Thus, in England, comparison of the 1971 and 1981 Censuses shows a clear pattern of highest growth in small towns of England and in the less heavily urbanised standard regions without major metropolitan centres, such as East Anglia, the East Midlands, and the South West (Congdon and Shepherd, 1986; Robert and Randolph, 1983). All metropolitan counties in England underwent major population losses in the 1970s, with London and Merseyside showing the highest annual rates of population loss in the subperiod 1971–77 (1.2% and 0.9%, respectively) (Britton, 1986).

However, by the late 1970s metropolitan population losses were slackening, and London in fact witnessed slight increases in population over the years 1983 to 1986. A revival of natural change has had some influence on this, but the major component has been improvements in the metropolitan net migration balance (table 1). The net migration loss

Table 1. Components of population change (in thousands), for London and the South East region, 1971–87.

Region	1971–76			1976–81			1981–87		
	nat.	net mig.	total	nat.	net mig.	total	nat.	net mig.	total
G. London	48	−487	−440	42	−325	−283	116	−151	−35
ROSE	104	186	290	62	255	317	94	248	343
South East	152	−301	−149	104	−70	34	210	97	307
England and Wales	381	−74	307	150	25	175	395	214	609

Note: ROSE rest of South East, nat. natural, net mig. net migration and other changes, G. London Greater London.

from London fell from 100 000 annually in the early 1970s to under 20 000 in the mid-1980s. The South East standard region as a whole is distinctive from other British regions containing a metropolitan centre, both in the extent of metropolitan population revival and in the degree to which population growth has continued in the nonmetropolitan remainder despite greater metropolitan population retention.

Our purpose in this paper is to set the pronounced population and migration turnaround in London in the wider context of population change in the functional settlement hierarchy of Britain. Data both for administrative divisions and for local labour market areas are used to this end. Particular focus is on the extent to which there is a general metropolitan population revival and how far this can be explained in terms of employment structure and change, by the housing market and by the winding down of policies of planned decentralisation in Britain.

This analysis of recent trends in British population therefore parallels, to some extent, the earlier 'turnaround' to counterurbanisation observed in nonmetropolitan regions in several countries: a shift from net migration loss to gain (Fielding, 1982). However, the scope of the present analysis is broader in the sense that we consider the attenuation of the high population losses of metropolitan regions in Britain, without necessarily implying a reversal to pronounced metropolitan growth. Such attenuation is apparent in other countries (Courgeau, 1986), though in the USA there are even signs of a complete reversal—to metropolitan growth rates in excess of nonmetropolitan growth rates (Engels, 1986).

2 Migration shifts in London and the South East of England

A comparison of population growth in the early 1980s with that in the 1970s over the counties of South East England (table 2) shows both the waning of migration loss from London and the continuation of growth through net migration in the rest of the region. At first sight, there is support for the notion that growth is 'rippling out' from the metropolitan hinterland, and that extended decentralisation from London—involving either a move outside the metropolitan 'daily urban system'[1] or perhaps long-distance commuting to fixed London workplaces—is increasingly prevalent. Thus net migration gain the outer metropolitan area (OMA) has turned to migration loss, and the quinquennial net migration gain of the outer South East has increased.

However, examination of the changing sources of the migration balances of London and the rest of the region points to a more complex picture. Table 3 shows a waning of decentralisation from London to the rest of the South East, particularly in the 1970s and early 1980s, and the emergence of net inflow to the capital both from Britain outside the

[1] An urban employment core together with the noncore commuter hinterland defined by significant journey-to-work flows to the core.

South East and from abroad (Champion and Congdon, 1987). In the rest of the region an improved international balance has offset reduced inflow from Greater London; net migration with respect to the rest of Britain (a slight loss) has remained at the levels observed in the 1970s. The result of these shifts—reduced migration loss from London combined with continued growth in the outer parts of the region—is that the South East as a whole, although accounting for 34% of the population of England and Wales in 1987 has accounted for 50% (307000 out of 609000) of the population growth in England and Wales in the period 1981–87 (OPCS, 1988).

A review of net migration rates at the disaggregated district level in the 1970s and 1980s confirms the lack of any simple trend to extended decentralisation [figures 1(a) and 1(b)]. A map of migration turnaround [figure 1(c)] between the periods 1971–81 and 1981–87 indicates the extent of (a) revival of net in-migration, from loss to gain or lesser loss, or accelerated net gains (in the case of positive values) or (b) enhanced net migration losses or reduced net migration gains (in the case of negative values). The attenuation of net migration losses in inner London, and to a lesser extent outer London, is apparent. This revival even extends to some districts in the outer metropolitan area which are on the

Table 2. Components of change in population (in thousands) for the South East counties and zones for the periods 1971–81 and 1981–87.

Area	1981 pop.	1971–81			1981–87		
		tot. ch.	nat.	net mig.	tot. ch.	nat.	net mig.
County							
Beds	510.3	42.8	32.7	10.1	15.6	19.4	−3.8
Berks	693.8	46.6	32.3	14.3	47.0	21.5	25.5
Bucks	571.8	91.1	28.0	63.1	49.6	17.6	32.0
East Sussex	665.3	12.7	−49.2	61.9	32.8	−23.9	56.7
Essex	1483.0	117.3	38.3	79.0	38.9	16.3	22.6
Hants	1488.5	88.0	44.1	43.9	48.2	23.8	24.4
Herts	964.8	31.8	30.2	1.6	21.8	15.9	5.9
Isle of Wight	118.1	10.9	−5.9	16.8	8.8	−3.4	12.2
Kent	1484.3	73.2	15.3	57.9	26.2	6.1	20.1
Oxon	541.8	25.7	21.5	4.2	36.3	11.8	24.5
Surrey	1016.8	2.8	4.9	−2.1	−16.4	1.3	−17.7
West Sussex	666.2	65.9	−21.6	87.5	33.9	−12.3	46.2
Zone							
OMA	5450.9	242.3	177.7	64.6	62.0	94.2	−32.2
Outer SE	4753.8	366.5	−7.1	373.6	280.7	−0.1	280.8
G. London	6805.7	−723.7	90.6	−814.3	−35.3	115.9	−151.2

Note: pop. population, tot. ch. total change, nat. natural change, net mig. net migration, Beds Bedfordshire, Berks Berkshire, Bucks Buckinghamshire, Hants Hampshire, Herts Hertfordshire, Oxon Oxfordshire, OMA outer metropolitan area, Outer SE outer South East, G. London Greater London.

boundary of London (such as Watford and Dartford). However, several districts in the OMA have moved from net migration gain to loss or much reduced gain (Sevenoaks, Horsham); this category includes new towns such as Bracknell and Basildon. Other districts in the OMA have, in contrast to those in London, undergone increased net migration losses (including another new town, Harlow). In the outer South East, the typical pattern is for continued growth in both periods but without any acceleration. There are some examples of increased growth through net migration in the 1980s (for example, in some southern coastal districts) but these are counterbalanced by net migration slowdowns in new towns (Milton Keynes, Basingstoke) and net out-migration from some heavily urbanised districts (Eastleigh, Southampton).

These trends in net migration gains in zones and districts of the South East do indicate some shifts in intraregional migration since the early 1970s: for example, they imply that the migration gain of the outer South East is increasingly drawn from the OMA, as net inflow from Greater London has declined. They also give an indication of the changing distribution of opportunities for and constraints on migrants to the South East from outside (from the rest of Great Britain or from foreign countries), and for potential migrants from London to the rest of the region.

Table 3. Components of migration (in thousands) for the period 1971–86: censal (1970/71 and 1980/81) and quinquennial (1976–81 and 1981–86).

Region	Source/ destination	1970–71[a]			1980–81[a]		
		in from	out to	net	in from	out to	net
G. London	ROSE	73	166	−93	54	94	−41
G. London	ROGB	67	81	−14	54	52	2
G. London	ROW	105	nd	nd	66	nd	nd
ROSE	G. London	166	73	93	94	53	41
ROSE	ROGB	149	150	−1	112	111	1
ROSE	ROW	92	nd	nd	66	nd	nd
		1976–81[b]			1981–86[b]		
G. London	ROSE	364	647	−283	359	601	−242
G. London	ROGB	400	410	−10	419	371	48
G. London	ROW	293	260	34	312	232	80
ROSE	G. London	647	364	283	601	359	242
ROSE	ROGB	727	758	−32	715	761	−45
ROSE	ROW	185	222	−37	235	217	18

nd no date: Census date for ROW is for inflow only.
[a] Source: Censuses, 1971 and 1981.
[b] Source: National Health Service Central Register (NHSCR) and International Passenger Survey (IPS).
Note: G. London Greater London, ROSE rest of the South East, ROGB rest of Great Britain, ROW rest of the World.

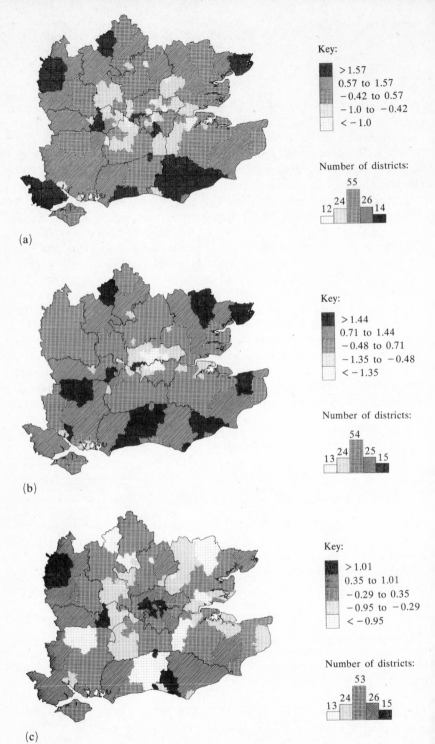

Figure 1. The South East districts: (a) annual net migration rate, 1981–87; (b) annual net migration rate, 1971–81; (c) turnaround in net migration, 1981–8 versus 1971–81. Rates are expressed as percentage of population.

One feature, further discussed below, is the much reduced net migration gains of new town districts, particularly in the metropolitan hinterland (OMA), following the winding down of planned decentralisation policies. The increased attractiveness of London to immigrants, and to some extent an increased retentiveness in terms of reduced levels of out-migration, are also evident.

3 Explanations of metropolitan migration turnaround

Other metropolitan counties have seen their rate of decline in population slacken in the 1980s, but to a less striking extent than London's. Moreover, the South East is somewhat exceptional among regions containing a metropolitan county in that high growth was maintained in the nonmetropolitan part of the region (table 4). Other nonmetropolitan remainders such as those in the West Midlands and the North have seen reduced growth or even increased losses in the 1980s (Britton, 1986). The average growth rate of 1% in the period 1981–86 of nonmetropolitan remainders (administratively defined) other than in South East England, is in contrast to one of 5.6% in the South East nonmetropolitan remainder.

These differences point towards explanations of migration turnaround in metropolitan counties. All metropolitan counties have gained through a reduction in planned decentralisation to new and expanded towns (NETs). It will be argued below that this is a major source of slowdown in population growth in satellite towns in metropolitan hinterlands. Similarly, intercensal evidence shows a larger fall in out-migration from London to NET districts in the rest of the South East (ROSE) than to districts not containing NETs (Congdon and Champion, 1989).

Population decentralisation from metropolitan areas, particularly that involving short-range moves, is related to the supply of new private housing and to the house price differential between metropolitan areas and their hinterlands (Buck et al, 1985). Models of housing-linked decentralisation from the capital conform to traditional theories of residential location which posit residential adjustment in relation to fixed metropolitan workplaces (and by implication extended commuting to London). It is true that the slowdown in new private house building in the nonmetropolitan parts of regions, particularly during the recession years of the early 1980s, will have reduced the opportunities for housing migrants; and that the revival in private-sector house building in the mid and late 1980s may have contributed to some upturn in out-migration from the capital (see Barlow, this volume). However, there is evidence to suggest that fluctuations in private house building are not a complete explanation of changes in metropolitan net migration.

For example, building society surveys show that most new houses in the South East outside London are taken by local households rather than longer distance migrants (84% from within 25 miles according to the surveys in 1986 and 1987 by the Nationwide Anglia Building Society,

Table 4. Average annual rates (expressed as numbers per thousand people) of population growth, natural change, and net migration 1971 to 1986, in the English metropolitan counties and nonmetropolitan remainders.

Area	1971–74	1974–77	1977–81	1981–86
Population growth				
Metropolitan counties				
Greater London	−12.0	−11.7	−7.5	−0.9
West Yorkshire	−0.3	−1.6	−1.4	−1.3
South Yorkshire	−0.8	−2.0	−0.6	−2.9
West Midlands	−3.1	−6.8	−5.1	−3.1
Tyne and Wear	−5.8	−4.1	−5.7	−3.4
Greater Manchester	−4.9	−5.1	−4.7	−3.0
Merseyside	−10.7	−8.0	−7.9	−7.1
Nonmetropolitan remainders				
All	7.2	3.9	5.0	3.5
South East	7.1	4.4	6.7	5.6
West Midlands	9.5	6.0	6.8	2.9
Yorks/Humberside	6.6	2.5	2.0	1.8
North West	8.7	2.5	2.2	0.8
North	4.0	1.6	−0.6	−1.8
Natural change				
Metropolitan counties				
Greater London	2.1	0.2	1.4	2.6
West Yorkshire	2.1	−0.1	0.8	1.3
South Yorkshire	2.6	−0.5	0.3	0.5
West Midlands	4.3	1.4	2.1	2.7
Tyne and Wear	1.0	−1.3	−0.2	−0.0
Greater Manchester	2.2	−0.3	0.6	1.2
Merseyside	1.8	−0.5	0.2	0.8
Nonmetropolitan remainders				
All	2.7	0.5	1.1	1.0
South East	3.0	0.8	1.4	1.4
West Midlands	4.2	1.5	1.9	1.6
Yorks/Humberside	1.9	−0.5	−0.2	−0.1
North West	1.3	−1.1	−0.2	0.1
North	1.9	−0.1	0.6	0.6
Net migration				
Metropolitan counties				
Greater London	−14.0	−12.0	−8.9	−3.5
West Yorkshire	−2.4	−1.5	−2.2	−2.9
South Yorkshire	−3.3	−1.5	−0.9	−3.4
West Midlands	−7.4	−8.2	−7.2	−5.8
Tyne and Wear	−6.8	−2.8	−5.5	−3.4
Greater Manchester	−7.2	−4.9	−5.2	−4.3
Merseyside	−12.5	−7.6	−8.1	−7.9
Nonmetropolitan remainders				
All	4.5	3.5	3.9	2.5
South East	4.2	3.6	5.3	4.2
West Midlands	5.2	4.5	4.8	1.2
Yorks/Humberside	4.7	3.0	2.2	1.9
North West	7.4	3.6	2.4	0.6
North	2.1	1.7	−1.2	−2.4

Table 5. Population and employment change (expressed in thousands and percent quinquennial change) in counties of the South East over the years 1971 to 1986.

County	E	ΔE		P	ΔP		A	ΔA		E^{surp}	
	1971	number 1971–81	%	1971	number 1971–81	%	1971	number 1971–81	%	number 1971–81	%
Bedfordshire	185.3	7.1	1.9	467.5	10.1	1.1	221.1	7.0	1.6	-10.7	-2.5
Berkshire	272.9	39.1	7.2	647.2	14.3	1.1	298.2	13.4	2.3	6.4	1.1
Buckinghamshire	151.4	45.5	15.1	480.7	63.1	6.6	226.0	30.4	6.8	16.8	3.7
East Sussex	191.3	11.4	3.0	652.6	61.9	4.7	269.8	16.0	3.0	7.8	1.5
Essex	435.2	22.5	2.6	1365.7	79.0	2.9	622.6	30.4	2.5	-13.2	-1.1
Hampshire	479.6	76.4	8.0	1400.5	43.9	1.6	620.8	15.7	1.3	-10.9	-0.9
Hertfordshire	381.0	19.0	2.5	933.0	1.6	0.1	446.8	-0.8	-0.1	-29.2	-3.3
Isle of Wight	35.9	2.3	3.2	107.2	16.8	7.8	43.8	3.5	4.2	1.3	1.5
Kent	472.3	29.6	3.2	1411.1	57.9	2.1	609.1	22.2	1.8	-7.1	-0.6
Oxfordshire	190.1	9.6	2.6	516.1	4.2	0.4	229.8	-12.4	-2.7	-21.9	-4.8
Surrey	309.4	23.9	3.9	1014.0	-2.1	-0.1	467.7	0.0	0.0	-1.4	-0.2
West Sussex	200.8	36.8	9.2	600.3	87.5	7.3	253.5	37.1	7.3	33.1	6.5
Rest of South East	3305.2	323.1	4.9	9595.9	438.2	2.3	4309.2	162.5	1.9	-29.0	-0.3
Greater London	3937.3	-426.7	-5.4	7529.4	-814.3	-5.4	3824.1	-346.0	-4.6	-385.1	-5.0

County	E	ΔE		P	ΔP	
	1981	number 1981–84	%	1981	number 1981–86	%
Bedfordshire	192.5	12.6	10.9	510.3	-3.8	-0.7
Berkshire	312.0	11.1	5.9	693.8	20.9	3.0
Buckinghamshire	196.9	25.8	21.8	571.8	27.8	4.9
East Sussex	202.6	17.2	14.1	665.3	47.1	7.1
Essex	457.6	-11.3	-4.1	1483.0	17.8	1.2
Hampshire	556.0	10.4	3.1	1488.5	30.3	2.0
Hertfordshire	400.0	21.4	8.9	964.8	9.2	1.0
Isle of Wight	38.2	3.1	13.4	118.1	9.8	8.3
Kent	501.8	-9.1	-3.0	1484.3	17.9	1.2
Oxfordshire	199.7	5.8	4.9	541.8	19.1	3.5
Surrey	333.3	20.1	10.0	1016.8	-3.4	-0.3
West Sussex	237.6	15.9	11.1	666.2	39.7	6.0
Rest of South East	3628.3	122.9	5.6	10204.7	232.0	2.3
Greater London	3510.6	-36.9	-1.8	6805.7	-121.7	-1.8

Note: E employment; ΔE employment growth (expressed as a number and as a percentage of E); P population; ΔP total net migration (expressed as a number and as a percentage of P; A economically active population (expressed as a number and as a percentage of A); E^{surp} employment surplus, expressed as a number and as a percentage of A.

with a median distance moved of only 4.4 miles). Moreover, the correlation between annual fluctuations in private house building in the South East outside London and net migration from London since the early 1960s has been relatively weak (Congdon and Champion, 1989). The correlations between gross migration from London according to the National Health Service Central Register (NHSCR) (after 1975) and private building are also low (SERPLAN, 1986). Finally, the level of new building is small in relation to the absolute size of the immigrant inflow to the nonmetropolitan parts of regions.

The somewhat exceptional nature of population turnaround in London and the continued growth in the ROSE has been related by some analysts to the strength of the South East economy in the early 1980s (Tyler and Rhodes, 1986). The South East outside London has continued to receive net immigration at levels similar to those of the 1970s, despite housing pressures and high costs of housing in the region; this reflects immigration from overseas or from the rest of the United Kingdom for primarily job-related reasons. By contrast, other nonmetropolitan parts of regions in the North, some with much above the national level of unemployment, have not replaced the fall in net inflow owing to the ending of planned decentralisation. In London itself, total employment is now growing (a sharp contrast to earlier decades) particularly in certain services. London's employment grew by 14% between 1984 and 1987, and in 1987 the growth rate of London's gross domestic product exceeded that of the national economy.

Intercensal analysis using labour market accounts for counties in South East England confirms an association between population growth and employment growth within the region. There is a positive association in the 1971–81 period between (a) total net migration and employment growth and (b) net in-migration by the economically active and the employment surplus—the excess of job growth (workplace based) over increases in the local labour force, as derived from labour market accounts (see table 5 and Congdon and Champion, 1989). This association continues in the 1980s, as evidenced by data from the Annual Census of Employment and midyear estimates (figure 2).

Analysis over time also supports the link between shifts in (net) out-migration from London and employment availability in the capital. A time series regression was undertaken of the annual percentage rate of net out-migration from London (NETOM) over 1966–67 to 1986–87 on relevant predictors in the labour and housing markets. These are (a) the ratio of house price to family incomes in London (RATIO), (b) annual rates of employment growth in London (ΔEMP), and (c) the number (in thousands) of new private houses in the ROSE (ΔPRHOU); all three predictors are lagged by a year. This gives the following equation (*t*-ratios are given in brackets):

$$\text{NETOM} = -0.335 + 0.204 \text{ RATIO} - 0.148 \Delta\text{EMP} + 0.016 \Delta\text{PRHOU} ,$$
$$\qquad\quad (0.9) \qquad (1.9) \qquad\qquad (4.1) \qquad\qquad (3.4)$$
$$R^2 = 0.75 .$$

All effects are as would be expected, and housing market influences on migration are clear. But also apparent is the role of job availability as an equilibrating influence on migration fluctuations over time. Indeed, given that net migration from the capital is a balance between immigration

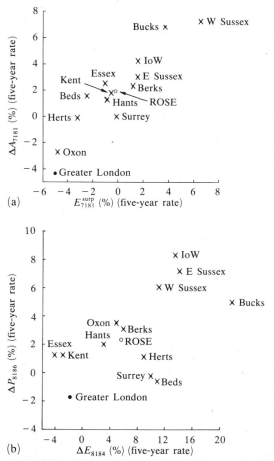

Figure 2. The South East counties: (a) net economically active migration, ΔA_{7181} (as a percentage of economically active population in 1971) versus employment surplus in 1971–81, E_{7181}^{surp} (as a percentage of economically active population in 1971); and (b) total net migration over the period 1981–86, ΔP_{8186} (as a percentage of 1981 population) versus the percentage employment change over the period 1981–84, ΔE_{8184}.

to the capital (primarily for job-related reasons) and out-migration (which at least to some extent will be reduced by an improvement in job supply in London), the employment growth effect is not surprising. In practice, the extent of housing-linked migration from the capital to the rest of the region (that is, residential decentralisation while retaining a fixed London workplace) is constrained by the problems of labour and housing market stress in the South East discussed in other chapters of this volume. These include (a) limitations on the supply of new housing for migrants in the ROSE (associated, for example, with competition between potential in-migrants and newly forming local households and with the limited supply of land for new building) and by (b) the increasing costs of long-distance commuting and transport infrastructure limitations on further growth of in-commuting to the capital.

4 Implications for counterurbanisation and reurbanisation
How do recent population shifts in South East England relate to the wider issue of counterurbanisation and reurbanisation? In some studies it is argued that the high losses in metropolitan population of the late 1960s and early 1970s were a temporary phenomenon and that current trends point towards a new equilibrium between metropolitan and nonmetropolitan areas in terms both of population and of employment (Richter, 1985). This may in turn be related to a new spatial division of labour with certain large metropolitan centres and their hinterlands containing disproportionate concentrations of high order corporate functions, and of growing financial and information services (Fielding, 1989). Both London and the South East region have disproportionate concentrations of high growth producer services (Hepworth et al, 1987; Gillespie and Green, 1987).

These sectors contribute disproportionately to the revival of London's economy and also to the expansion of employment in the rest of the region. Between 1981 and 1987, jobs in banking, insurance, and finance in London grew by 154000 (or by 27% of the 1981 total in this sector and other sectors declined by 204000 (SERPLAN, 1988, page 93). In the ROSE this sector contributed 60% of the total growth in jobs over the period 1981-87 (namely 169000 out of 322000). In some instances, growth or revival of metropolitan areas and their hinterlands may also reflect the location of 'hi-tech' manufacturing, often boosted by military spending—Boston and its New England hinterland, and Bristol in the United Kingdom being possible examples.

A further issue highlighted by recent population shifts in London and the South East is the role of international migrant flows in enhancing or offsetting intranational flows, whether the latter are predominantly urbanising or counterurbanising. Earlier work on counterurbanisation suggested that international migration of (primarily) low-skill workers masked population losses in larger and metropolitan settlements, and concealed the true extent of deconcentration (Fielding, 1982). The evidence of recent trends, at least for the London metropolitan region and its environs, is that international migration is increasingly biased towards professional and managerial workers (Champion and Congdon, 1987), and that it has boosted growth in both the metropolitan core and the less densely populated nonmetropolitan parts of the South East.

Such changes in the nature and direction of international migration can be related to changes in the international spatial division of labour for producer and information services, insofar as they have affected London and South East England. The revival of London's economy is part of an urban polarisation associated with the enhanced economic dominance of a small number of 'world cities' at nodal points in corporate financial and information networks (Gillespie and Green, 1987, page 401). The producer-service effect is not confined to the metropolis as there is evidence of decentralisation of growth in this sector to elsewhere in the region (including the 'Greater South East'). International migration to the region, primarily job-linked and by increasingly higher-income and higher-skill groups, appears to have responded to the new division of labour.

5 The functional context of metropolitan population revival

In this section we consider the relation between these recent patterns of population and employment redistribution with the local labour market framework as our unit for analysis. The use of the administrative divisions of counties and standard regions in the previous sections may be criticised on the grounds that such divisions do not correspond to meaningful functional criteria. For example, standard definitions of metropolitan regions do not take account of the dependence of commuter hinterlands on large urban cores, and so may 'underbound' the true metropolitan region (Champion et al, 1983).

Labour market regions are intended as far as possible to be self-contained entities, based on the 'daily urban system' concept of interdependence between an employment core and its commuting hinterland. Employment cores are here differentiated between 'dominant' metropolitan centres (such as London and Brighton within the South East); subdominant or satellite towns which are employment cores but also have high commuting to a metropolitan centre (for example, Slough in relation to London); and freestanding centres, separate from other major employment cores in commuting terms. The definition of local labour market also includes rural centres, self-contained but with too little employment to constitute a functional region.

It has been argued that labour market regions are the most appropriate unit for the analysis of migration in that moves within such regions are expected to represent (housing) adjustments to changed socioeconomic or family status, whereas moves between regions can be regarded as labour

oriented (Korcelli, 1986). Although not all counterurbanising moves can
be regarded as employment moves, the use of the concept of local labour
market for analysing reurbanisation or counterurbanisation can also be
supported. Use of such regions for analysis will reduce confusion
between counterurbanisation and urban decentralisation (Kontuly and
Vogelsang, 1985).

Table 6 shows patterns of population growth for local labour market
areas (LLMAs), by functional status, in different standard regions or groups

Table 6. Population change and turnaround (expressed in thousands and as
quinquennial growth rates) in the standard regions, by labour market region.

Labour market region	Pop. 1981	Pop. change 1971–81	Quin. 1971–81	Pop. change 1981–85	Quin. 1981–85	Turn.
South East						
Metropolitan	8437.6	−757.4	−4.06	−48.3	−0.72	3.35
Satellite	4832.6	324.8	3.56	97.7	2.53	−1.04
Freestanding	3252.9	296.7	4.92	131.2	5.04	0.13
Rural	61.9	3.4	2.87	2.3	4.57	1.70
South West						
Metropolitan	1600.5	−5.0	−0.15	8.4	0.65	0.81
Satellite	1026.4	26.7	1.32	−3.3	−0.40	−1.72
Freestanding	3427.6	228.4	3.48	94.5	3.45	−0.04
Rural	1025.4	80.9	4.16	22.7	2.77	−1.39
Midlands						
Metropolitan	2591.1	−87.5	−1.62	−6.9	−0.33	1.29
Satellite	2217.9	76.9	1.78	9.0	0.51	−1.28
Freestanding	4921.0	327.9	3.52	77.5	1.97	−1.55
Rural	730.7	79.4	6.01	26.3	4.50	−1.51
North						
Metropolitan	5174.8	−331.4	−2.98	−98.0	−2.37	0.62
Satellite	4790.2	90.4	0.96	−18.0	−0.47	−1.43
Freestanding	4156.1	25.7	0.31	−14.2	−0.43	−0.73
Rural	258.8	15.8	3.17	10.4	5.02	1.86
Scotland						
Metropolitan	1862.5	−170.3	−4.13	−44.3	−2.97	1.16
Satellite	695.7	−9.4	−0.66	−14.6	−2.62	−1.95
Freestanding	1829.5	32.3	0.88	6.7	0.46	−0.42
Rural	657.2	48.2	3.80	5.2	0.99	−2.81
Britain						
Metropolitan	19666.5	−1351.6	−3.18	−189.0	−1.20	1.98
Satellite	13562.9	509.4	1.93	70.9	0.65	−1.28
Freestanding	17587.1	911.0	2.68	295.8	2.10	−0.58
Rural	2734.0	227.7	4.42	66.9	3.06	−1.36

Note: Pop. population; Quin. quinquennial growth rate; Turn. turnaround.

of standard regions[2]. Population changes at the small area (ward) level estimated during the period 1981–85 have been aggregated to functional local labour markets (Bracewell and Dugmore, 1988). In the subsequent commentary, nonmetropolitan local labour markets are taken to include

Table 7. Employment change and turnaround (expressed in thousands and as quinquennial growth rates) in the standard regions, by labour market region.

Labour market region	Emp. 1981	Emp. change 1971–81	Quin. 1971–81	Emp. change 1981–84	Quin. 1981–84	Turn.
South East						
Metropolitan	4 168.0	− 366.0	− 4.04	− 41.9	− 1.68	2.36
Satellite	1 710.5	171.4	5.57	52.1	5.07	− 0.49
Freestanding	1 236.0	133.5	6.06	50.4	6.80	0.75
Rural	24.0	− 4.0	− 7.18	1.8	12.30	19.49
South West						
Metropolitan	644.3	− 20.8	− 1.57	− 43.3	− 11.19	− 9.63
Satellite	320.0	− 20.5	− 3.01	− 17.8	− 9.29	− 6.28
Freestanding	1 197.4	93.0	4.21	17.8	2.48	− 1.73
Rural	302.0	23.2	4.15	− 0.1	− 0.05	− 4.20
Midlands						
Metropolitan	1 090.5	− 126.4	− 5.19	− 38.3	− 5.85	− 0.66
Satellite	838.7	− 52.3	− 2.93	− 15.4	− 3.07	− 0.14
Freestanding	1 913.9	65.8	1.78	46.7	4.07	2.29
Rural	235.1	16.8	3.84	13.4	9.53	5.69
North						
Metropolitan	2 108.5	− 262.1	− 5.53	− 121.5	− 9.60	− 4.07
Satellite	1 679.6	− 77.3	− 2.20	− 86.1	− 8.54	− 6.34
Freestanding	1 523.2	− 79.6	− 2.48	− 29.9	− 3.27	− 0.78
Rural	72.3	5.9	4.43	7.6	17.46	13.03
Scotland						
Metropolitan	799.0	− 60.6	− 3.52	− 30.5	− 6.35	− 2.83
Satellite	227.3	− 38.3	− 7.21	− 12.8	− 9.38	− 2.17
Freestanding	736.3	45.2	3.27	− 17.7	− 4.01	− 7.28
Rural	214.1	20.8	5.37	− 5.7	− 4.41	− 9.78
Britain						
Metropolitan	8 810.4	− 835.9	− 4.33	− 275.4	− 5.21	− 0.88
Satellite	4 776.2	− 17.0	− 0.18	− 80.1	− 2.80	− 2.62
Freestanding	6 606.8	257.8	2.03	67.4	1.70	− 0.33
Rural	847.6	62.6	3.99	17.0	3.35	− 0.64

Note: Emp. employment; Quin. quinquennial growth rate; Turn. turnaround.

[2] Standard regions apart from South East England and Scotland are grouped. The 'North' contains the North West, Yorkshire and Humberside, and the North standard regions; the 'South West' combines Wales and the South West standard region; and the 'Midlands' combines the East and West Midlands with East Anglia.

both freestanding and rural towns, as they are by definition beyond the metropolitan sphere of economic influence (specifically, commuting linkage). Satellite towns are distinguished both from metropolitan centres and from nonmetropolitan towns, as although having commuting linkages with the associated metropolis, they have in the past gained population through net in-migration from metropolitan cores, even if such growth is generally classified as decentralisation rather than deconcentration.

Table 6 confirms the analysis for administrative regions, namely of a revival of metropolitan population in most standard region groups, but most pronounced in South East England. Growth rates remain high in nonmetropolitan labour markets, but have fallen, between the periods 1971–81 and 1981–85, in most standard region groups. Only in the South East and freestanding towns of the 'South West' has growth in nonmetropolitan towns not fallen in the 1980s as the metropolitan centres

Table 8. Population change and turnaround (expressed in thousands and quinquennial growth rates) in the standard regions by policy type.

Policy status	Pop. 1981	Pop. change 1971–81	Quin. 1971 –81	Pop. change 1981–85	Quin. 1981 –85	Turn.
South East						
New Town	867.4	133.1	8.99	34.1	4.91	−4.08
Expanded town	832.5	90.7	6.02	39.6	5.95	−0.07
Other	14885.1	−356.3	−1.15	109.2	0.92	2.07
South West						
New town	141.8	6.4	2.35	−0.2	−0.19	−2.54
Expanded town	701.8	58.5	4.47	25.7	4.58	0.12
Other	6236.3	266.0	2.18	96.8	1.94	−0.24
Midlands						
New town	745.9	132.1	10.66	38.2	6.41	−4.25
Expanded town	571.5	94.7	9.82	20.5	4.48	−5.34
Other	9143.3	169.9	0.94	47.3	0.65	−0.29
North						
New town	551.1	30.0	2.85	1.3	0.31	−2.55
Expanded town	* 72.0	4.6	3.37	1.1	1.95	−1.42
Other	13756.8	−234.1	−0.83	−122.2	−1.11	−0.28
Scotland						
New town	271.0	3.1	0.58	−1.1	−0.53	−1.11
Expanded town	0.0	0.0	0.0	0.0	0.0	0.0
Other	4774.0	−102.3	−1.03	−45.8	−1.20	−0.17
Britain						
New town	2577.2	304.7	6.65	72.3	3.51	−3.14
Expanded town	2177.9	248.5	6.34	87.0	4.99	−1.35
Other	48793.9	−256.7	−0.26	85.3	0.22	0.48

Note: Pop. population; Quin. quinquennial growth rate; Turn. turnaround.

have revived (the accelerated growth in northern rural towns being from a low population base). Thus as in the analysis of administrative regions (table 4), the distinctiveness of the nonmetropolitan remainder in the South East is apparent.

Changes in employment depicted in table 7 (drawing from the 1981 and 1984 Censuses of Employment) are, however, less clear cut. Only in the South East is there a clear metropolitan revival in employment. In other standard region groups, most notably the 'Midlands', there are even signs of an acceleration in the growth of nonmetropolitan employment in the 1980s, and an increase in the losses of metropolitan employment. The discrepancy between increased population retention by metropolitan regions but an absence of a general employment revival may be seen as a source of the higher than average increases in metropolitan unemployment over the period concerned.

Table 9. Employment change and turnaround (expressed in thousands and quinquennial growth rates) in the standard regions by policy type.

Policy status	Emp. 1981	Emp. change 1971–81	Quin.	Emp. change 1981–84	Quin.	Turn.
South East						
New Town	351.2	63.3	10.98	12.0	5.69	−5.29
Expanded town	283.3	36.5	7.39	13.4	7.89	0.50
Other	6 504.0	−164.8	−1.24	36.9	0.95	2.18
South West						
New town	47.8	1.5	1.62	−1.4	−4.73	−6.35
Expanded town	203.8	12.1	3.16	11.9	9.73	6.57
Other	2 212.1	61.2	1.42	−53.9	−4.06	−5.48
Midlands						
New town	286.8	30.2	5.90	13.3	7.76	1.86
Expanded town	184.2	18.5	5.58	13.4	12.10	6.53
Other	3 607.3	−144.9	−1.93	−20.3	−0.94	0.99
North						
New town	197.4	−6.0	−1.47	−9.4	−7.93	−6.45
Expanded town	26.6	2.5	5.26	1.8	11.13	5.87
Other	5 159.7	−409.8	−3.68	−222.3	−7.18	−3.50
Scotland						
New town	89.9	−0.5	−0.25	−1.2	−2.22	−1.97
Expanded town	0.0	0.0	0.0	0.0	0.0	0.0
Other	1 886.9	−32.4	−0.84	−65.4	−5.78	−4.93
Britain						
New town	973.0	88.5	5.01	13.4	2.29	−2.71
Expanded town	698.0	69.6	5.54	40.5	9.66	4.12
Other	19 369.5	−690.7	−1.72	−325.0	−2.80	−1.07

Note: Emp. employment; Quin. quinquennial growth rate; Turn. turnaround.

Examination of population and employment growth in NETs in tables 8 and 9 points to one reason for this differential in the extent of metropolitan population as against employment revival in most standard region groups. (It may be noted that only those NETs which are cores of local labour markets are the subject of this analysis, thereby excluding several NETs which are subdivisions of metropolitan labour markets, but do not constitute the core.) Most standard region groups show a reduced rate of population growth in NETs, and a revival in other types of town. The slowdown in population growth in NETs is concentrated in satellite and freestanding towns within the urban hierarchy. These functional categories account for all but one of the 21 new towns and all but two of the 19 expanded towns. By contrast, employment growth in the expanded towns category increased in the early 1980s, and although employment growth in new towns has generally slowed, the quinquennia growth rates remain high in the South East and the 'Midlands'. Thus the advantage of employment growth of policy designated towns, especially expanded towns, has continued, but population migration to such towns has slowed considerably.

The slowdown in population growth is most marked in satellite new towns, from 5.5% quinquennial growth in 1971–81 to 1.5% in 1981–85 a compared with freestanding new towns (a slowdown from 7.8% to 5.4%) Satellite expanded towns also show a greater deceleration of population growth (from 9.8% to 5.0%) than freestanding expanded towns (from 4.8% to 4.6%). Contraction of population growth in satellite NETs is one cause of the reduced growth in the outer metropolitan ring around London, evident in table 2 and in the analysis of figures 1(a) to 1(c).

6 A model of growth and turnaround in local labour markets of South East England

The data on population and employment change at the level of the individual local labour market demonstrate the continuing tendency to deconcentration within the 'greater South East', albeit with a redistribution in the sources of migrants in the case of population change, as discussed above. Thus LLMAs more distant from London show the highest growth rates in the period 1981–85, examples including Milton Keynes, Huntingdon, Newmarket, Bishop's Stortford, Peterborough, Andover, and Weston-super-Mare. However, comparison of annual rates of change between the periods 1981–85 and 1971–81 highlights the population shifts which have occurred in the 1980s, such as the stemming of high losses of metropolitan migration. The London LLMA emerges as having one of the biggest turnarounds in growth rate, alongside LLMAs which reflect a selective rippling out across the 'greater South East'—with Andover, Wells, Weymouth, Hastings, and Canterbury among those showing the largest gains in growth. Figure 3 shows the generally positive association between shifts in population and employment.

To investigate formally the links between population and employment turnaround, a simultaneous-equations model is proposed for the 59 local labour markets in South East England, and for the 103 local labour markets in the 'greater South East' (including the South West and East Anglia standard regions). In this model the postulated interdependence between employment and population turnaround and growth is expressed (see table 5)[3]. It also includes the influences of structural characteristics (such as employment specialisation), of selective migration (such as retirement migration), and of regional and urban policy. For example, turnaround in population would be expected to be negatively related to NET status, on the basis of the above results. Employment growth and turnaround would be expected to be positively related to concentrations of, and growth in, producer services and high-technology manufacturing. The former sector is as defined in Gillespie and Green (1987), the latter as in Townsend (1986).

The spatial distribution of producer services in particular is marked by considerable urban and regional differentiation (in contrast to consumer services). Producer services have, moreover, been seen as a contributor to the 'export base' of (functional) regions, and to overall economic growth (Gillespie and Green, 1987; Townsend, 1986). Several studies show a spatial concentration of producer services in the South East, especially in London and its surrounding 'subdominants'. There is evidence also that although concentration has been increasing in terms of corporate control, a deconcentration of lower order 'back office' functions has taken place within the South East. Hence variations in concentration and growth of producer services within the local labour markets of the South East may be seen as a source of differences in their overall employment growth and revival. There are several reasons why such reasoning may not be applicable to the same extent beyond the South East (for example, the gains in rent and wages flatten out

[3] There are four endogenous (dependent) variables and eleven exogenous (independent) variables in the system to be estimated by two-stage least squares. The endogenous variables are annualised rates of population and employment growth (ΔPOP8185 and ΔEMP8184, respectively), and turnaround in these two annualised rates, that is, later period minus earlier period growth rates (POPTURN and EMPTURN, respectively). The exogenous variables are first-period annualised rates of growth (ΔPOP7181 and ΔEMP7181); percent indices of economic structure from the 1981 Annual Census of Employment for the high-technology and producer-service sector (HITECH and PRODSERV, respectively); annualised rates of growth in percent points in these sectors between 1981–84 (ΔPRODSERV and ΔHITECH); NET dummy indicators, crossed in equation (1) with a dummy for satellite LLMAs (NEWEXP and NEWEXP $\times$ SATELL); rates of retirement migration from the 1981 Census (immigrants over retirement age expressed as a percent of total population), crossed with a dummy for nonmetropolitan status (RETMIG $\times$ NONMET); ratios of child to women of reproductive age from the 1981 Census (CHLDRAT); and a dummy for nonmetropolitan status (NONMET).

after a certain distance), so that the impacts of specialisation in producer services will be expected to be particularly marked in the South East.

The estimated model coefficients for the South East (table 10, see over) show the expected positive effects of population and employment turnaround on each other and on overall growth. It is noticeable that although both coefficients are significant (at the 10% level), the coefficient expressing the dependence of population turnaround on that of employment is smaller than that expressing the dependence of employment on population turnaround (the latter being virtually a one-to-one relationship). In turn this difference reflects the much greater variability of employment than of population shifts, an indication of the wide range of economic fortunes in local labour markets. It is also

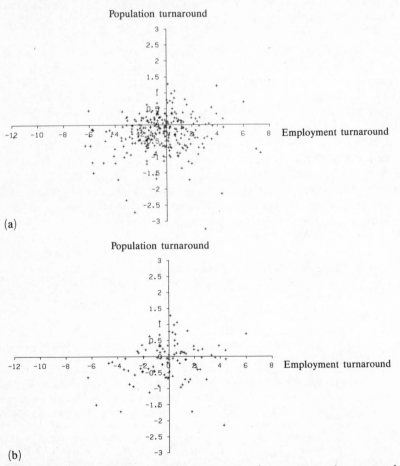

Figure 3. Annual turnaround in population growth versus annual turnaround in employment growth, in local labour market areas of (a) Britain, and (b) the South East.

Table 10. Two-stage least-squares regression estimates of simultaneous model for local labour markets (t-ratios in parentheses).

Equation	R^2

South East Standard Region

(1) POPTURN = 0.144 + 0.086 EMPTURN + 0.332 RETMIG × NONMET − 0.304 NEWEXP × SATELL − 0.396 ΔPOP7181 − 0.147 NONMET   0.50
           (1.4) (1.4)   (1.5)   (1.2)   (5.5)   (0.5)

(2) ΔPOP8185 = −5.003 + 0.190 EMPTURN + 0.154 CHLDRAT + 0.792 RETMIG × NOMET + 0.473 NEWEXP − 0.541 NONMET   0.38
              (3.4) (2.5)   (3.6)   (2.6)   (2.1)   (1.4)

(3) EMPTURN = −2.883 + 0.947 POPTURN + 0.119 PRODSERV + 0.031 HITECH + 0.748 ΔPRODSERV + 0.488 ΔHITECH   0.26
           (1.7) (1.5)   (2.2)   (0.5)   (1.6)   (0.7)
                  −0.429 NEWEXP − 0.364 ΔEMP7181 + 0.023 NONMET
                   (0.5)   (2.0)   (0.03)

(4) ΔEMP8184 = −1.969 + 1.055 POPTURN + 0.113 PRODSERV + 0.0113 HITECH + 0.619 ΔPRODSERV + 0.360 ΔHITECH   0.15
             (1.1) (1.5)   (1.9)   (0.2)   (1.2)   (0.5)
                 + 0.416 NEWEXP − 0.005 NONMET
                  (0.5)   (0.01)

Greater South East

(1) POPTURN = 0.175 + 0.049 EMPTURN + 0.362 RETMIG × NONMET − 0.370 NEWEXP × SATELL − 0.421 ΔPOP7181 − 0.250 NONMET   0.47
           (1.9) (1.1)   (2.1)   (1.7)   (7.3)   (1.1)

(2) ΔPOP8185 = −4.326 + 0.075 EMPTURN + 0.135 CHLDRAT + 0.789 RETMIG × NONMET + 0.332 NEWEXP − 0.513 NONMET   0.35
            (3.9) (1.4)   (4.3)   (3.4)   (2.2)   (1.7)

(3) EMPTURN = −1.462 + 1.099 POPTURN + 0.088 PRODSERV − 0.038 HITECH + 0.370 ΔPRODSERV + 0.844 ΔHITECH   0.24
          (1.2) (2.1)   (2.1)   (0.8)   (1.4)   (1.8)
               + 0.720 NEWEXP − 0.420 ΔEMP7181 − 0.023 NONMET
               (1.3)   (2.8)   (0.05)

(4) ΔEMP8184 = −1.216 + 0.961 POPTURN + 0.096 PRODSERV + 0.0034 HITECH + 0.409 ΔPRODSERV + 0.861 ΔHITECH   0.18
          (0.9) (1.7)   (2.2)   (0.7)   (1.4)   (1.7)
               + 1.158 NEWEXP + 0.074 NONMET
               (2.0)   (0.1)

Note: For elucidation of variables, see footnote 3.

apparent that employment and population recovery (or acceleration) are more likely to occur in local labour markets with low growth or loss in the 1970s; this represents a convergence or 'negative feedback' effect.

Population growth by natural increase, as proxied by the ratio of young children to women of reproductive age in 1981, has the anticipated positive effect on overall increase in population. This indicator is also a surrogate for past patterns of family migration—for example, to NETs during the 1970s. NET designation itself has a positive impact on growth, reflecting the continued influence of such schemes in promoting decentralisation and deconcentration from London (Congdon and Shepherd, 1986). However, as expected, it is associated [see the results of equation (1) of table 10] with a deceleration of growth as compared with the 1970s, particularly in satellite NETs. This primarily reflects the recent downturn in net migration to these towns. Nonmetropolitan status lacks a positive effect on growth and turnaround in the early 1980s—a striking contrast to earlier decades. The age selective migration effect (represented by the term RETMIG × NONMET) in raising population growth in nonmetropolitan LLMAs is, however, apparent (Kontuly and Vogelsang, 1985; McCarthy and Morrison, 1977).

Employment growth and turnaround are positively and significantly related to concentrations of employment in the producer services, and growth in this sector is also associated with growth in total employment. This tends to confirm the nature of producer services as a 'basic' sector. It may be noted that growth in producer services is expressed in terms of differences in percent points (1984 percent of total employment in this sector minus corresponding 1981 percent), so that the producer-service effect in equations (3) and (4) (see table 10) is indicative of structural change rather than of absolute growth in the number of jobs in the producer services.

The growth effect of specialisation in high technology is less pronounced than that of specialisation in producer services in the local labour markets of the South East. However, in the 'greater South East' (including East Anglia and the South West) growth in high-technology employment is a significant source of overall employment growth and turnaround. Growth in this sector has continued in most LLMAs in East Anglia despite the recession and in many such areas in the South West; examples include LLMAs in the M4 corridor and a cluster of towns in the Cambridge subregion. Even in these growth zones with a concentration of high-technology jobs, growth in jobs in the producer services may be comparable or faster (Boddy and Lovering, 1986).

Employment growth and acceleration in the 'greater South East' are also differentiated from the South East standard region by the greater positive impact of NET designation. Expanded towns in East Anglia and the South West have, if anything, seen faster growth in employment in the 1980s than in the 1970s. However, the deceleration of population growth in (satellite) NETs is apparent both for the 'greater South East' and for the South East. This tends to confirm the possibility, also suggested in tables 8 and 9, of discrepancy between employment and population trends in NETs.

7 Conclusions

In our analysis in this paper we have considered components of recent population change in the South East and London, comparing the 1980s with the early and late 1970s. We have found evidence both of a revival of London's population as net out-migration has declined, and of continuing high levels of net migration to outer parts of the South East region. As a result, the contribution of the entire region to national population growth currently exceeds its relative size. These shifts reflect a waning of deconcentration from the metropolitan centre combined with increases in net foreign inflow both to London and to the rest of the region, and an increased net inflow to the capital from Britain outside the South East.

This relative increase in the South East's share of national population growth has obvious implications for the planning of housing and other infrastructure provision. An example is the recent upward revision in projected households for London and the rest of the region, and the problems caused by matching increased demand with new dwellings (SERPLAN, 1988). The problems associated with metropolitan employment revival including adequate provision for car and rail commuting to the capital, together with emergent skill shortages, are discussed by Palmer in this volume.

Population turnaround in metropolitan regions, whether administratively or functionally defined, is apparent throughout Britain, albeit to a less marked extent than for London. Metropolitan employment turnaround is, however, less general in the early 1980s. A winding down of new town expansion has increased the retention of metropolitan population throughout Britain, but the South East is distinctive both in its association with the recovery of metropolitan employment and in the continuation of growth in the nonmetropolitan part of the region.

A simultaneous-equations model of population and employment growth in the local labour markets of the South East confirms the interplay between population revival and employment revival, and further demonstrates the importance of urban type and sectoral economic specialisation to overall growth. These findings lend support to those by researchers in other countries that the process of population redistribution is not only a matter of population density and metropolitan or nonmetropolitan status. This is only the basic level of counterurbanisation or reurbanisation. Rather growth and shifts in growth are more fundamentally a reflection of urban type (policy status or retirement town, for example) and the economic structure and growth of different functional regions. Changes in economic growth are in turn linked to shifts in the spatial division of labour—intranationally and, to some extent, internationally—for different sectors such as producer services. The contrast between London and other metropolitan centres in the United Kingdom is one example which confirms such a conclusion.

References

Boddy M, Lovering J, 1986, "High technology industry in the Bristol sub-region: the aerospace-defence nexus" *Regional Studies* **20** 217–232

Bracewell R, Dugmore K, 1988, "Small area population estimates: 1982–85" *BURISA Newsletter* **82** 11–12; availabe from School of Advanced Urban Studies, University of Bristol, Grange Road, Bristol BS8 4EA

Britton M, 1986, "Recent population changes in perspective" *Population Trends* **44** 34–41

Buck N, Gordon I, Young K, 1985 *The London Employment Problem* (Clarendon Press, Oxford)

Champion A, Congdon P, 1987, "An analysis of the recovery of London's population change rate" *Built Environment* **13** (4) 193–211

Champion A, Coombes M, Openshaw S, 1983, "A new definition of cities" *Geographical Magazine* (November) 305–307

Congdon P, Champion A, 1989, "Trends and structure in London's migration an their relation to employment and housing markets", in *Advances in Regional Demography* Eds P Congdon, P Batey (Belhaven Press, London) pp 180–204

Congdon P, Shepherd J, 1986, "Modelling population changes in small English urban areas" *Environment and Planning A* **18** 1297–1322

Courgeau D, 1986, "Vers un ralentissement de la 'déconcentration urbaine'" *Population et Société* **41** 1–4

Engels R, 1986, "The metropolitan/nonmetropolitan population at mid-decade", paper presented to the Population Association of America, Annual Meeting, California; copy available from Bureau of the Census, Washington, DC

Fielding A, 1982, "Counterurbanisation in Western Europe" *Progress in Planning* **17** 1–54

Fielding A, 1989, "Population redistribution in Western Europe: trends since 1950 and the debate about counterurbanisation", in *Advances in Regional Demography* Eds P Congdon, P Batey (Belhaven Press, London) pp 167–179

Gillespie A E, Green A E, 1987, "The changing geography of producer services employment in Britain" *Regional Studies* **21** 397–412

Hepworth M E, Green A E, Gillespie A E, 1987, "The spatial division of information labour in Great Britain" *Environment and Planning A* **19** 793–80

Kontuly T, Vogelsang R, 1985, "Counterurbanisation and age selective migration in the Federal Republic of Germany", paper presented to the 25th European Conference of the Regional Science Association; available from Department Geography, University of Utah, Salt Lake City, UT 84112

Korcelli P, 1986, "Migration and urban change", in *Migration and Human Settleme* Eds A Rogers, F Willekens (D Reidel, Dordrecht) pp 323–354

McCarthy K, Morrison P, 1977, "The changing demographic and economic structure of non-metropolitan areas in the United States" *International Region Science Review* **2** 123–142

OPCS, 1988 *Mid-1987 Population Estimates for England and Wales* Office of Population Censuses and Surveys (Population Monitor PP1 88/1)

Richter K, 1985, "Nonmetropolitan growth in the late 1970s: the end of the turnaround" *Demography* **22** 245–263

Roberts S, Randolph W, 1983, "Beyond decentralization: the evolution of population distribution in England and Wales, 1961–1981" *Geoforum* **14** 75–102

SERPLAN, 1986, "Regional trends in the South East" *SERPLAN Monitor 1985–86* London and South East Regional Planning Conference, 50–64 Broadway, London SW1H 0DB

SERPLAN, 1988, "Regional trends in the South East" *SERPLAN Monitor 1987–88* RPC 1060, London and South East Regional Planning Conference, 50–64 Broadway, London SW1H 0DB

Townsend A R, 1986, "The location of employment growth after 1978: the surprising significance of dispersed centres" *Environment and Planning A* **18** 529–545

Tyler P, Rhodes J, 1986, "South East employment and housing study", DP-15, Department of Land Economy, Cambridge University, Cambridge

South East England in the Eighties: Explanations for a House Price Explosion

A W EVANS
University of Reading

1 Introduction

In this paper the evidence relating to house prices in South East England is reviewed and it is shown that house prices have been rising rapidly, that this has occurred as land prices have risen, and that this appears to be due to the restricted availability of land for housing. It is then shown that house prices in the South East and the other regions in the south of the country have risen more rapidly than elsewhere, particularly in the last three years or so. This differential effect is attributed to three factors which are discussed in turn. First, a reduction in migration out of the country has led to an unanticipated increase in the population to be housed; second, the effectiveness of regional policy has decreased as controls such as Industrial Development Certificates have been eliminated and as the financial resources put into regional incentives have been reduced; third, policies affecting the local authority housing sector— increases in rents, reduction in the number of dwellings built, sales of existing stock—have increased the potential mobility of the population.

2 House prices and the supply of land

It seems clear from the evidence that restrictions on the availability of land for development in the southern part of England have caused, and are causing, house prices to be higher there than they otherwise would be. The evidence for this has already been made available, for example, in a paper published by the House Builders Federation (Evans, 1987) and in papers resulting from a recent study of the costs of the planning system (Cheshire et al, 1985). It has also been summarised in a recent paper (Evans, 1988).

In brief the argument is that the demand for property and, in particular, for land in southern England has increased in the years since the planning system was initiated in 1947 because of increasing incomes, an increasing population, and reduced travel costs (which allowed people to live away from the main built-up areas) but that the amount of land released for development through the planning system has not increased commensurately. As demand has risen so the price of land for development has also risen, to levels well above the price of agricultural land without planning permission for development. Because the argument is fundamental to an understanding of the situation it is summarised here.

existing supply of land is determined, and that so is the price of land, and also to agree that, by definition, the existing supply of land is fixed. Suppose new houses are built on a new area of land not contained within the existing supply. Buyers of houses will now have a greater range to choose from as they seek the best buy not only amongst the houses built on the existing supply of land but also amongst new houses built on the new land. It is clear that the demand for houses on the existing supply of land will fall because of the increased supply of competitive products and so, as a result, their price will fall as will the price of the housing land.

In practice both land and house prices are determined simultaneously, by demand and by supply. Restricting the supply of land will raise the price of both. The high price of housing land is therefore due to the restrictions on the supply of land. If the supply were increased the price would be lower. This is the correct interpretation of the relevant economic theory.

4 The operation of the market—the supply of land

Rising prices in a market, any market, are a signal to suppliers to provide more of the product. The rising price of housing land in the South East should therefore cause more land to be brought to the market to be sold for development. But the evidence is that the amount of land which could be brought forward for development is now very restricted indeed. Figure 2 shows the number of hectares sold to private developers in the South East (outside Greater London) with planning permission for four dwellings or more. As we have stressed, prices are signals, and a price rise should bring out an increased supply. The figure shows that the market did indeed respond to the land price boom of 1972/73. More land was sold for development as the price rose, and less when it fell. But over the ensuing period land sales have failed to respond in the same way to the increasing price of land in real terms. Even less land was sold each year in the four years of rising

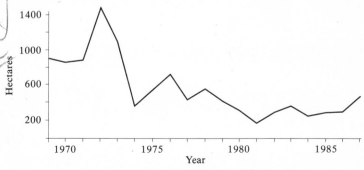

Figure 2. The number of hectares sold in the ROSE with planning permission for four dwellings or more. Source: DoE, 1980, table 100; 1988, table 10.1.

land prices between 1982 and 1987 than was sold in 1974, after the collapse of the 1972/73 land price boom. The price of land is increasing, but land sales are declining, presumably because the land which could have been sold has now been sold and relatively little now remains for sale, whatever the price.

More direct evidence of the position is provided by a study carried out by Roger Tym and Partners (1987) for the Department of the Environment and SERPLAN, published in July 1987. They analysed a representative sample of five-hundred housing sites on which construction was started in the first half of 1984. It was found that only 35% of sites were on open land formerly used for agriculture or forestry. Of the remaining 65%, 21% of starts were on vacant or derelict land, 18% on residential land (including garden space), and 26% on land in a variety of other uses (industry and commerce 8%, defence 7%, outdoor recreation 6%, community services 4%, and transport or utilities 1%). Thus most housing development in South East England results from the intensification of use in existing urban areas or from taking over land from other, nonrural uses. Further, over a fifth of all sites in the sample were adventitious in that they had never been identified in any planning document, whether statutory or nonstatutory, but had been found and identified as suitable for development by developers or land owners. At that time Roger Tym and Partners found that purchases from local authorities and other public bodies were the most common source of housing sites for large builders. But this source must dry up in due course as the available supply is sold.

5 The operation of the market—the demand for housing

Just as rising prices in a market are a signal to suppliers to supply more of the product, so rising prices are a signal leading consumers to economise on their purchases of a product. So if house prices and land prices rise one would expect people to adjust to the situation by 'trading down', buying smaller houses occupying smaller sites. This does not mean, of course, that they necessarily spend less (because the house or site is smaller); nor does it mean they necessarily spend more (because the price of the house or site has risen). The outcome can only be determined empirically and the econometric evidence suggests that in practice the total amount spent on housing by households does not vary very much when house prices change.

The position is made more complicated by the fact that incomes change over time as well as land and house prices, and as people's incomes change so their expenditure on housing changes. As people's incomes increase this leads them to spend more on housing, attempting to buy bigger houses on bigger sites. Econometric work suggests that on average if the income of a household increases by, say, 1% its expenditure on housing will also increase by about 1%. So as household incomes change over time, households will still spend an almost constant proportion of their incomes on housing.

This analysis explains why the relationship between house price and income stays fairly constant as shown in figure 1. As incomes rise people buy more housing; as the price per unit of housing rises so they buy less housing. In particular, if the price of land rises (or falls) one would expect less (or more) land to be purchased but the amount spent on housing to remain approximately the same. For example, if someone moves from London to Glasgow the family might move out of a two-bedroomed flat and into a three-bedroomed bungalow. The price of both may be approximately the same, but the price of housing is not the same. It is cheaper in Glasgow, but this cheapness allows more housing to be bought. So, people adjust their purchase of housing to changing economic circumstances and these adjustments ensure that the relationship between incomes and house prices remains very stable.[2]

Evidence that households shift towards buying cheaper house types is given in table 1 in which the average price of dwellings in the South East mortgaged by Building Societies in the period 1975–87 is shown as an index (equal to 100 in 1975). This is compared with a house price index for the same period, derived from the same data, but weighted to give the change in prices which would have resulted if the same mix of dwelling types had been sold in each year throughout the period. The weighted index rises faster than the unweighted because the latter is biassed downwards as households trade down into less-expensive dwelling types.

Table 1. Weighted and unweighted house price indices for the rest of the South East (1975 index = 100). Source: DoE, 1986, table 10.8; 1988, table 10.8.

Year	Unweighted	Weighted	Year	Unweighted	Weighted
1975	100	100	1982	202	226
1976	106	107	1983	230	256
1977	112	114	1984	255	290
1978	129	133	1985	276	320
1979	168	177	1986	331	375
1980	203	214	1987	391	461
1981	204	224			

[2] There is also an administrative relationship which ensures that house prices and incomes stay aligned. Building societies and other housing finance institutions will not lend more than fixed multiples of borrowers' incomes. As the advance is a large proportion of the price of the house, particularly for a first-time purchaser, this is likely to act as a constraint on large changes in the relationship between house prices, advances, and incomes.

Of course, it could be said that this was a response to a shift in demand as people came to prefer more high-density living. This is not borne out by the data on the prices of different kinds of housing. Figure 3 shows the price indices for different kinds of homes over the same period for the whole of England and Wales, as separate figures for the South East are not published. It can be seen that the more land used up by a dwelling type in proportion to capital, the faster the rate of price increase. If the shift in types of dwelling built has occurred because of a shift in demand we should have expected flats to have risen in price faster than terraced or semi-detached houses and these would have risen in price faster than bungalows or detached houses (and land prices would not have increased relative to incomes). As this did not occur, the shift in types of dwelling constructed did not come about because of a shift in demand, but because of the increasing price of land.

The differential impact of the house price boom in the South East region and its relationship to land availability are indicated in table 2. This is taken from figures collected by the National House-Building Council (NHBC) and shows the proportion of different kinds of dwellings constructed in different parts of the country. In London and the South East a far higher proportion of new dwellings are flats, maisonettes, and terraced homes. Whilst one might possibly expect this to be so in an urban area such as London, the figures indicate that the rest of the South East (ROSE), which consists of the outermost suburbs of London and a number of small towns, is also being developed in the land-economising way that one would normally expect in the inner area of a large conurbation.

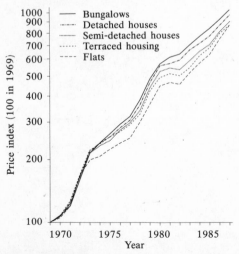

Figure 3. Dwelling price by type of dwelling mortgaged in the United Kingdom. Source: DoE, 1980; 1988.

The difference between the pattern of development in southern England and in the rest of the country also indicates that the shift towards flats is not occurring for demographic reasons. True, households are smaller than they used to be, but there is no reason at all to suppose that this demographic change should differentially affect Southern England. The fact that dwellings appear to use land more intensively in the ROSE is therefore evidence that the change is a response to changing supply conditions rather than changing demand conditions. .

Moreover, these data also suggest that the rise in land prices did not come about because of a shift in demand towards more land per house. Rather, people responded to the rise in the price of development land by accepting less land per house. As land prices have risen so the planned density of development has increased, because developers have used land more intensively. This process was constrained by planning controls but has clearly occurred. There is some evidence that dwelling sizes may be smaller in the South East. For example, the Nationwide Building Society recently reported that the average house size in Bedfordshire was 852 square feet and cost nearly £43 000, whereas in Lancashire the average house size was 987 square feet and cost only £27 000 (*Chartered Surveyor Weekly*, 1987).

Table 2. Percentage of 'starts' of dwelling types by region, 1987. Source: National House-Building Council.

Region/area	Det. Bung.	Att. Bung.	Det. House	Semi-det. House	Terr. House	Flats and Mais.
North	16	7	40	16	10	11
North West	11	7	47	15	6	14
Yorkshire and Humberside	21	8	39	17	7	7
West Midlands	10	3	54	16	6	11
East Midlands	17	5	49	17	8	4
East Anglia	12	5	36	15	20	12
South West	8	3	35	18	20	12
South East[a]	4	2	34	11	18	30
Greater London	1	1	6	5	18	69

[a] Excluding Greater London.
Note: Det. detached, Att. attached, semi-det. semi-detached, Terr. terraced, Bung. bungalows, Mais. maisonettes.

6 House prices and the regions

It is, of course, well known that house prices in the southern, and particulary the southeastern, part of the country are higher than elsewhere. Table 3 illustrates this, showing that average prices are higher in the regions to the south and southeast of the country. But the table also

shows that house prices appear to have risen far more rapidly in these
regions than elsewhere in the period 1986/87.

This pattern has not always been evident. Table 4 shows the weighted
index of house prices for each of the regions over the period 1975–87.
It can be seen that, on average, prices doubled between 1976 and 1980
and that the rate of increase was more or less the same in each of the
regions. Since then, particularly since 1983, the rate of increase in the
southern regions has been much faster than that in the remainder of the
country. The rate of increase has been fastest in Greater London, followed
by the ROSE, East Anglia, the South West, and the East Midlands.
The other regions—Yorkshire and Humberside, North, North West, and
the West Midlands—have lower rates of house price increase, as do
Scotland, Wales, and Northern Ireland.

Why should there have been this acceleration in house prices in the
southern and eastern part of the country in the last four years or so?
After all, average house prices have always differed between regions.
Table 3 shows the average price of houses mortgaged with the Building
Societies in each of the regions in 1969, 1977, 1986, and 1987. Regional
differences have always existed, but it is clear both from table 3 and table 4
that these differences have increased substantially in the last few years.

The increase in house prices must occur because of an increase in
demand or because of a reduction in supply. But given the nature of
the housing market with a given housing stock at the beginning of any
period it is obvious that the supply of housing has not been reduced.
It follows that the demand for housing must have increased in the South
East faster than the available supply of housing has increased. I showed
earlier that the supply of housing land is restricted and that this has
resulted in rising house and land prices, but the data do not indicate

Table 3. Average price of dwellings mortgaged by building societies. Source:
DoE, 1980, table 105; 1988, table 10.11.

Region/area	1969	1977	1986	1987	Change (%) 1986 to 1987
Greater London	6195	16745	54863	66024	20
Rest of South East	5792	16466	48544	57387	18
East Anglia	4298	12176	36061	42681	18
South West	4496	13555	38536	44728	16
East Midlands	3791	11367	28463	31808	15
West Midlands	4348	12528	28437	32657	11
Yorkshire and Humberside	3436	10722	25607	27747	11
North West	3922	11523	27503	29527	11
North	3714	11773	24333	27275	11
Wales	4168	11673	27354	29704	11
Scotland	4609	14236	28242	29591	10

any sharp deterioration on the supply side in the early 1980s. There are, then, two possibilities if the change has occurred on the demand side. The first is that demand has increased throughout the country but supply is more restricted in the south and southeast. This is possible, of course, but appears unlikely in that the rate of new building has also increased fastest in the southeast. The second possibility is therefore the most likely—the demand for housing has increased faster in the south and southeast than elsewhere in the country.

But why should this have been? It might be the nature of the present boom and the previous recession. The 'smoke stack industries' of the northern and midland regions were hit harder in the recession of 1980/81.

Table 4. Regional weighted house price indices (1975 index = 100). Sources: CSO, 1982; DoE, 1986, table 10.8; 1988, table 10.8.

Year	Greater London	Rest of South East	East Anglia	South West	East Midlands
1975	100	100	100	100	100
1976	107	107	106	107	108
1977	115	114	110	114	116
1978	137	133	127	131	131
1979	183	177	164	123	165
1980	223	214	207	216	204
1981	230	224	219	223	220
1982	234	226	227	232	226
1983	263	256	248	255	251
1984	306	290	273	275	275
1985	348	320	307	303	295
1986	424	375	357	349	328
1987	529	461	427	409	366

Year	West Midlands	Yorkshire and Humberside	North West	North	Wales	Scotland
1975	100	100	100	100	100	100
1976	108	113	110	112	111	120
1977	118	120	121	127	116	131
1978	136	135	140	142	135	147
1979	174	169	181	174	171	176
1980	206	207	221	206	205	202
1981	215	233	235	219	222	220
1982	219	235	242	229	234	236
1983	238	264	266	254	257	264
1984	254	281	282	268	267	281
1985	267	297	295	276	287	297
1986	291	325	324	299	306	313
1987	334	350	345	326	339	339

Moreover, in the present boom, the service industries of London and the south—finance, tourism, etc—and the 'high-tech' industries of the south are those which are growing fastest. But the decline of the old 'metal bashing' industries has been going on for decades, as has the rise of electronics and high tech. Other booms and other recessions have occurred in the past without this differential impact on the regions. Some factors must distinguish this boom from previous ones to explain the differential impact on house prices in the south.

The first, and in my view, the primary reason is a substantial change which has occurred in the pattern of international migration. Far fewer people have left the south than in the past; as a result, most of any increase in the housing stock has had to be used to accommodate the increase in the existing 'indigenous' population, and less of this increase is available to accommodate migrants from elsewhere.

Additional, secondary, reasons are the winding down of regional policy and the increased potential mobility of former local authority tenants. The first means that growth is deterred in, or steered away from, the south to a lesser extent than in the past. The second means that a sector of the population which was relatively immobile is now more able and willing to attempt to migrate.

7 International migration

The dramatic change which has occurred in the pattern of international migration since 1983 deserves to be better known. International migration is monitored through surveys of passengers arriving at and departing from Britain's ports and airports, and these surveys have been carried on since 1963. In the following twenty years there was always a net outflow—with the single exception of 1978/79 when there was a small net inflow—so that emigration exceeded immigration, usually by substantial numbers. In 1983 the situation changed and there has been a substantial inflow over the three succeeding years for which figures have been published. The pattern of migration over the years is indicated in table 5, which is reproduced from *OPCS Monitor* MN 87/3 (OPCS, 1987).

This change has not occurred because of any substantial increase in immigration by non-British citizens. As table 5 shows, though this has increased, the primary cause has been a substantial fall in the rate of emigration by British citizens; this almost halved from a peak outflow of 186 000 in 1982/83 to 105 000 in 1983/84.

This change in the direction of net migration would anyway affect the demand for housing in the country, but its total impact is greater because it is felt mainly in the South East. As table 6 shows, of a net inflow of 67 000 in 1985/86 to the United Kingdom, the desired place of residence of 51 000 people was South East England, or nearly 80% of the total. Because total housing completions in the region at that time amounted only to about 50 000, this population inflow would have had a substantial impact on the demand for housing in the region. If 51 000 represents about some 20 000 – 25 000 households, the implication is that between a half and a third of new dwellings were necessary to accommodate the increase in the population or, rather, to accommodate the households which might have been expected to leave the country but did not.

Table 5. International migration in thousands by citizenship for the United Kingdom. Source: OPCS, 1987.

	Midyear ending										
	1976	1977	1978	1979	1980	1981	1982	1983	1984	1985	1986
All citizenships											
Inflow	197	181	162	194	203	156	171	200	199	214	244
Outflow	220	210	198	187	209	235	257	222	167	177	176
Balance	− 23	− 29	− 36	6	− 6	− 79	− 86	− 21	32	37	67
British citizens											
Inflow	87	80	70	77	76	58	78	102	90	104	113
Outflow	154	136	136	122	139	158	186	156	105	114	106
Balance	− 67	− 56	− 65	− 45	− 63	− 100	− 108	− 54	− 15	− 9	7
Non-British citizens											
Inflow	109	100	91	117	126	98	94	98	109	110	130
Outflow	66	74	62	66	69	77	71	66	62	63	70
Balance	43	26	29	51	57	21	22	32	46	46	61

Table 6. International migration (in thousands) by area of next or last residence in the United Kingdom. Source: OPCS, 1987.

Country or region of next or last residence	Mid-1985 to mid-1986		
	inflow	outflow	balance
United Kingdom	244	176	67
England	219	150	69
North	6	4	2
Yorkshire and Humberside	11	10	1
East Midlands	8	7	1
East Anglia	11	8	3
South East	136	85	51
Greater London	80	42	38
Remainder of South East	56	43	14
South West	17	10	7
West Midlands	14	10	4
North West	15	15	0
Wales	9	6	3
Scotland	14	18	− 4
Northern Ireland	2	2	0

Why the direction of migration changed, on balance, is not clear. It might be because of changes in the personal tax structure (although the Budget of 1983 was not notable for this), because of increased confidence in Britain's future following the 1983 election, because the British economy improved relative to other economies in 1983 as Britain pulled out of deep recession and countries such as West Germany began to suffer from unemployment, or because of the tightening of migration restrictions imposed by the 'old commonwealth' and the United States of America. Therefore, we do not know whether the change is permanent or temporary and likely to be reversed if say, the economies of other countries improve whilst the rate of British economic growth slows. Furthermore, because we do not know the reasons for the change, we cannot identify the extent to which it is exogenous, for example, owing to restrictions on immigration by other countries, or endogenous, as the rising demand for labour in the South East causes people to remain who would otherwise have left. To the extent that it is a response to rising labour demand, the effect on the supply of labour on the South East is the same as an increse in in-migration from elsewhere in the country. But the effect, so far as the rest of the country is concerned, is different. Because the increase in the housing stock is taken up by the existing population staying put, fewer houses are available for migrants from other regions. In-migration from elsewhere therefore has to fall, even though the rising demand for labour in the South East makes migration to jobs located there attractive. The pressure of demand on the available supply causes house prices to rise in order to choke off migration from elsewhere in the country. If this is so it explains the passion which the problem causes, as the increase in the number staying is preventing others from moving in from elsewhere who would otherwise have done so.

Since the first version of this paper was circulated the hypothesis above has been tested in a paper by Muellbauer and Murphy (1989). They found, as expected, that migration into the South East was negatively correlated with the level of international in-migration.

8 Regional policy

A secondary factor which is likely to have given further impetus to the rise in house prices in the South East is the winding down of regional policy over the last decade or so. It has been true for half a century or more than the southern part of the country has been the favoured area as regards growth and development, and the regions to the north and west have been assisted by some form of regional policy. But the strength with which these policies have been applied has been reduced over the years. This reduction in the emphasis put on policies to steer employment north and west to the assisted areas began in the mid-1970s. first, as their effectiveness began to be questioned and, second, as concern over the problems of the inner cities grew, so that the problems of cities such as London and Birmingham began to be considered as of equal importance to those of cities in the assisted areas, such as Glasgow or Newcastle.

This winding down of regional policy had been in progress for many years before the election of the Conservative government in June 1979, but the commitment of the government to a reduction in government intervention in industry meant that changes after that date became more formal. The Location of Offices Bureau was abolished in 1979. Enterprise zones, of which thirteen were designated in 1981, including one in the Docklands in inner London, were further evidence of a decline in a purely regional approach to spatial problems, as were the creation of the London Docklands Development Corporation, and the Merseyside Development Corporation in 1980, and further urban development corporations in 1986. By implication, development was favoured whether in the South East or the North West.

The areas affected by what is usually regarded as regional policy—the provision of incentives for firms to locate or expand in these areas and the control of expansion in other areas—were also reduced in two stages, in August 1982 and November 1984. Office development permits, which had been required for firms wishing to develop offices in the South East, were abolished in 1980, and industrial development certificates (IDCs), required for the development of factories in the nonassisted areas, were abolished in 1981, so that since then the only limitations imposed on development in the southern part of the country have been planning controls and the availability of land. Industrial development certificates had been required for more than thirty years, since they were introduced in the 1947 Town and Country Planning Act, so that their abolition was a fundamental change. It is also agreed that "IDCs were generally effective in diverting manufacturing industry to the depressed regions" (Balchin and Bull, 1987, page 43). For example Twomey and Taylor (1985) found that "approximately 70 per cent of all the moves estimated to have been caused by regional policy were due to restrictions on the location of industry" (page 274). The suspension of IDCs meant, presumably, that industry which might have gone to the assisted areas no longer did so after 1981.

But regional policy was most effective in steering development to the assisted areas when economic growth was high, and was least effective during periods of recession. When the economy is growing, sales and profits of firms increase so that they need to expand and may be willing to move to, or open a branch factory in, another area. On the other hand, when the economy is depressed, the sales of firms fall, as do their profits, so that they have no need to move elsewhere and no money to finance such a move. Neither the stick of IDC control nor the carrot of grants for capital expenditure has much effect at these times.

So, during the 1970s there were fewer moves to the assisted areas both because of the recession which began after the oil price increase of 1973, and also, probably, because of an increasing reluctance to refuse IDCs in the nonassisted areas. In the even deeper recession which occurred in the early 1980s it is clear that regional policy would have little impact even if it had never been reduced in effectiveness, so that the various measures such as the suspension of IDCs in 1981 would have had little immediate effect.

Only as the economy turned round in the mid-1980s would the absence of a strong regional policy be noticeable. Firms wishing to expand were no longer explicitly discouraged from doing so in southern England, and the financial inducements to move elsewhere are now less than they were, as are the number of places which are assisted by these inducements. Over most of the country the market is therefore allowed to determine the location of employment. If firms wish to expand production they are expected to do so at what they regard as the most favourable location, and if this is in southern England—because of proximity to markets or the existence of other similar firms, leading to agglomeration economies— then so be it. The pattern of employment growth since 1979 is shown in table 7. It can be seen that this is very similar to the pattern of increase in house prices during the period.

The difficulty is that land availability and planning controls impose constraints on development in southern England which are quite separate from the controls of regional policy. The expansion of firms in southern England must lead to an increased demand for labour in the region, resulting in higher wages and in-migration (or less out-migration) and an increased demand for property which is itself limited by planning controls. Although local authorities seem to have been reluctant to limit industrial development, where they could be seen as deliberately stifling economic growth, the supply of housing land has been deliberately limited on environmental grounds, so that an increased demand for labour by firms results in higher property prices as the larger labour force bids for the limited available supply.

Table 7. Percentage change in labour force (including self-employed) in the regions 1979–86. Source: DE, 1987a; 1987b.

Region	Change (%)	Region	Change (%)
South East	2	Yorkshire and Humberside	−6
East Anglia	13	North West	−12
South West	5	North	−10
East Midlands	0	Wales	−13
West Midlands	−7	Scotland	−8

9 Local authority housing

Three factors have had an impact on local authority housing since the Conservatives came to power in 1979, and are likely to affect the private-sector housing market. The first is the reduction in the rate of construction of housing by the public sector. Table 8 shows that the number of dwellings on which construction for local authorities was completed in 1976 was nearly 130 000, but by 1987 the number had fallen to under 20 000. For new towns the number fell from 16 104 to 571, and the same fall is evident in other parts of the public sector.

The fall in the number of houses built by the public sector affects the system in two ways. First, the provision of local authority housing in southern England has, in the past, eased problems of labour supply for firms by providing housing to which people can move from the rest of the region or the rest of the country. This has been most evident with respect to the new towns. Particularly in the case of the earliest new towns the availability of housing was regarded as a crucial factor in their development. Turok (1989) documents the development of Bracknell and shows how employees were attracted to the town by the possibility of obtaining housing, and firms were attracted because they could place their employees in Bracknell's houses. Although this role of the new towns became less important over time as adequate housing became more widely available, it has not completely disappeared. Milton Keynes has been seen as a place where firms can expand in southern England *and* where their workers can find reasonably priced homes. The decline in the construction of local authority, new town, and other public-sector housing therefore shifts the burden back to the private sector. But the private sector may find it difficult or more expensive to fill the gap for two reasons. First, local authority planning committees may be more

Table 8. Public-sector housing completions—Great Britain 1976–87. Source: DoE, 1987, table 6.1; 1988, table 6.1.

Year	Local authorities	New towns	Housing associations	Government departments	Total
1976	129 202	16 104	15 770	1 930	163 006
1977	119 644	15 930	25 127	1 810	162 511
1978	96 196	10 463	22 771	1 309	130 739
1979	75 573	9 476	17 835	1 139	104 023
1980	76 991	8 470	21 097	560	107 118
1981	54 956	10 324	19 249	295	84 824
1982	33 163	3 902	13 015	131	50 211
1983	32 742	2 044	15 823	248	50 857
1984	31 689	2 130	16 692	225	50 736
1985	26 074	985	12 869	117	40 045
1986	21 320	943	12 178	369	34 810
1987	18 880	571	11 898	738	32 087

willing to give themselves planning permission for new developments than they would be to give permission to private developers. Second, local authorities may use their powers of compulsory purchase to acquire land when a landowner is unwilling to sell, whereas the private developer has to search further for sites or pay more. The result is less housing in total and a higher price for land and private-sector housing. In this respect one may note that in Mayes' (1979) econometric model of the housing market in the United Kingdom, the number of house completions in the public sector is significantly and *negatively* related to house prices in the private sector. The fall in public-sector completions should therefore be expected to lead to higher private-sector house prices.

The second and third factors which might be expected to have an impact on house prices in the private sector, particularly in southern England, are the increase in the cost of local authority houses to tenants and the sales of local authority houses to tenants under the 'right to buy' legislation. As to the first of these, table 9 shows the average weekly unrebated rents over the period 1976 to 1986. It can be seen that rents were shifted up sharply between 1980 and 1982. Of course, many tenants would be entitled to rebates, but for the rest local authority housing became less economical and private-sector housing looked a better buy.

The shift into the private sector was further encouraged by the right to buy under the Housing Act (1980) which came into effect in October 1980. Table 10 shows that sales of local authority housing were increasing even before the Conservatives came to office in 1979, but sales leaped in 1982, and even though numbers have fallen somewhat since then, the result has been a substantial shift towards owner-occupation.

Table 9. Average weekly unrebated rents—Great Britain. Source: DoE, 1987, table 11.1; 1988, table 11.1.

Year	Greater London		ROE&W		England&Wales		Scotland	
	£	inc. (%)	£	inc. (%)	£	inc. (%)	£	inc. (%)
1976	5.78		4.57		4.77		3.47	
1977	6.50	12.5	5.31	16.2	5.52	15.7	4.02	15.9
1978	6.99	7.5	5.62	5.8	5.85	6.0	4.46	10.9
1979	7.93	13.4	6.04	7.5	6.40	9.4	4.92	10.3
1980	9.42	15.8	7.42	22.8	7.71	20.5	5.88	19.5
1981	13.16	39.7	11.07	49.2	11.43	48.2	7.69	30.8
1982	15.24	15.8	13.17	19.0	13.50	18.1	9.02	17.3
1983	15.98	4.9	13.62	3.4	14.00	3.7	9.86	8.5
1984	16.87	5.6	14.27	4.8	14.71	5.1	10.46	6.1
1985	17.49	3.7	15.21	6.6	15.59	6.0	11.55	10.4
1986	18.10	3.5	16.08	5.7	16.41	5.3	12.99	12.5
1987	18.86	4.2	16.92	5.2	17.24	5.1	14.58	12.2

Note: ROE&W Rest of England and Wales, inc. increase.

The effect of sales to sitting tenants is neutral as far as total demand and supply in the housing market is concerned, but the increase in the cost of local authority housing should result in an increase in the demand for private-sector housing, and, given a restricted supply, an increase in its price. The shift into private-sector housing is not, however, neutral as regards the mobility of households. It has been well documented that local authority tenants are less likely to migrate. Johnson et al (1974) noted from their surveys of migrants to four areas in 1970 and 1971 that "people renting from the local authority were much less likely to be labour migrants than the average" (page 133) and this is confirmed in the econometric study by Hughes and McCormick (1981). Using data from the 1973 General Household Survey they found that local authority tenants were the least likely to migrate of any house group. Indeed "the rate of migration between regions for owner-occupiers is predicated to be 6.5 times that for council tenants" whereas the latter are most likely to move houses within their region (page 936). Thus the shift out of local authority housing into owner-occupancy is likely to free households to migrate, and migration in the United Kingdom is likely to increase. Of course the restriction which, in effect, prevents tenants who buy from moving for five years, delays the impact of this change, but the 200000 who bought in the peak year of 1982 are now free to sell and move if they wish. Some support for this view is given in the paper by Muellbauer and Murphy (1989) mentioned earlier. They found that migration into the South East was positively correlated with increases in household mobility largely resulting from shifts out of local authority housing.

Table 10. Sales of public-sector dwellings by local authorities[a] in England and Wales. Source: DoE, 1987, table 9.6; 1988, table 9.6.

Year	Sales to sitting tenants, including 'right to buy'	Other sales of existing dwellings
1976	–	4102
1977	–	12020
1978	–	29100
1979	–	40595
1980	–	79390
1981	96965	4215
1982	196855	3825
1983	133665	6600
1984	98185	3410
1985	87735	3259
1986	84264	2894
1987	93826	2083

[a] Figures exclude shared ownership sales and sales of houses built for sale.

10 Summary

In this paper I have demonstrated that house prices have been rising substantially faster in the South East than in the rest of the country and that, on the supply side, a major cause has been the restriction on the supply of land for development. These restrictions have resulted in a process of intensification of land use in the South East, and households have been forced into buying smaller homes than they would have done otherwise.

The increase in house prices must also have been caused by an increase in the demand for housing in the South East, and three reasons were put forward why, in the 1980s, the demand for housing in the South East should have risen faster than elsewhere. First, international migration out of the South East has fallen considerably so that since 1983 there has been net international in-migration leading to a substantial increase in the demand for housing, and to price rises which serve to choke off interregional migration. Second, the winding down of regional policy has meant that firms needing to expand in southern England are now free to do so, subject only to constraints owing to planning controls and the availability of land, and so are more likely to do so than in the past thus increasing the demand for labour (and hence the demand for housing). Third, changes in the local authority sector mean that households which might have sought local authority tenancies in the past are now more likely to bid for housing in the private sector, so increasing the demand for housing.

Acknowledgements. I am indebted to the Nuffield Foundation for financial suppor and to Paul Cheshire and others for extensive discussion and comment.

References
Balchin P N, Bull G H, 1987 *Regional and Urban Economics* (Harper and Row, London)
Chartered Surveyor Weekly 1987, "Price surge heightens divide", 23 April, page 2●
Cheshire P C, Sheppard S, Hooper A, 1985, "The economic consequences of th British planning system", DP-29, discussion paper in urban and regional economics, Department of Economics, University of Reading, Reading
CSO, 1971 *Economic Trends* Central Statistical Office, number 208 (February) table 4, page xlviii (HMSO, London)
CSO, 1982, "A new index of average house prices", Central Statistical Office *Economic Trends* number 348 (October) 134–138 (HMSO, London)
DE, 1965–1986 *Family Expenditure Survey* (annual) Department of Employment (family expenditure for the years 1963 to 1985) (HMSO, London)
DE, 1987a *1984 Census of Employment* and revised employment estimates, Department of Employment, Caxton House, Tothill Street, London SW1
DE, 1987b *Employment Gazette* January **95**(1) 31–37; available from Department of Employment, Caxton House, Tothill Street, London SW1
DoE, 1980 *Housing and Construction Statistics 1969–1979* Department of the Environment (HMSO, London)
DoE, 1986 *Housing and Construction Statistics 1975–1985* Department of the Environment (HMSO, London)

DoE, 1987 *Housing and Construction Statistics 1976–1986* Department of the Environment (HMSO, London)

DoE, 1988 *Housing and Construction Statistics 1977–1987* Department of the Environment (HMSO, London)

Evans A W, 1987 *House Prices and Land Prices in the South East—A Review* The House Builders Federation, 82 New Cavendish Street, London W1

Evans A W, 1988 *"No Room! No Room!"* (Institute of Economic Affairs, London)

Eversley D E C, 1987, Tillingham Hall Inquiry: Proof of Evidence on Behalf of the Council for the Protection of Rural England; copy available from CPRE, 4 Hobart Place, London SW1

Grigson W S, 1986 *House Prices in Perspective: A Review of South East Evidence* SERPLAN, 50–64 Broadway, London SW1H 0DB

Housing Act, 1980 *Public General Acts—Elizabeth II* chapter 51 (HMSO, London)

Hughes G, McCormick B, 1981, "Do council housing policies reduce migration between regions?" *Economic Journal* **91** number 364 (December) 919–937

Johnson J H, Salt J, Wood P A, 1974 *Housing and Migration of Labour in England and Wales* (Saxon House, Farnborough, Hants)

Mayes G, 1979 *The Property Boom* (Martin Robertson, Oxford)

Muellbauer J, Murphy A, 1989, "Housing and regional migration to and from the South East", paper presented at a conference on Housing and the National Economy, National Institute of Economic and Social Research, December 1988

OPCS, 1987 *OPCS Monitor* MN 87/3, Office of Population Censuses and Surveys, St Catherine's House, Kingsway, London WC2

Property Market Report 1987, number 46 (Autumn) The Inland Revenue Valuation Office (Surveyors Publications, 12 Great George Street, London SW1)

Roger Tym and Partners, 1987, "Land used for residential development in the South East", Roger Tym and Partners, 25 Craven Street, London WC2

Town and Country Planning Act, 1947 *Public General Acts—George VI* chapter 51 (HMSO, London)

Turok I, 1989 *Development Planning and Local Economic Growth: A Study of Process and Planning in Bracknell New Town* (Pergamon Press, Oxford)

Twomey J, Taylor J, 1985, "Regional policy and interregional movement of manufacturing industry in Great Britain" *Scottish Journal of Political Economy* **32** 257–277

Housing Land Availability in the South East

A HOOPER, P PINCH, S ROGERS
University of Reading

1 Introduction

Throughout the 1970s land availability for private housebuilding became
an increasingly sensitive political issue, yet its resolution in practice
remained an essentially technical exercise conducted with relatively little
sophistication. Lacking, in general, detailed monitoring systems, local
planning authorities tended to approach the issue by matching the number
of planning permissions for private housing granted each year against
the number of dwellings built, with the overall aim of ensuring a surplus
at the county level to allow a consistent rate of building for the plan period.
Some authorities, particularly those with growth areas designated in the
Strategic Plan for the South East (*SPSE*), had earlier appreciated the need
for some kind of control over the rate of release of housing land, but the
findings of the *SPSE* review in 1976 that the regional population would
remain more or less stable until 1991 (with the consequent downgrading
of 'major' growth areas') tended to remove some of the urgency from
the need to exercise a firmer control over the process of land release.

Indeed, the first three circulars on land availability (DoE, 1970,
circular 10/70; 1972, circular 102/72; 1973, circular 122/73) had had
the effect of ensuring an automatic continuation of past trends in house
building, for under their provisions, planning authorities were urged to
ensure that there was sufficient building land identified for a continuation
for five years of the building rate of the previous year (or the last five
years' average if that were greater). Circular 102/72 assumed a close
relationship between land available in planning terms and land actually
available for development (under the then existing development conditions).
Research has demonstrated (DoE, 1978a) that land with outstanding
planning permission has a 70% probability of being developed within a
two-year period, and hence it is not surprising that the stock of land
with outstanding planning permission has often been used as a measure
of land supply, to be matched against the demand for land which is
normally expressed in terms of past rates of housing completions.
However, land with outstanding planning permission is only one, albeit
important, element of land available for residential development in
planning terms. Such land has been defined (DoE, 1975, page 2) as
"the stock of land which local planning authorities consider is sufficient
to meet the demands for housing land over the next 5 years", and includes
planned allocations as well as outstanding permissions. Research carried
out by JURUE (1977) has stressed the close relationship between 'stock'
and 'flow' approaches in any comprehensive understanding of the concept
of 'land availability', and since the mid-1970s the question of allocations of

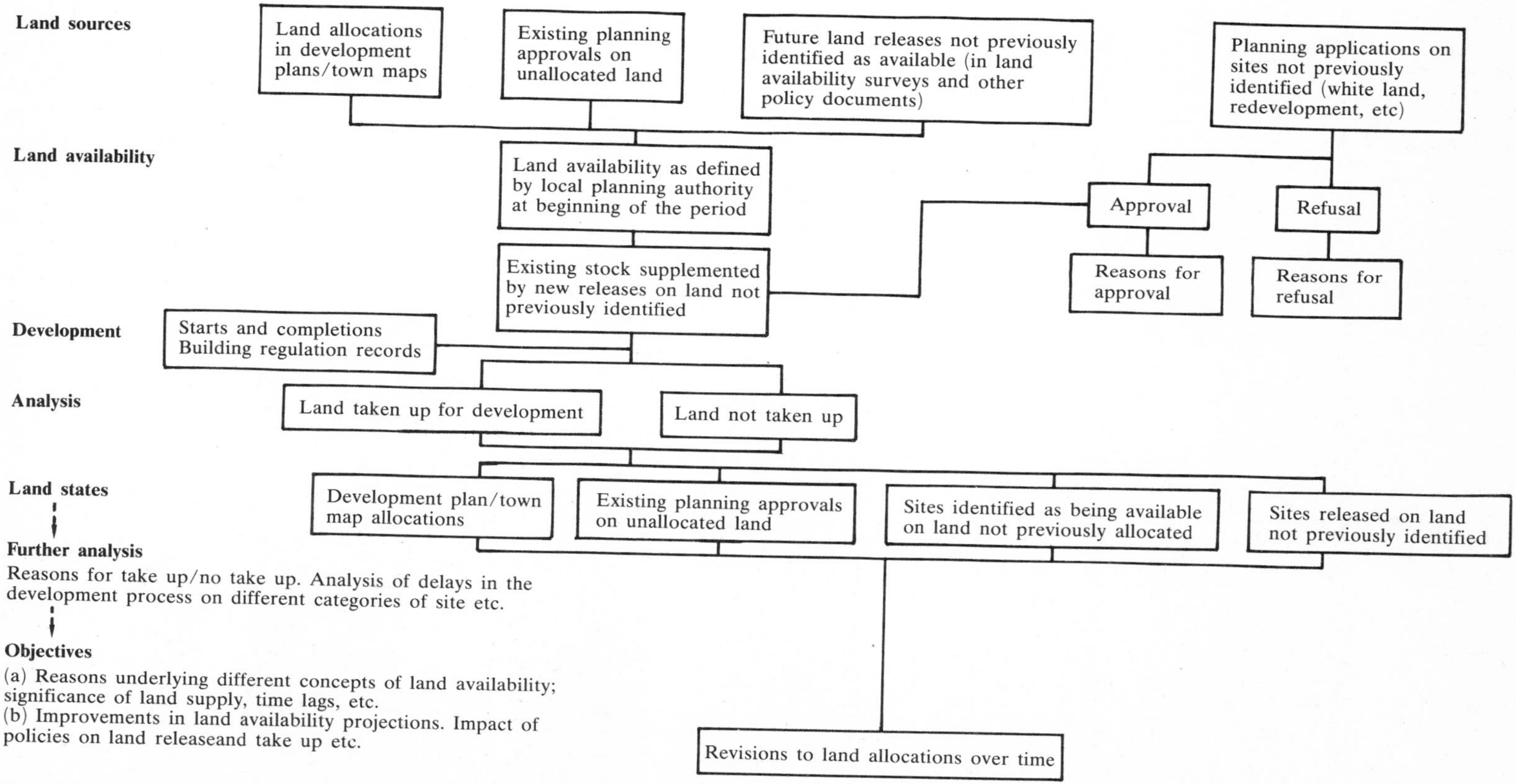

Land sources
Land allocations in development plans/town maps
Existing planning approvals on unallocated land
Future land releases not previously identified as available (in land availability surveys and other policy documents)
Planning applications on sites not previously identified (white land, redevelopment, etc)
Land availability
Land availability as defined by local planning authority at beginning of the period
Approval
Refusal
Reasons for approval
Reasons for refusal
Existing stock supplemented by new releases on land not previously identified
Development
Starts and completions
Building regulation records
Analysis
Land taken up for development
Land not taken up
Land states
Development plan/town map allocations
Existing planning approvals on unallocated land
Sites identified as being available on land not previously allocated
Sites released on land not previously identified
Further analysis
Reasons for take up/no take up. Analysis of delays in the development process on different categories of site etc.
Objectives
(a) Reasons underlying different concepts of land availability; significance of land supply, time lags, etc.
(b) Improvements in land availability projections. Impact of policies on land releaseand take up etc.
Revisions to land allocations over time

Figure 1. The process of residential land conversion: analysis framework. Source: JURUE, 1977.

land in development plans (a 'stock' matter) and the progress of this
allocated land through the planning system to completed dwellings (a
'flow' issue) have been more closely interrelated.

Interestingly, however, both the 1975 DoE study and the 1977
JURUE study found that a considerable proportion of land developed
for residential purposes was unallocated in formal planning terms (more
than half and two-fifths respectively). Unfortunately, most of the research
and policy effort over the last decade has been focused upon improving
the efficient operation of the development control system (sometimes in
terms of speed of operation), that is, the identification and measurement
of land flows into the system (as defined primarily by planning permissions)
and out of the system (as measured by housing starts and completions
or lapsed permissions) (JURUE, 1977, page 6). Little attention has
been given to the problem of identifying the stock of land available in
various categories at the beginning and end of the relevant period, and
therefore the improvements in land accounting procedures that have
occurred have generally been in the direction of 'comparative statics'
rather than a deeper understanding of the dynamics of land supply and
its relationship to demand and other policy objectives. Although there
has been, therefore, an improved understanding of the process of land
conversion for private residential development in terms of the volume
and rate of land flows through the development pipeline, together with
the spatial distribution of such flows, less attention has been given to the
factors which determine the basic structural features of the pipeline and
pressures to which it has been obliged to accommodate itself (see figure 1).

2 Current housing land accounting procedures
The 1980s witnessed availability of housing land, particularly in the
southeast of England, emerging as an acutely significant political issue.
Accompanying this political sensitivity, accounting procedures for housing
land improved apace, partly reflecting new central government advice, but
also in response to the need to exercise closer control of residential land
release in alterations to structure plans and to defend such strategies on
appeal against the refusal of planning permission. In 1978 the DoE and
the Housebuilders Federation instigated a pioneering joint study of housing
land availability in Greater Manchester. One of the aims of this was "to
devise, with the benefit of experience, a simple method of appraisal for use
by other local authorities and builders, without needing direct Department
of the Environment support" (DoE/HBF, 1979, volume 1, page 2).

Under the terms of reference of the study, authorities were asked not
simply to provide a list of sites with outstanding residential planning
permission (and hence 'available' in a planning sense) but to list sites
expected to sustain new private house completions during the study period
(three and a half years). Noting that this concept of 'availability' was
relatively new to many of the authorities, an annex to the study

recommending a suggested simplified methodology for future studies indicated that normally the study period should be five years. Furthermore, it suggested that sites below a certain size should be excluded, although their contribution to the total amount of land available for private housebuilding should be agreed. It was explicitly noted that such studies would constitute essentially a 'snapshot', relating land availability to a quantitive statement of the housing requirements of local authorities.

In circular 9/80 all local authorities were subsequently urged to undertake studies along the lines of the Greater Manchester study. It reiterated the requirement in circular 102/72 to maintain a five-year supply of land at all times, but related this requirement to the provisions of approved development plans—"However, the amount and location of land required to make up that supply should now be derived from the housing policies and proposals in approved structure and local plans, and not at current building rates" (DoE, 1980a, paragraph 4). A footnote indicated that, where a plan had not yet been approved, the proposals in the latest draft plan could be used as a temporary guide. The 'simple method' set out in the annex to the Greater Manchester study was reproduced as an appendix to the circular.

Although, superficially, the provisions of circular 9/80 appeared to relate the supply of housing land to the planning considerations contained in approved development plans, in practice the relationship was more complicated. The key problem stems from the failure in circular 9/80 to address the central question of the relationship between the process of planned allocation of land in relation to housing requirements (that is, relating the five-year land supply *requirement* to the housing *provision* figures of approved structure and local plans) and the process of land release through the system of development control. Indeed as early as 1982 one observer noted that the effective operation of circular 9/80 was dependent upon existing structure plans containing detailed information on the number of new houses the authority expects the structure plan area will need over the next five or ten years, and the relevant number of years that the plan provisions are to run (Mackie, 1982, page 10). In many cases, existing structure plans did not contain such information, and the derivation of the five-year supply proved problematical. As Mackie noted also, the problem of deriving the five-year requirement is not confined to the initial years of a structure plan, for the five-year housing requirement (derived from the housing provision) has to be compared with the level of land availability derived from a joint study on an intermittent basis as the plan progresses. It is noted in circular 9/80 that authorities may well find it necessary to repeat land availability exercises 'periodically', but no specific guidance is given. This was first acknowledged in a number of planning appeals following circular 9/80, resulting in the recommendation by the DoE of a formula known as the 'residual method'. This method operates by deducting the number of dwellings completed since the beginning of the plan period from the original level of housing land required, and this 'residual requirement' is then divided by the number of years the structure plan has left to run. The resultant annual residual requirement is multiplied by five to give the five-year requirement. Mackie has noted that in practice the effect is to discourage land release where rates of housebuilding are higher than expected as the plan progresses, whereas in areas where the rates are below projections enough land to provide for rates even higher than the projections will be released. He locates the basic flaw in the fact that

"while the Department of the Environment insists that current building rates should *not* be used for determining the 5 year land supply requirement it is itself recommending the use of a method which not only uses current building rates as one of its main elements, but uses it in such a way as to make it inevitably distort the housebuilding policies contained in approved structure plans" (Mackie, 1982, page 12

The appropriate spatial scale to which the five-year land requirement should apply was also unclear in circular 9/80, but the DoE's interpretation was that a five-year supply of housing land should exist not only at structure plan level but also for each district. Clearly this implied the need for an associated requirement to disaggregate the overall housing provision in approved structure plans to the district level, itself problematical when some plans dealt with policy areas which spanned district boundaries

Annex A of circular 22/80 (DoE, 1980b) reinforced the significance of studies on housing land availability by indicating that, in the absence of an identified five-year supply of land, there should be a presumption in favour of granting permission for housing except where there are clear planning objections which in the circumstances of the case outweigh the need to make the land available for housing.

Circular 15/84 (DoE, 1984) reiterated the important contribution that the joint studies on land availability introduced by circular 9/80 can make in ensuring that suitable land is made available for development and clarified the general approach to be adopted in the compilation and use of such studies. It was advised that plans should indicate in broad terms the scale of provision to be made for housing in the area as a whole and in each district, and that they should identify those locations where provision for substantial growth is to be made. As well as restating the requirement for a minimum five-year supply of land, it is indicated that the aim should always be to ensure at least two-years' supply available on which development can start straight away, though no method is advised on which to base this estimate. Joint studies by local authorities and housebuilders undertaken after circular 9/80 are commended, and annex B sets out a method for preparing studies on land availability, which local authorities and housebuilders are asked to adopt.

This method includes the establishment of figures in approved plans of housing provision for counties and individual districts, and local authorities should indicate whether the housing provision in plans includes gains from redevelopment, conversions, and building on small sites. For the first time, the residual method is expressly recommended (two years after the first published criticism!). It is noted that when the housing provision in approved and adopted plans covers only part of the period of the land availability study, published modifications to proposed alterations to the structure plan may be used for land supply calculations. When there are no such modifications then the average annual provision for the last five years of the time covered by the policy should be extrapolated to give an estimate of the land required. It will only be appropriate to base the calculation of the required housing land supply on an unapproved alteration to a structure plan or on unapproved local plans when there are no figures for housing in the approved structure plan, or when the time period of the plan has expired. The studies are not expected normally to attempt to identify small sites (for less than ten dwellings), infill, or similar sites that are not specifically allocated for development or redevelopment, but local authorities and housebuilders may agree an allowance in the overall assessment where appropriate.

It is noted that the DoE's regional offices will be ready to help facilitate such studies and to advise on methodology and other matters dealt with in this circular, and it is recommended that such studies be regularly jointly reviewed and revised, normally every two years or so. Annex A to the circular is a reprint of that attached to circular 22/80, indicating its continued relevance.

Circular 15/84 thus compounded many of the problems implicit in the methodology recommended following the Greater Manchester study of 1979 (Hooper, 1979; 1980; 1982; 1983; Rydin, 1986), not least the issue of the residual method. Not surprisingly, therefore, several local planning authorities pointed out that the strict application of the methodology gave rise to anomalous results. In particular, following the advice in circular 15/84 to allow flexibility in the rate at which land is made available for housing in structure and local plans, many local authorities increased the levels of housebuilding recommended in their structure plans. As Rydin notes (1986, page 108), "These levels were intended to indicate the theoretical maximum housing need and not to be housebuilding targets." Yet authorities such as West Yorkshire, Norfolk, and Merseyside experienced, as a result of circular 15/84, the effect of regarding revised structure plan figures as achievable and inflexible housing targets, unrelated to actual annual housing completions. A seminar at the end of 1986 (Doak et al, 1987) chronicled the enduring character of the methodological problems associated with the joint studies on housing land availability.

The increasing demand for a more flexible interpretation of the methodology outlined in circulars 9/80 and 15/84 on the part of local planning authorities was accompanied by an increasingly confused and complicated treatment of the issues in planning appeals, requiring clarification by the courts (Hooper et al, 1988). The courts established that local planning authorities had little, if any, flexibility as to the manner in which they undertook land availability calculations, but retained a greater measure of discretion in the way in which they related these calculations to strategic housing provisions.

Subsequently, in May 1987, a press release from the DoE set out new procedures on the supply of housing land, contained in a written answer from the Secretary of State to a question in the House of Commons, which has subsequently been codified in Planning Policy Guidance (PPG) Note 3 issued in January 1988 (DoE, 1988b). Once again the residual method is recommended as "normally" providing a reliable yardstick against which the adequacy of land availability can be measured, but departures from the residual method may be permissible where there is a very substantial discrepancy between recent rates of building and the assumptions made in development plans. It will be necessary to follow the detailed application of this new apparent flexibility in relating land availability studies to structure and local plan housing provisions through a number of planning appeals before a reliable evaluation can be made, but its effect seems to be to remove the automatic trigger or ratchet effect of land availability studies in terms of land release, and to place a renewed significance upon the housing provisions of constantly updated development plans.

Yet the context of present and future development plans is far from providing an appropriate vehicle for this task. As well as the uncertainty arising from the proposals outlined in the "The Future of Development Plans" (DoE, 1986), the programme of preparation of local plans is beginning to have a significant impact upon the housing provision figures contained in approved structure plans, at the same time as these latter are being amended in the light of contemporary development pressures. The requirement, reiterated in PPG3 (annex B) that the housing provisions should be based on approved and adopted plans or on published modifications to proposed alterations to structure plans seems to pose difficulties for local planning authorities in keeping their land supply adjusted to contemporary needs, given the administrative timetable associated with the process of reviewing the structure plans. This problem has received considerable recent attention in the wake of the release of the 1985-based projections of household formation published in February 1988 (OPCS, 1988). Also, a recent discussion paper prepared by the DoE includes the suggestion that where counties have submitted proposals awaiting 'examination in public' (EIP), the EIP panel should be invited to take account of the new figures, something that has been advocated by local planning authorities since 1985 (*Planning* issue 613, 12 April, page 2).

One method of avoiding the problems arising from the residual method, namely the proposal for an annual target rate of completion for each district for which land provision should be made (but with no fixed end-date) has not received favour. In PPG3 it is stated clearly that development plans should not specify the precise number of acres or houses to be developed each year, though broad programming over the period of the plan may be acceptable in areas where there are strong pressures for development. Clearly, the residual need methodology continues to embody all the contradictions which marked its birth in the Greater Manchester study, reflecting a failure at the level of planning policy to relate the 'stock' and 'flow' aspects of the supply of housing land.

3 Assessing housing land supply

The requirement in circular 15/84 (DoE, 1984, paragraph 5) and PPG3 (DoE, 1988b, paragraph 16):

"sites must not only be free, or easily freed, from planning, physical and ownership constraints, but must also be capable of being developed economically, be in areas where potential housebuyers want to live, and be suitable for the wide range of housing types which the housing market requires",

ensures that a considerable proportion of potentially 'available' land is not recorded as being available, under the terms of the circular, for private residential development.

In principle, the studies record all 'available' sites of 0.4 ha or more, whether or not they have planning permission. Studies on land availability should not usually attempt to identify small sites of less than 0.4 ha (one acre) or infill sites;[1] nor should they identify small sites which are not specifically allocated for development or redevelopment. It is recognised that such sites, together with the conversion of larger houses into smaller units or the adaptation of nonresidential buildings for use as housing, can make a useful contribution to total housing provision, and if on the basis of past experience and realistic appraisal of future potential it seems likely to meet a significant part of the future demand the local planning authority and housebuilders should agree an allowance in the overall assessment. The actual methods for estimating the capacity of small sites varies from a simple extrapolation of existing planning permissions for such sites or projection of past completion rates to calculations of an annual average for each district, subarea, and county

[1] It is interesting that small sites are defined as less than 0.4 ha in PPG3 and as less than ten dwellings in circular 15/84. The problem of defining large and small sites is reflected in the wide variability found in the accounting procedures of different counties, and makes the aggregation of land supply data across county boundaries problematical.

as a whole, with construction of 35% rising to 75% of the annual average from the second to fifth years (as in West Sussex). The calculation for such small sites may achieve strategic significance, as in the recent decisions relating to Berkshire County Council's alteration to their Structure Plan. Once again definitional problems bedevil the interpretation of land availability surveys across counties. Typically, estimates for small identified sites and small unidentified sites are made, with widely varying definitions of 'small' (up to nine dwellings per site in some cases, whereas some counties define a large site as six or more dwellings).

Some ambiguity arose over the interpretation of paragraph 8 of annex B to circular 15/84 concerning the treatment of large (that is, more than 0.4 ha) unidentified sites. Some counties chose to include an estimate for such sites within their overall calculation. In paragraph 10 of annex A to PPG3 it is argued that the incidence of such sites is likely to be highly variable and their contribution to the supply of housing land is inherently unpredictable. It is argued that to attempt to take such sites into account is likely to introduce too great an element of uncertainty into the overall assessment and local planning authorities are therefore advised that no allowance should normally be made for this factor. However, as West Sussex County Council (WSCC, 1987) have pointed out, some counties when preparing their alterations have elected to incorporate housing development on unidentified sites within the total requirement for dwellings in the plan, and have included an estimate of completions on unidentified sites based on past experience of their occurrence on small and large sites. The advice in PPG3 on the treatment of large unidentified sites (to exclude them in the overall assessment) compromises the relationship between the components of the figures on dwelling requirements of approved plans and those in the assessments of land availability.

This serves to highlight the increasing importance in recent years of estimates of land on 'unidentified' sites. 'Unidentified' sites are those new sites appearing in surveys of land availability as a result of the grant of planning permission in the period since the last survey—in the case of counties with annual surveys, only those new sites appearing as a result of the grant of planning permission in the year preceding the survey base date fall into this category. Such sites are sometimes termed 'windfall' or 'unforeseeable' sites in land availability surveys.

West Sussex County Council have classified unidentified sites into four main categories: (1) new sites (where there were no previous buildings), (2) redevelopment sites, (3) change of use of buildings, (4) conversions (changing the number of units in a residential building). In West Sussex, the first two categories share equally in making up 80% of dwelling provision on unidentified sites. Analysis of data on the development of unidentified sites in West Sussex indicates that the contribution of such sites is an increasing trend, particularly for private-sector development, and that although national and local policies continu to encourage the maximum use of urban land a significant reduction in the level of unidentified sites is not likely to occur. Differing assumptions in this regard result in some counties adopting a trend line whereas others take an annual average over a period of ten years or more. Regarding the size composition of unidentified sites, West Sussex point out that the size of the site is less important than its dwelling product, but that, whereas 90% of sites are of less than 0.25 ha and only 5% are over 0.5 ha, under one-third of the dwellings permitted on previously unidentified sites are on sites for less than six dwellings. The effect of advice in PPG3 to exclude large unidentified sites from estimates of land availability will be, therefore, to create apparent rather than real shortages in land supply, with the consequent release of additional land on appeal as well as large unidentified sites, so that the dwelling provision figures in approved plans will be significantly exceeded.

It is interesting to note that DoE statistics (DoE, 1988a) indicating the proportion of housebuilding taking place on 'brown-field' sites (previously classified as 'urban') was 45% in 1985, 46% in 1986, and 44% in 1987, and that only 20% of housing land in 1987 was previously vacant, against 23% in the preceding years. This seems to bear out the significance of urban land in the total land supply, and a considerable proportion of this land would presumably fall into the 'unidentified' category in land availability surveys. Research by Roger Tym and Partners (RTP, 1987) confirms the significance of 'adventitious' sites in the supply of land for housebuilding in the South East (one fifth of all sites) and the significance of 'urban' sites (just over half of all starts).

The report noted that over a third of starts occurred on sites which were not identified for housing in land availability studies prior to detailed consent (in the first six months of 1984) and concluded:

"Although these studies typically allow for an extra 10 per cent from unidentified sources such as very small sites and other windfall sites and although some of the sites not identified prior to detailed consent will appear in later land availability publications, the overall conclusion is that land availability studies underestimate the amount of land available for housebuilding" (RTP, 1987, page 38).

A final problem in assessing the supply of housing land is the procedure for assessing the production of dwellings from sites. Circular 15/84 and PPG3 require an assessment in each of the study years of the likely output from sites, that is, estimates are required not only of the number of dwellings to be produced and when they will be produced but also the rate at which they will be produced. As Williamson and Parks (1985, page 8) noted "Any housing land which is not expected to be developed within the five-year study period under this assessment is not regarded as being 'available' and is discounted as though it did not exist. In some cases this will be parts of housing sites which are under development."

It is essential, therefore, that local planning authorities monitor, preferably annually, the effect of unforeseen factors on the number of dwellings achieved, as compared with the numbers expected. The degree of flexibility built in to housing allocations for particular districts will be to a large extent determined by the 'slippage' allowance arising from factors such as ownership constraints and marketing conditions, and this may be significant especially in areas of restraint. The tendency in district plans to allocate slightly more land than would appear necessary on a straightforward numerical basis in order to be sure that sufficient dwellings are built to fulfill the structure plan policies is largely accounted for by this factor.

4 Joint land availability studies and land release

The emergence of joint studies on land availability is a pragmatic response to the lacunae left by the demise of regional strategic planning and land policy. In this last respect it is worth noting that circular 10/70 ("Land Availability for Housing") was issued as part of the Conservative alternative to 'socialist' land policy instruments such as the Land Commission (McKay and Cox, 1979). This Conservative alternative abjured direct institutional involvement by governments in land markets, and sought instead to build a cooperative coalition between local authorities and private housebuilders which would be responsive to changing patterns of demand for housing. Even circular 44/78 (DoE, 1978b), issued by a Labour government, sought to buttress this coalition, for it was (wrongly) thought that the problem of development values had been resolved by the Community Land Scheme, which provided the context for circular 44/78 (and, paradoxically, coincided with the effective termination of the Scheme). This developing 'corporatist' approach to land release operated after 1979 in a new political and economic context of reprivatisation, yet within the constraints of the existing planning system (Rydin, 1986, pages 83–84). A key element of the new corporatism is that it operates from day-to-day at the local level, but that the key parameters are set by central government.

The first of these parameters is the ability of central government, through the Secretary of State for the Environment, to establish and revise the proposed levels of housebuilding in structure and local plans. The present administration has not produced a national strategy within which such proposals can be made, but in the South East of England the regional guidance prepared by SERPLAN and agreed by the Secretary of State provides broad 'guidance figures' for each county up to the year 2001. Recently these guidance figures have been revised upwards as a response to the latest forecasts on household formation, but at every EIP of alterations to structure plans for the South East counties the Housebuilders Federation has contested the level of house building provided for in the county strategy. In the case of only one county (Hertfordshire) has the approved alteration resulted in a level of housebuilding not exceeding the proposed strategy. But, as Rydin (1986, pages 105 – 106) has pointed out, the land availability studies are themselves acting as an input to the structure planning process, with inflationary effects upon the process of land release. That the South East counties are under significant pressure of housing demand is revealed by the recent publication by SERPLAN of the South East Regional Monitor for 1987/88, which indicates that from 1984 to 1986 nearly half of the 150 000 growth in population of England and Wales took place in the South East.

The second parameter which central government controls is the advice which it issues on the methodology to be adopted in compiling the joint studies. Not only is this methodology partial in favour of the housebuilders (Hooper, 1979; 1980; Rydin, 1986), but it has been progressively amended to exclude from real availability land which is available in planning terms but which is unsuitable for ownership or marketing reasons. Some local planning authorities have made determined efforts to take into account assessments of market demand following the reports by Coopers and Lybrand (CL, 1985; 1987), but the practical difficulties have inhibited progress to date. At the district level, allocations in plans are sometimes deliberately generous in order to provide a degree of flexibility in response to factors of differential market demand, and to 'protect' the local planning authorities position at appeal.

It is in this last respect that central government controls the 'rules of the game' through the role of the Secretary of State and the Planning Inspectorate in the planning appeals which involve issues of land availability. The courts have clearly established the heavily circumscribed discretion which local planning authorities have in compiling joint studies on land availability and in relating them to the housing strategies of structure plans (Hooper et al, 1988). The nonsensical outcomes which derive from an inflexible application of the methods recommended in successive circulars on land availability have resulted in the more flexible advice contained in PPG3, but this serves only to direct attention back to the housing provision figures in statutory development plans.

The net effect of the procedures recommended by the DoE for accounting for land supply is to severely curtail the discretion of local planning authorities in assessing sources of real availability by excluding in a rather arbitrary fashion sites which are deemed to be unavailable or difficult to predict, and at the same time comparing the assessed outcome with the residual rate of need calculated according to generous assumptions (depending, since PPG3, on the context). As Williamson and Parks noted in 1985 "Needless to say, the final results bear little relation to reality and are very heavily biased in favour of finding an inadequate—less than five years—supply" (Williamson and Parks, 1985).

In consequence, in areas of high market demand the response of the current system of land release is a slow 'bleeding' of planning permissions toward the final stages of a given plan period, followed by a haemorrhaging as a new plan 'regime' is established. Because of a lack of effective phasing powers, the degree of planned control of development which results is often retrospective in its strategic effect, and is chiefly concerned with tactical planning of the 'mopping-up' variety. In the absence of more comprehensive strategic planning instruments, joint studies on land availability are left as the most significant practical planning vehicle for relating the processes of land allocation and land release. This is a role for which they were never intended, but which they have been forced by circumstances to assume.

5 Strategic and tactical land release: case studies

The latest national assessments of availability of housing land (DoE, 1987; CPOS, 1988) indicate that in the majority of counties there is an adequate supply of housing land as defined by land availability circulars. The DoE survey indicates that certain counties in the South East with less than five years of approved plans remaining have a technical deficiency, though the survey of the County Planning Officers' Society nonetheless concludes that there is an excess of available land at the structure plan five-year requirement for the region as a whole. Both studies indicate, however, that there were localised shortfalls within individual counties. The broad balance at county level may thus hide a complex process whereby pressure from residential developers responds to the different planning regimes it encounters at district level.

Thus the planning response to pressure for residential development can be detected at both the county and the district level, and it is not always the case that this response is unified in relation to strategic planning objectives. This can best be demonstrated by briefly considering the experience of two counties in the South East which have struggled in different ways to manage this development pressure. Essex and Kent are both situated in the eastern sector of the South East where current strategy is to encourage economic development (diverted from the western sector). Both contain large areas of land protected by area designations, including the London Green Belt, and both have recently experienced the impact of major new developments (the expansion of Stansted Airport in Essex and the Channel Tunnel development in Kent).

6 Planning for restraint in a growth area: the case of Essex
6.1 Introduction
The County of Essex provides a useful illustration of the housing development pressures faced in the South East of England and the problems associated with the attempts of local planning authorities to restrain this process.

6.1.1 *The postwar planning experience*

A quite dramatic population and housing growth characterised Essex between the years 1951 and 1976 (see table 1). Over this period the annual average rate of population increase was 23 600, accommodated by an average annual rate of housebuilding of 12 133 dwellings.

Within this context, the restraint-oriented planning policies pursued by Essex County Council frequently conflicted with much of the postwar regional planning guidance (see Rydin, 1986, pages 99 – 108). In 1969 for example the County extended its metropolitan green belt, despite *The South East Study 1961 – 1981* (MHLG, 1964) which identified south Essex as a major growth area within South East England. Consequently, central government formally refused this extension to the green belt. It was, however, granted interim status, as although Rydin (1986) remarks, between 1964 and 1982 numerous appeals over sites within this area were approved by central government.

The *Strategic Plan for the South East* (SEJPT, 1970), in which it was planned to cover the period from 1967 to the end of the century, again directed growth towards South Essex. It was approved in principle by the government in 1971. South Essex was one of five major growth areas identified by the *Plan*, which was aimed at accommodating a regional population growth of 3 500 000 people to the end of the century.

During the revision of this plan in the early 1970s, Essex County Council argued strongly for a revised estimate of population growth on the basis of several factors, including the cancellation of Maplin Airport, the downturn in the national economy, lower regional population forecasts, and plans to redevelop the London Docklands. It was partly successful in its demands. The revised plan, the *Strategic Plan for the South East: Review* (SEJPT, 1976), proposed the progressive introduction of restraint on development in the 'rest of the South East' (the South East excluding Greater London) to help promote the development of inner London. Growth areas such as south Essex were still recognised, however, although at a reduced but unspecified level.

Table 1. Population and housing growth in Essex, 1951 – 76. Source: ECC, 1982b.

Year	Population	Population increase			Houses completed 1961 – 76	Implied annual HB rate
		total	% of total increase in SE	implied annual increase		
1951	830 000					
1961	1 100 000	270 000	25	27 000		
1971	1 364 000	264 000	27	26 400		
1976	1 420 000	56 000	na	11 200	182 000	12 133

Note: SE South East of England, HB housebuilding, na data not available.

During the process of preparing the *Essex Structure Plan* (ECC, 1982a) the 1975 'issues' stage and the 1976 'alternatives' stage reflected this changing regional strategy, and progressively proposed increased restraint on development within Essex. In the 'alternatives' stage, however, mindful of past experience, the possibility of some extra growth was envisaged; a potential extra 24 000 dwelling sites in addition to an identified 95 000 sites available within the County were highlighted.

The public reaction to the 'alternatives' stage, however, strongly favoured further retrenchment, and consequently the *Draft Essex Structure Plan* (ECC, 1977) further reduced these growth proposals. Changing regional guidance backed up Essex's position. In the 1978 "Strategic Plan for the South East Review: Government Statement", Essex's regional role was more clearly located. In this statement the estimated number of households needed for the South East until 1991 was increased to 750 000, owing primarily to single-person households. However, in the light of the abandoned Maplin Airport and the proposed Docklands redevelopment it noted the "government consider, therefore that Basildon New Town should provide adequately for most of the presently foreseen needs of growth in South Essex" (quoted in ECC, 1982b, page 2). The County therefore was successful in establishing restraint in its previously designated growth area.

In the submitted *Essex Structure Plan*, following yet more public demands for restraint and in the light of the 1978 Government Statement (available from the DoE), the level of proposed growth was further reduced. In south Essex, even the plans for limited additional growth beyond existing commitments were dropped.

6.2 Planning policy and practice at the county level
Having examined the context within which the *Essex Structure Plan* was prepared, its more detailed housing provisions, their subsequent amendment through the *Essex Structure Plan: First Alteration* (ECC, 1987) and its relationship to continued development pressure can be examined.

The *Essex Structure Plan* is quite explicitly restraint oriented. The Written Statement (ECC, 1982b, page 8) refers to the "lack of balance between people, jobs, environment and services" in the county. Whereas "in the past development has been led by the growth in population and housing", it suggests that the "County's existing local problems and commitments to considerable development make the addition of further housing growth undesirable."

The original housing provisions estimated in the *Structure Plan* covered the period from April 1977 until December 1990, some thirteen years nine months. In the plan submitted to the Secretary of State the aggregate housing provision was 82 000 dwellings, implying an average annual completion rate of 5964 dwellings. In order to encourage this implied 'slowdown' in average annual rates of housing completion, a phasing programme was included to restrain the supply of land for housing.

The Secretary of State, in approving the plan on 30 March 1982, deleted the County's phasing proposals and increased the total housing provision by 11 840 (14%) to 93 840 dwellings. This implied a new average annual rate of completions of 6825 dwellings. Interestingly, the Secretary of State, in adding 11 840 dwellings to the aggregate figure, made it clear that of this figure some 6640 dwellings could be met through 'intensification' of the existing land supply. This generic term had four components: the subdivision of the existing dwelling stock; conversions to residential use; redevelopment to achieve net housing gain; and minor infilling.

The (then) Secretary of State's belief, that the County had under-estimated potential population increase in and migration into the County, supposedly inspired this modification. With regard to these factors the Written Statement to the approved *Structure Plan* makes some reference to population forecasts "as a guide to the amount of change which should be accommodated" (ECC, 1982b, page 9). Thus in 1977 the Office of Population Censuses and Surveys (OPCS) forecast a growth of 134 000 over the period 1976 – 91, whereas the Greater London Council (GLC) forecasts ranged from 34 000 to 98 000 people for the same period. Yet it also stresses that these forecasts "have not been used to assess the general amount of development necessary but instead the general statements of regional strategy, the estimates of the future number of households and the housing supply which is already committed in the County have been used as a basis" (page 9).

In relation to rates of household formation reference is made to a DoE forecast of a potential increase of 100 000 households between 1976 and 1991. This was a product of both local demand and inward migration. The County's own estimate based on purely local demand was 90 000 households by 1991.

Against such demands the Written Statement refers to an identified land availability of some 90 000 dwelling sites at April 1977. This housing land availability, it suggested, would increase to 100 000 dwellings up to the period 1991 if existing stock vacancies and normal turnover was allowed for. Clearly then, for "the County as a whole the number of dwellings both existing and to be built should ... be sufficient to meet both estimated local requirements and allow some provision for inward migration" (ECC, 1982b, page 9). Central to the *Structure Plan*, therefore, was a restriction on future housing development to existing commitments.

Given the implied average annual completion rate of housing provisions in the *Structure Plan*, the Written Statement 'wishfully' noted that the "general effect will be gradually to reduce the rate of housebuilding in the County as land becomes less freely available and as pressures from people wanting to move into the County lessen as a result of regional policies" (page 9). Given, however, the actual rate of house completions at the beginning of the plan period, the Written Statement goes on to note that "the reduction in rate will not be immediate but would be a gradual tapering" and recognises that quite a high level of activity for some years remains inevitable. In addressing this point, a table allocating the general rate of housing development to three five-year periods under the heading "County Strategy" was included. This implied an average annual completion rate of 9306 dwellings up until 1980, 6838 dwellings from then until 1985, and 4950 dwellings in the final five years of the plan period.

The relationship between the *Structure Plan* policy and actual development practice is revealing. Although the *Plan* was not approved until 1982, in the County Strategy in the early years the existing level of completions of dwellings was essentially recognised. Thereafter it was progressively sought to curb this acknowledged high level of completions. Between 1980 and 1984, completion rates actually failed to match the County Strategy, reflecting the general economic recession in this period. Completion totals were nevertheless still in excess of the implied average annual completion rate of 6825 dwellings derived from the aggregate provision described in the *Structure Plan*.

However, from 1984 onwards, completion rates increased together with the divergence between planned development and the actual process itself. Although in the County Strategy it was sought to 'tail off' the average annual rate of completions, in practice the rate increased quite profoundly. By April 1987 completions had reached 83 613 dwellings, almost 90% of the total provision of the *Structure Plan*, some 10 000 above the County Strategy, and over 15 000 greater than the total average annual completion rate implied in the *Structure Plan*.

It is this 'slippage' that the *Essex Structure Plan: First Alteration* (ECC, 1987) is an attempt to control. This *First Alteration* addresses the period from 1986–2001. It is an attempt to roll forward the existing housing provision but, unlike the previous plan, proposes a more explicit policy for housing rather than merely a rationalisation of existing commitments.

The proposed *First Alteration* makes reference to the changing planning context and the nature of the reformulated regional planning guidance. It cites as most significant locally the decision by central government in 1985 to expand Stansted Airport by the addition of a new terminal which will increase use to 15 000 000 passengers per annum. The main regional guidance noted by the *Plan* is the letter from the Secretary of State, 19 June 1986, to the chair of SERPLAN. This basically endorsed SERPLAN's "South East England in the 1990s: A regional statement" and in particular the housing projections for each county contained within its appendix. In the case of Essex the addition of 39 500 dwellings between 1991 and 2001 was envisaged. In the letter it was also noted that the phased development of Stansted Airport would need to be considered when proposing the amount and location of development in Essex and Hertfordshire.

The first key component of the *First Alteration* housing allocations is an estimate of the number of dwellings that could be built in the County between the years 1986 and 1991. It was estimated that a total of 38 100 dwellings could be completed during this period, broken down into the components shown in table 2. In the *Plan* it is noted that this forecast "was not carried out jointly with the House Builders Federation [HBF] ... [but] does nevertheless result from consideration of the methodology set out in Department of the Environment Circular 15/84 'Land for Housing'". Beyond this the *Plan* accepts the need to accommodate the indicative regional guidance figure of 39 500 for the period 1991–2001 but that any more "should be considered elsewhere with particular regard to the economically more buoyant areas to the west of the region" (ECC, 1987, page 6).

The *First Alteration* also refers to existing household projections and assorted housing needs. In 1983, using OPCS population projections, the DoE predicted a need for 69 100 households for the period 1986–2001. This projection when modified by Essex County Council in the manner shown in table 3 produced an estimated gross dwelling requirement of some 78 000. However, it is noted in the plan that these recent "DOE household projections show significant differences in the numbers of forecast households for similar time periods. Therefore, whilst useful in demonstrating a broad indication of change, based on certain assumptions, they do have their limitations for Structure Plan purposes" (ECC, 1987, page 6).

No reference is made in the plan to these alternative household projections, however, instead it is noted that these "are not definitive targets which have to be achieved: they provide guidance to be set alongside other planning policy objectives" (ECC, 1987, page 6).

The *First Alteration* then goes on to note that the DoE (OPCS) 1983 household projections for the 1990s and the regional planning guidance determine a net increase in dwelling stock of some 40 000 units. When conversions and changes of use are considered this produces a figure of net aggregate housebuilding of 43 000 dwellings. This figure, it is

Table 2. Estimated housing development, 1986–1991. Source: ECC, 1987, explanatory memorandum, page 5.

Committed sites (dwelling capacity six or more units)	30 500
Small sites (five or less units) within towns and villages	5 600
Recycled urban land and new sites	1 950
Total (estimated and adjusted)	~ 38 100

Note: Data includes development of about 1000 houses on new large sites at Harlow and West Thurrock.

suggested, will still permit some acceptance of net migration to the County. If this figure of 43 000 is added to estimated completions in the period 1986–91 then some 81 000 dwellings are projected for the period 1986–91. This is the basis of the plans allocations, and is proposed as a "scale of development which represents a reasonable view on development which is likely to take place in the short term, as well as conforming to regional guidance for the 1990s" (ECC, 1987, page 6).

Against this identified housing requirement the proposed *First Alteration* then positions estimates of the existing housing land supply within each district so that "decisions relating to 'new' housing areas can be clearly identified" (ECC, 1987, page 11).

Four components of land supply are identified in this process. First, there are small sites of five or less dwellings. At 5 April 1986 it was estimated that within Essex there were an estimated 4100 such dwelling sites with planning permission. It is noted that "experience has shown that these sites are continuously being brought forward although not identified in a previous residential land survey" (ECC, 1987, page 12). Consequently, as was the procedure in the 1984 study *Housing Land Availability in Essex*, conducted jointly by the County with the HBF, an allowance is made for this process (ECC, 1985). For the period 1986–91 an allowance of 5600 dwellings on such small sites is assumed, and for the period 1991–2001 the number is 8050 dwellings. In total, therefore, for the whole *Plan* period, land available for some 13 650 dwelling units on small sites is assumed. Only 30% of this figure, that is, 4100 dwelling sites, are identified in terms as having planning permission.

The remaining three categories of land supply relate to large sites, these being sites capable of accommodating six or more dwellings. The first aspect of this component is large committed sites with planning

Table 3. Estimated gross dwelling requirements, 1986–2001. Sources: DoE, 1983; ECC, 1987, page 6.

	Projection
Housing projections	
1986–91	29 600
1991–96	25 000
1996–2001	14 500
Total	69 100
Allowances	
Dwelling loss and change of use	5 100
Dwelling vacancy	2 600
Reduction in number of shared dwellings	1 300
Total	9 000
Total overall (1986–2001)	78 100

permission. At April 1986 it was suggested that there were an estimated 40 950 such sites. The next component is 'safeguarded sites' which refers to land set aside in some local plans for development after 1991 and which are assumed to be utilised. In total this component provides 2150 sites. The final component is 'recycled urban land'. This relates to the "dwelling capacity of sites occupied by non residential land uses, situated within existing built up areas, which have not been specifically identified by the local planning authorities in the April 1986 residential land data" (ECC, 1987, explanatory memorandum, page 12). This includes derelict land, underused land, mineral workings, and obsolete industrial/commercial areas. Justification of the inclusion of such an allowance for these unidentified large sites is made by reference to DoE circulars which "have emphasised the need to maximise the use of existing urban sites, by the recycling of land within existing built up areas, before considering the release of new sites on previously undeveloped land" (page 12). The total for this component is 7350 dwelling sites.

Considered together these components of land supply represent a total capacity of 64 100 dwellings. Of this total, 70% are existing commitments with planning permission, but 30%, that is 19 050 sites, are predictions of future land supply. The proposed *First Alterations*, by accepting this 64 100 dwelling capacity as 'available', consequently identifies the need for 17 100 dwellings on what are essentially green-field sites in order to meet the 81 200 housing allocation in the period 1986–2001. This submitted provision, however, has not as yet been statutorily approved. Indeed, the examination in public (EIP) in February 1988 of the provision, which resulted in Essex revising its provision totals, is indicative of the continued pressures destabilising this policy approach.

Immediately prior to this EIP the DoE released a revised estimate of household formation rates for Essex for the period 1986–2001, based on 1985 OPCS population projections. This new projection revised upwards the previous forecast of 69 000 households by 17 000 (25%) to 86 100 households. This move clearly served to undermine many of the arguments central to the County's submitted level of housing provision. Perhaps not surprisingly the County's representative at the EIP suggested rather drily that this move had demonstrated a 'superb timing'.

In the light of these revised DoE household forecasts a number of other estimates were circulated at the EIP. Indicative of the housebuilders view and at the uppermost extreme was a projection of 93 700 house-holds, produced by Chapman Warren by means of the 'Chelmer Model' applied to 1985 OPCS population projections. Essex County Council, alternatively, revised their previous estimate of 71 000 households by 7000 (10%) to 78 000.

The revised context provided by these new projections in part perhaps contributed to the County's decision to revise its housing allocations.

Such a move was also empowered by an updated land availability study conducted by the County (ECC, 1988). This revealed the current situation as regards completions and identified land availability. The HBF did not participate in this study however. The housing provision was increased by 7800 (10%) to 89000 dwellings for the period 1986-2001. This implied a new average annual completion rate of 5933 dwellings.

At the County level of analysis, therefore, the *Structure Plan* process has continued to be an attempt to curb an actual rate of dwelling of completions that in practice has varied little since the starting date of the original *Structure Plan*. If anything, current completion rates appear to be increasing. More generally, revisions to household projection estimates have destabilised the impact of restraint-oriented policy.

6.3 Development policy and practice at the district level

If one examines the experiences of individual district councils[2] in Essex more profound indications of a mismatch between policy and practice are revealed. A comparison, for each district, of the level of actual dwelling completions at 31 March 1987 (ten years into the *Structure Plan*) with the level of completions anticipated by the implied average annual completion rate of the total housing provisions stated in the original county *Structure Plan* some interesting findings are produced. By 31 March 1987, given the average annual completion rate implied in the *Structure Plan*, the actual level of dwelling completions should amount to 73% of the total provision for each district. In practice, all districts except Maldon exceed this level. The difference between predicted and actual totals in percentage terms is also interesting. Most noticeably in the districts of Uttlesford, Southend, Thurrock, Epping Forest, and Brentwood, the actual level of completions already exceeds the total provision up to 1991. At one extreme the level in Brentwood is some 122% greater than that anticipated from the implied average annual rate of completions.

A mapping of the percentage extent to which the level of completions exceeds that anticipated illustrates the geographical distribution of development pressure. Currently, pressure appears to be greatest within those districts nearest to London and to be contained within the extent of the metropolitan green belt falling within Essex. In the more rural districts outside the green belt such as Braintree, Tendring, and Maldon the pressure to date seems to be less developed. The situation within Uttlesford district, although in part reflecting development pressure relating to the expansion of Standsted Airport, is also indicative of the 'spillover' effect of development pressure from within the green belt districts closest to London.

[2] Basildon; Braintree; Brentwood; Castle Point; Chelmsford; Colchester; Epping Forest; Harlow; Maldon; Rochford; Southend; Tendring; Thurrock; and Uttlesford.

By comparing the two most extreme examples, the evolving relationship between *Structure Plan* policies and completion rates can be shown more clearly. An examination of the experience of Brentwood, a district near to London and within the metropolitan green belt, is illustrative of the most extreme example of actual completion rates outpacing housing provisions. The *First Alteration* is clearly an attempt to redress a level of completions already (31 March 1987) 1097 dwellings (57%) above the total *Structure Plan* provision of 1920 by 1991.

At the other extreme is the experience of Maldon district. This predominantly rural area, outside the metropolitan green belt, was the only district in Essex at 31 March 1987 where actual completions had not reached the level implied in the *Essex Structure Plan.*

In the submitted *First Alteration* it was sought to maintain this relatively stable level of completions. In order to conform with the original total provision for 1991 of the *Structure Plan*, the County Strategy proposed that initially there should be a higher level of average annual completions which should later 'tail off' to the 2001 provision total. However, the revised district total that was suggested at the EIP considerably increased the total provision figure for 2001.

Although Maldon was then a relatively 'stable' district, the discussions at the EIP emphasised Maldon's vulnerability to the 'spillover' effects of development from the explicitly more pressurised districts nearer to London. The current experience of such districts, notably Brentwood, serves to illustrate the potential future effects that relatively uncontrollable rates of housing completion could have upon the district of Maldon.

The outcome of Essex's submitted *First Alteration* housing provisions currently lies with the Secretary of State. Of crucial importance, however, will be the situation of assessed availability of housing land in the County. The importance of such studies as a basis for the derivation of strategic housing provisions has been indicated in this summary. Such land availability assessments will equally be important to the County's resistance to development pressure as acted through future planning appeals.

7 The policy and practice of residential development in Kent
7.1 Introduction
Planning for residential development within Kent has operated through the process of structure plans for just over a decade. The original *Kent Structure Plan* was prepared in 1977 and approved with modifications in 1982 (KCC, 1977). Since then policies have been reviewed twice, a first set of *Alterations* (KCC, 1981a) approved in December 1983 (KCC, 1984) and a further second set now submitted for approval (KCC, 1987a). A brief review of the development and revision of housing policies reveals key policy themes running through the *Structure Plan* and illustrates changes in the strategy made over time. Use of housing completions

data for both the county as a whole and selected planning subareas
allows the relationship between policy and practice to be demonstrated.

7.2 Policy review: the *Kent Structure Plan*

The original *Kent Structure Plan* gave firm housing provision figures for
a five-year period (1977–82) distributed between eleven policy areas.
This initial provision reflected primarily a high level of then existing
housing land commitments estimated as being sufficient to sustain eight
years of housebuilding at average annual rates experienced during the
1966–76 period of housebuilding 'boom'. As a result and in accordance
with policies for countryside conservation and general restraint of
growth, except at the county growth point of Ashford, no releases of
fresh land for housing were considered necessary prior to the first
review of the *Plan*. A major emphasis of the *Plan* was the need to
control and phase 'limited' reserves of available land and to give priority
to locally generated housing demand. Existing commitments were to be
made to last for as long as possible to minimise the take of 'fresh' (green-
field) land. In pursuance of this, it was emphasised that maximum use
should be made of potential housing land within existing built-up areas.

The 'strategy' of the original *Structure Plan* was therefore based on
the concept of 'growth' (at Ashford) and restraint elsewhere and was
largely 'commitments' based with little need to make further land
releases in the then short to medium term.

7.2.1 *First review and first alterations*

The first review of the *Plan* was undertaken in 1980 and first alterations
to selected policies prepared and submitted in April/May 1981. Based
on revised population, household, and subsequent dwelling requirement
projections these alterations implied a 25% reduction on past (1974–79)
building rates for the 1979–86 period for the County as a whole.

Drawing on the conclusions of the 1980–84 residential land availability
study (KPOG, 1981), revisions were also made to estimates of existing
(committed) available housing land. A comparison of these with the
revised dwelling requirement figures shows that the existing stock of
dwellings together with land then available was almost sufficient numerically
to meet the projected requirements for the County as a whole (table 4).

An analysis of the relationship between revised dwelling requirement
projections, revised estimates of existing land supply, and recent building
rates showed that housing provision for Kent as a whole should be made
on the presumption that building rates will be lower in the future compared
with the past (see tables 4 and 5). In addition, it was felt there should
be a presumption in favour of making provision for dwellings in localities
where demand is locally generated and also of redistributing housing
pressures which could not be met in situ to areas with employment
potential and an available supply of housing land.

Against a framework of general 'strategic policies' housing provision quantities were rolled forward in two 'blocks'—1979–86 and 1986–91— for each of eighteen 'functional' policy subareas (based on the main urban areas within the County). Overall, the submitted provision figures implied a gradual decline in annual building rates compared with those of the past (see table 6). Only at Ashford did the revised figures imply an increase in annual building rates, whereas marked reductions were implied at Maidstone/Malling and the Medway towns, reflecting the 'restraint' and 'redistribution' policy decisions taken there. It was expected that *intensification* of development within existing built-up areas would make a considerable contribution to meeting the provision quantities.

On approval, the revised housing provision figures were adjusted downwards by the Secretary of State for the 1979–86 period (by 2200 dwellings) and were increased (by 400 dwellings) for the 1986–91 period.

Table 4. Dwelling supply and requirements, 1979–86 and 1986–91. Source: KCC, 1981a, table 5.

Planning areas	Dwelling supply		Dwelling requirements		Surplus	
	1979 –86	1986 –91	1979 –86	1986 –91	1979 –86	1986 –91
Dartford	600	100	0	100	600	0
Gravesham	1 300	0	2 700	400	– 1 400	– 400
Sevenoaks	800	0	– 300	– 300	1 100	300
Swanley	1 100	400	2 500	1 000	– 1 400	– 600
Tonbridge	300	100	500	– 100	– 200	200
Tunbridge Wells	1 400	100	2 800	900	– 1 400	– 800
Subtotal	5 500	700	8 200	2 000	– 2 700	– 1 300
Ashford	4 100	1 700	3 400	1 500	700	200
Maidstone/Malling[a]	4 700	2 400	7 400	3 300	– 2 700	– 900
Medway Towns[b]	6 400	2 100	11 700	6 500	– 5 300	– 4 400
Faversham	600	300	400	– 100	200	400
Sittingbourne	1 500	2 300	1 000	600	500	1 700
Sheppey	1 200	100	900	100	300	0
Subtotal	18 500	8 900	24 800	11 900	– 6 300	– 3 000
Canterbury	1 500	200	3 000	900	– 1 500	– 700
Herne Bay/Whitstable	1 800	500	2 300	400	– 500	100
Dover	700	200	– 300	– 700	1 000	900
Deal/Eastry/Sandwich	1 200	500	– 600	– 1 200	1 800	1 700
Thanet	2 300	500	4 200	1 400	– 1 900	– 900
Shepway	3 400	800	200	– 1 300	3 200	2 100
Subtotal	10 900	2 700	8 800	– 500	2 100	3 200
Kent total	34 900	12 300	41 800	13 400	– 6 900	– 1 100

[a] Excludes Walderslade area. [b] Includes Walderslade area.

The effect of the modifications was to imply an overall decline in building rates, but to apportion the decline slightly more evenly between the two plan periods.

The first alterations became operative in January 1984 and together with unaltered policies from the 1980 approved *Plan* constitute the current approved *Kent Structure Plan*. A number of policy 'themes' that were developed in the original plan are carried forward. First, the overall strategy of 'growth' at Ashford and general 'restraint' elsewhere is continued and supplemented by 'redistribution' policies to enable the conservation of established countryside, and the restraint policies in demand pressure areas are to be maintained. Second, 'phasing' of housing land reserves continues as a supported policy and is made more explicit in an attempt to rationalise planning consents in accordance with provision figures. Third, providing for the local element of demand is still important but a specific 'local needs' policy (HEC2) was deleted by the Secretary of State. Maximising the use of potential housing land within built-up

Table 5. Building rates (completions per year): past and trend requirements. Source: KCC, 1981a, table 6.

Planning area	Past rates, 1974–79	Trend requirements	
		1979–86	1986–91
Dartford	210	0	20
Gravesham	410	390	80
Sevenoaks	160	−40	−60
Swanley	470	360	200
Tonbridge	120	70	−20
Tunbridge Wells	460	400	180
Subtotal	1830	1170	400
Ashford	510	490	300
Maidstone/Malling[a]	1130	1060	660
Medway Towns[b]	1310	1670	1300
Faversham	160	60	−20
Sittingbourne	240	140	120
Sheppey	220	130	20
Subtotal	3570	3540	2380
Canterbury	280	430	180
Herne Bay/Whitstable	280	330	80
Dover	420	−40	−140
Deal/Eastry/Sandwich	200	−90	−240
Thanet	790	600	280
Shepway	400	30	−260
Subtotal	2370	1260	−100
Kent total	7770	5970	2680

[a] Excludes Walderslade area. [b] Includes Walderslade area.
Note: Figures (including totals) are rounded separately to nearest 10.

areas is carried forward by a new policy (HEC3) allowing additions to
the provision totals so long as they are from an urban source. The
presumption is still against the release of 'fresh' (green-field) land.

Table 6. Policy housing provisions and implications for building rates. Source:
KCC, 1981a, explanatory memorandum, page 15.

Planning areas	Dwelling provision		Implied annual building rates		Past building rates 1974–79
	1979 –86[a]	1986 –91[b]	1979 –86	1986 –91	
Dartford	700	400	100	80	210
Gravesham	2 500	700	360	140	410
Sevenoaks	1 100	500	160	100	160
Swanley	1 500	800	210	160	470
Tonbridge	1 000	300	140	60	120
Tunbridge Wells	2 800	1 000	400	200	460
Subtotal	9 600	3 700	1 370	740	1 830
Ashford	4 000	3 000	570	600	510
Maidstone/Malling[c]	6 200	2 900	890	580	1 125
Medway Towns[d]	8 100	3 400	1 160	680	1 305
Faversham	700	300	100	60	160
Sittingbourne	1 700	1 200	240	240	240
Sheppey	1 600	700	230	140	220
Subtotal	22 300	11 500	3 190	2 300	3 560
Canterbury	2 000	800	290	160	280
Herne Bay/Whitstable	2 300	500	330	100	280
Dover	1 000	700	140	140	420
Deal/Eastry/Sandwich	1 200	500	170	100	200
Thanet	3 000	1 400	430	280	790
Shepway	2 000	900	290	180	400
Subtotal[e]	11 500	4 800	1 640	960	2 370
Kent total[e]	43 400	20 000	6 200	4 000	7 760

[a] Mid-1979 to mid-1986. [b] Mid-1986 to mid-1991. [c] Excludes Walderslade
area. [d] Includes Walderslade area. [e] The error in total is in the original table:
source of error unknown.

7.2.2 *Second review and alterations*

A second review of the *Plan* has now been undertaken, and further
alterations which roll forward housing provision in three five-year bands
to the end of the century are now submitted for approval to the Department
of the Environment.

As a starting point to the revision of housing policies, population,
household, and dwelling requirement projections were reassessed with a
1986 base date, together with the most up-to-date land availability
information (KCC, 1987b). For the 1986–91 period a comparison of

revised projected dwelling requirements with land supply data showed
that, at the County level, requirements were slightly less than identified
land supply, leaving a small land 'surplus' overall. For the post-1991
period, the relationship deteriorates markedly owing to the fact that little
housing land was identified for the 1991 – 2001 period (see table 7).

For Kent as a whole, the revised projected dwelling requirements for
the 1986 – 91 period (29 500) is substantially higher than that projected
in the approved *Plan* (20 400). However, the quantity of land (then)
committed (for 32 800 dwellings), the 'replenishment rate' of new land
coming forward (windfall/incidental development), plus current building
rate data all point towards the approved provision figure for this period
being exceeded. For the 1991 – 96 period, however, the relationship
between projected dwelling requirements and estimated land supply implies
that significant land releases will need to be made to meet projected
requirements for the 1990s.

A new general strategic housing policy (policy S3) essentially repeats
the overall 'strategy' of earlier versions of the *Plan*. Ashford is to remain
the County growth point particularly in the context of the Channel Tunnel
whereas elsewhere requirements are in general to be met unless there

Table 7. Projected dwellings requirements and housing land supply, 1986 – 2001
(Figures shown in thousands.) Source: KCC Planning Department.

	1981 – 86 est. comps.	1986 – 91		1991 – 96		1996 – 2001 req.
		req.	sup.[a]	req.	sup.[a]	
Maidstone/Malling area	3.8	4.0	4.7	4.5	0.5	4.5
Sevenoaks area	0.7	0.3	0.7	0.3	0	0.3
Swanley area	1.3	1.3	0.8	1.2	0.1	0.9
Tonbridge area	0.5	0.2	0.7	0.2	0.2	0.2
Tunbridge Wells borough	1.8	1.8	1.8	1.6	0.4	1.2
Dartford borough	0.9	0.6	1.4	0.6	0.3	0.6
Gravesham borough	1.1	1.0	1.4	1.0	0.1	0.7
Medway Towns area	5.1	5.4	4.9	5.0	1.6	4.6
Faversham area	0.4	0.5	0.6	0.5	0	0.5
Sheppey	0.5	0.4	1.2	0.3	0.1	0.2
Sittingbourne area	0.8	0.8	1.5	0.8	1.3	0.6
Ashford borough	2.9	3.0	2.7	3.1	1.6	3.2
Canterbury area	1.3	2.6	1.2	3.0	0.2	3.0
Herne Bay/Whitstable	1.5	1.9	1.6	1.9	0.2	1.8
Dover area	0.5	0.6	1.0	0.5	0.2	0.3
Deal area	0.9	0.8	1.3	0.7	0.1	0.7
Folkestone/Hythe area	1.3	1.7	1.7	1.7	0.2	1.8
Romney Marsh area	0.5	0.6	0.7	0.6	0.1	0.6
Thanet District	1.5	2.0	2.6	1.5	0.4	0.8
Kent County	26.9	29.5	32.8	29.0	7.6	26.5

[a] Derived from KCC (1986).
Note: Est. comps estimated completions, req. requirement, sup. supply.

are strong conservation or infrastructure contraints. One change, however, is that it is no longer intended to pursue an 'explicit' phasing policy, and it is proposed that the current approved phasing policy (SP3) is deleted. Against this general strategy, more specific housing policies are proposed. Policy HD1 quantifies the general strategy and rolls forward provision to 2001. Policy HD2 reaffirms the objective to make better use of existing housing stock and housing land within urban areas. Policy HD3 identifies the main areas where the release of fresh land is a significant issue and indicates the main alternative ways of making fresh land provisions. Alternatives proposed included edge-of-town peripheral expansion, new 'freestanding' communities, and the expansion of selected larger rural settlements.

During the consultation period for the proposed alterations, objections were made in relation both to the proposed housing quantities (HD1) and to the policy of fresh land release (HD3). Many districts and amenity groups felt the housing provisions were far too high in terms both of absolute and of implied average annual rates, particularly when compared with the existing approved rates of provision. In response, total provision was reduced by 6100 dwellings. In relation to HD3 there was considerable objection to the notion of 'freestanding' new communities and land releases at some of the larger rural settlements. After further consultation, in the finalised policy the references to 'free-standing' new communities are deleted and the list of locations and larger rural settlements regarded as strategically suitable for land releases are revised.

Even though the proposals carry forward a number of earlier policy themes (such as maximising urban land use and minimising the taking of fresh land), overall they imply a significant increase in housebuilding rates, particularly for the 1986–91 period when compared with the approved provision for this period. In addition, the provision proposed for the 1990s is substantially higher than that indicated by SERPLAN's (1985, RPC 450) regional guidance figures (51 100 compared with 35 500), although this is qualified in terms of the County's household and dwelling requirement projections. Even when compared with the most recent DoE (OPCS) 1985-based population and household projections, the reduced level of provision for the 1990s is still 4000 higher than the projected growth in households for Kent.

Perhaps the most significant feature of the *Second Alterations* (KCC, 1987a), however, is the introduction of a policy specifically related to the release of 'fresh land'. In earlier 'versions' of the *Structure Plan* there was generally sufficient land already committed together with the successful operation of an 'urban land' policy to minimise further release of green-field land. For the first time though, the relationship between projected dwelling requirements, land supply, and recent completion rates indicates that for the 1992 some significant land releases may need to be made. It is even more significant that now the different alternatives have been explored the rural settlements are being asked to make their contribution. In relation to this last point, it is also interesting to note the growing role that land availability studies are assuming in the revision and rolling forward of housing provision quantities in Kent. It is evident that, increasingly, land availability studies are being undertaken on a regular basis in order to update the information base on land supply for the purpose of monitoring the progress on housing provisions and for indicating the time for their review.

7.3 Policy in practice
7.3.1 *The county level*
The overall efficacy of Kent's housing provision policies can be demonstrated by comparing actual trends of housing completion with the implied rates of dwelling provision proposed in the *Structure Plan*.

From 1974–79, completion rates were highest, averaging approximately 7770 dwellings per annum. Over the two years 1979–81, rates dropped off to an average of 5552 dwellings per annum and fell further to 4500 per annum in the subsequent two years to 1983. Most of this reduction can be attributed to the severe downturn in the housing market as a result of general national recession. Completion rates recovered quickly, however, over the two-year period 1983–85, averaging approximately 6140 per annum, falling back to an average of 5600 per annum in the following year, 1985/86.

The provision rate in the current approved (1984) *Structure Plan* for the 1979–86 period is 5886 dwellings per annum. Over this period as a whole, completions averaged slightly less at approximately 5450 dwellings per annum.

By mid-1986, 92% of the provision in the approved plan for the 1979–86 period had been fulfilled, with total completions (37 990) only 3200 dwellings short of the approved provision (41 200). Although slightly below the 'strategy' provision for this period (which implies a higher rate than the average total rate of provision in the *Plan* largely as a consequence of high completion rates in the preceding years), completions were above the average annual implied building rate for the total plan period to 1991. Extrapolation of the completions trend indicates that a 'tapering off' of rate of build as implied by the 1986–91 strategy provision band (which implies a rate of 4080 dwellings per annum) is unlikely to occur and that this planned provision to 1991 is more likely to be substantially exceeded.

In response, in the *Second Alterations* higher rates of build are proposed for the 1986–91 period (5620 per annum) which accord more closely with the 1979–86 average rate of completion. A much more gradual tapering of build rates is envisaged by the two subsequent five-year provision bands which imply average annual rates of 5180 per annum for the 1991–96 period and 5040 per annum for the 1996–2001 period.

Overall, there has been a significant 'readjustment' and 'realignment' of policy at subsequent stages of the structure plan process as information concerning actual rates of housebuilding together with revisions of land supply and dwelling requirement projections becomes available.

7.3.2 *The district level*

An examination of the experience of individual policy subareas reveals further instances of policy/practice mismatch and subsequent readjustment.

Examining the 'residual' position of each policy subarea at mid-1986, some areas have substantially exceeded their 1979–86 provision (for example, Dartford Borough, Swanley, and Shepway) whereas in others building rates have remained stubbornly below the 1979–86 provision level (particularly Sheppey and Gravesham Borough). Some of these 'anomalies' can be examined further.

In Sheppey, one of the more remote rural areas of Kent, housing completions have remained substantially below the planned implied building rate (56% below provision at mid-1986). As a result, in the *Second Alterations* to the *Structure Plan* much lower rates of build are proposed, particularly in the first strategy period (1986–91) of the plan, as a means of bringing policy more into line with the reality of housebuilding rates on the Isle of Sheppey.

The reverse situation is demonstrated by the experience of Dartford Borough, predominantly urban and within easy access of Greater London. By 1986, 99% of the total approved provision had been achieved over only 60% of the plan period. The divergence between the planned provision rate and actual build is striking. To correct this 'slippage', substantially higher rates of housebuilding for the ensuing plan period are proposed in the *Second Alterations*. Indeed, for the 1986–91 period an increase of 117% on the approved provision for this period is proposed (2395 extra dwellings compared with 1100 extra dwellings by 1991).

The experience of Swanley, which lies within the metropolitan green belt, is interesting. Here housing completions have exceeded the approved implied annual building rate, and as a consequence three five-year strategy 'bands' of provision with successively declining implied building rates are suggested in the *Second Alterations* in an attempt to bring actual completions more in line with the original policy trend.

In the Ashford Borough, although Ashford itself is designated as a growth point for Kent, much of its surrounding rural area is protected by countryside conservation policies. Up to mid-1986 completions were largely in line with the planned rate of provision. Further growth, however, is proposed at a steady rate of 600 dwellings per annum to the year 2001 compared with the 800 per annum implied by the current approved provision. This reduced rate was largely the result of objections made during the consultation stage to the *Second Alterations*. Concern was expressed toward Ashford continuing as a growth point because of the implications for the surrounding countryside and the impact on rural settlements.

These examples illustrate how, for certain areas, the relationship between policy as formulated and policy as implemented can diverge quite markedly. It is also evident that in many instances the forward planning process works retrospectively, attempting to realign policy more favourably with market trends. This seems particularly so for initial 'strategy' periods subsequent to the review and revision of the approved *Structure Plan*.

References
CL, 1985 *Land Use Planning and the Market* Coopers and Lybrand, Plumtree Court, London EC4A
CL, 1987 *Land Use Planning and Indicators of Housing Demand* Coopers and Lybrand, Plumtree Court, London EC4A
CPOS, 1988 *Structure Plans and Housing Land* County Planning Officers' Society, Planning Department, The Shirehall, Abbey Foregate, Shrewsbury SY2 6ND
Doak J, Henderson B, Nadin V, 1987, "Joint housing studies: where do we go from here?" *Planning* (706) 20 February, 6–7
DoE
    1970, "Land availability for housing", Circular 10/70
    1972, "Land availability for housing", Circular 102/72
    1973, "Land availability for housing", Circular 122/73
    1975 *Housing Land Availability in the South East: A Consultants' Study* (HMSO, London)
    1978a *Land Availability: A Study of Land with Residential Planning Permission*
    1978b, "Private sector land—requirements and supply", Circular 44/78
    1980a, "Land for private housebuilding", Circular 9/80
    1980b, "Development control—policy and practice", Circular 22/80
    1983, "Household projections"
    1984, "Land for housing", Circular 15/84
    1986 *The Future of Development Plans*
    1987 *Land for Housing Progress Report*
    1988a *Land-use Change in England* Statistical Bulletin 5
    1988b, "Planning policy guidance: land for housing", Planning Policy Guidance Note 3 (January)
    Department of the Environment, 2 Marsham Street, London SW1
DoE/HBF, 1979 *Study of the Availability of Private Housebuilding Land in Greater Manchester (1978–81)* 2 volumes, Department of the Environment/Housebuilder Federation; copy available from DoE, 2 Marsham Street, London SW1
ECC
    1977 *Draft Essex Structure Plan*
    1982a *Essex Structure Plan*
    1982b, "Essex structure plan: approved written statement"
    1984, "Joint housing land availability study", ECC with the Housebuilders Federation
    1985, "Housing land availability in Essex—March 1984"
    1987 *Essex Structure Plan: First Alteration*
    1988, "Housing land availability in Essex—1st April 1987"
    Essex County Council, Globe House, New Street, Chelmsford CM1 1LF
Hooper A, 1979, "Land availability" *Journal of Planning and Environment Law* 752–756

Hooper A, 1980, "Land for private housebuilding" *Journal of Planning and Environment Law* 795–806

Hooper A, 1982, "Land availability in south-east England" *Journal of Planning and Environment Law* 555–560

Hooper A, 1983, "Land availability studies and private housebuilding", in *Land Policy: Problems and Alternatives* Eds S M Barrett, P Healey (Gower, Aldershot, Hants) chapter 6

Hooper A, Pinch P, Rogers S, 1988, "Housing land availability: circular advice, circular arguments and circular methods" *Journal of Planning and Environment Law* 225–239

JURUE, 1977 *Planning and Land Availability* Joint Unit for Research on the Urban Environment, Department of Architectural, Planning and Urban Studies, Aston University, Birmingham

KCC

1977 *Kent Structure Plan*

1981a, *Kent Structure Plan: 1981 Alterations*

1981b, "Kent structure plan: 1981 alterations. Housing requirements and land supply", WP-1/81

1984, "Kent structure plan: statement of policies approved by the Secretary of State for the Environment and explanatory memorandum—approved December 1983"

1987a *Kent Structure Plan: Second Review and Alterations*

1987b, "Housing land supply change in Kent 1985–86"

Kent County Council, County Planning Department, Springfield, Maidstone, Kent

KPOG, 1981, "Land supply in Kent 1980–84" (revised edition), Kent Planning Officers Group and the Housebuilders Federation; available from Kent County Council, County Planning Department, Springfield, Maidstone, Kent

KPOG, 1986, "Housing land supply in Kent mid 1985–mid 1991", summary report, Kent Planning Officers Group, Kent County Council, County Planning Department, Springfield, Maidstone, Kent

OPCS, 1988 *1985-based Projections of Household Formation* (February), Office of Population Censuses and Surveys, St Catherines House, 10 Kingsway, London WC2

McKay D, Cox A, 1979 *The Politics of Urban Change* (Croom Helm, Andover, Hants)

Mackie J W, 1982 *Goodbye Rural Berkshire: Development Pressures in Central Berkshire and South-East England* Binfield and Warfield Parish Councils

MHLG, 1964, "The South East study 1961–81", Ministry of Housing and Local Government (HMSO, London)

RTP, 1987 *Land Used for Residential Development in the South East* TP-2, Roger Tym and Partners, 9/10 Sheffield Street, London WC2A 2EY

Rydin Y, 1986 *Housing Land Policy* (Gower, Aldershot, Hants)

SEJPT, 1970 *Strategic Plan for the South East* South East Joint Planning Team (HMSO, London)

SEJPT, 1976 *Strategic Plan for the South East: Review* South East Joint Planning Team (HMSO, London)

SERPLAN, 1985 "South East England in the 1990s: a regional statement", RPC 450 (October), 50–64 Broadway, London SW1H 0DB

Williamson E, Parks A, 1985 "Strange side effects from central prescription" *Planning* issue 610 (March)

WSCC, 1987, "Housing land supply studies: housebuilding on unidentified sites", West Sussex County Council, County Hall, Chichester, West Sussex

Regionalisation or Geographical Segmentation? Developments in London and South East Housing Markets

J BARLOW
University of Sussex

1 Introduction

During the last three years there have been a number of media stories examining the presumed 'decentralisation' of lower-income households from London. These households are perceived to be moving out in order to buy cheaper housing outside the capital. The *Sunday Times Magazine*, for example, ran a dramatic story asking: "Why are ... people commuting from a London suburb 105 miles from the City? ... What is the connection between a shortage of London nurses and escalating house prices in north Norfolk?" The answer, the author concluded, "is that they are all caught up in the same upheaval—the nationwide fall-out from the London property boom" (McGhie, 1988, page 21). A few weeks later, *The Observer Magazine* ran an almost identical story (Brennan, 1988). In the 1960s it was observed that people were moving from London to commuter centres in the outer metropolitan area (OMA) for housing reasons (Craven, 1969), so this phenomenon is not necessarily new. Nevertheless, the extreme rates of house price inflation in London, relative to other regions, may have given renewed impetus to this process. Obtaining comprehensive evidence for the extent to which this is the case is another matter, though. There are certainly plenty of anecdotes[1] but, as yet, little direct empirical evidence, although a number of authors have examined the process of subregional population decentralisation (for example, Congdon and Champion, 1989; Gordon, 1987; Gordon and Vickerman, 1982; Hamnett, 1986). Most of these works have considered the relative balance between housing and labour market influences on population decentralisation. Rates of construction of new housing have frequently been used as a proxy for housing 'market' change. Clearly, given the substantial decline in the level of new housebuilding since the early 1970s (despite a slight upturn in recent years), as well as a shift the character of the output (from public to private, and 'up market'), house *building* can only be an approximate measure of housing market influences. Most work on intraregional population decentralisation therefore only tangentially makes reference to the housing market.

---

[1] Numerous media stories over the last few years are testimony to this, for example, *The Guardian* (1987), *The Independent* (1987), *The Observer* (1984; 1986; 1987).

In this paper I consider some recent trends in the owner-occupier housing markets of the South East in order to shed some light on the issue of decentralisation. The question is whether the housing market for London's work force is becoming 'regionalised', in other words 'spreading' throughout the South East as a whole. Five related trends are discussed. In section 2 I examine subregional variations in house prices within southern England [2]. This allows us to determine the extent to which particular areas within the region are significantly cheaper and whether there are price variations by *type* of housing. In section 3 I consider the characteristics of purchasers in different parts of the region: are there areas, for example, where the predominant purchaser is the first-time buyer? In section 4 I examine the socioeconomic characteristics of first-time buyers in the London housing market, with special reference to purchasers of converted flats, which form the main 'starter-home' sector, and to the question of access to the London housing market. Next I look at population and employment trends within the South East, together with alternative explanations for intraregional migration. In section 6 I consider the housebuilding 'boom' and the markets that developers are currently targeting. Finally, I attempt to draw some conclusions on the relationships between house price inflation, migration, and housebuilding.

2 House price variations in southern England
Since the early 1980s the cost of owner-occupier housing in southern England has risen rapidly. Annual rates of house price inflation of 20%–30% have not been uncommon, especially in the mid-1980s. Figure 1 shows the annual inflation rates for all house types combined in different parts of southern England, using data from the Department of the Environment/Building Societies' Association annual survey of mortgages (DoE, 1980; 1981; 1984; 1987; 1988) and from the Nationwide Anglia Building Society's house price indexes (NBS, various years). The average inflation rates in each series are not dissimilar, although the NBS index for London is slightly more cyclical than the DoE/BSA equivalent. Two points are clear from these indices: first, the annual rate of inflation in the current boom had returned to the level of the late 1970s by 1988 and, second, the rate of inflation today is not as great as that of the 1970–72 boom. However, these indices only provide us with an aggregate view of house price trends. The segmentation of the owner-occupier market by house type and location means that it is quite possible that rates of inflation will vary substantially according to these aspects of the market.

[2] Although much of the analysis is conducted at a relatively broad regional level, I do not wish to imply that this is the best areal unit for analysis. Unfortunately, house price data from building societies is not readily available at the district level, and there are problems over the representativeness of data at this scale.

Figure 2 shows the relationship between house prices in London and in the rest of the South East (ROSE), East Anglia, and the South West, using the DoE/BSA annual mortgage survey. East Anglia and the South West have been included in the analysis because parts of these regions are now falling into the London commuter belt as improvements to the

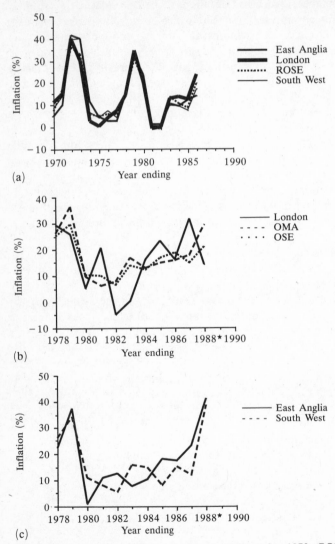

Note: The year ending 1970, for example, is 31 December 1970. ROSE rest of South East, OMA outer metropolitan area, OSE outer South East, ⋆ second quarter (Q2).

Figure 1. Annual house price inflation, (a) south of England, (b) London and South East, and (c) East Anglia and South West. Sources: DoE, 1981; 1987; NBS, various years.

transport infrastructure are made. It should be noted that because the index is based on a survey of mortgages granted, there may be broad problems of comparability from year to year because building societies have tended in the past to vary their lending policies. However, given the degree of intersociety competition, the lending policies should be broadly similar in any one year, so that data can be regarded as a reasonably accurate description of building-society-financed housing trends[3].

From figures 2(a) and 2(b) we can see that both for first-time buyers and for purchasers as a whole, relative house prices in each area have displayed a highly cyclical nature. During the 'interinflationary' period between the years 1973 and 1978 there was a convergence towards

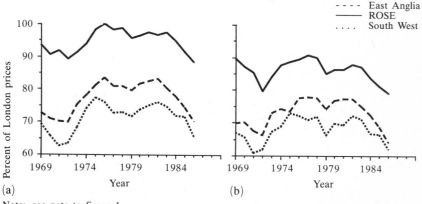

Note: see note to figure 1.

Figure 2. Regional house prices in relation to London, (a) all buyers, and (b) first-time buyers. Source: DoE, 1980; 1988.

[3] How representative of the owner-occupier market as a whole is building society data? The only comprehensive source of information on the characteristics of purchasers is provided by building societies, because banks and other institutional lenders tend not to release information on their mortgage lending. Of the building socities, the Halifax and Nationwide Anglia provide the most detailed information. Nationally, building societies account for over three-quarters of all mortgage lending, with banks taking about 21% and insurance companies under 1% of the business. We can be reasonably certain that the degree of competition between building societies means that their lending practices are similar, and hence there are no significant variations in purchaser characteristics between societies. However, it is clear that banks and insurance companies tend to lend on more expensive property, so we must bear in mind the possibility that a more expensive market segment is missed from the analysis by examining only building society data. This may be particularly relevant in London, given the high prices of dwellings, although a recent survey of purchasers of converted flats in London showed that only 17.6% had obtained a mortgage from a bank, finance company, or insurance company (Barlow and Hamnett, 1988).

average London prices. Divergences have occurred when inflation has
been high, during the early 1970s and early 1980s. This implies that
there is a time lag between London and other regions in the relative
rates of growth in house prices. During periods of rapid inflation hous
prices in London tend initially to increase faster than in other regions,
which then subsequently 'catch up'. This was the conclusion of Hamne
(1983; 1984), who argues that although it is true that there have been
persistent regional differences in *absolute* house prices and distinct
fluctuations in the level of house prices in cheaper regions in relation t
those in London, there has not been a *growing* divergence between the
South East and the rest of Britain. Figure 2(b) also shows that althoug
the prices paid by first-time buyers in the South vary cyclically in relation
to London, they are nevertheless considerably lower outside the capital

Unfortunately the data available from the DoE/BSA survey cannot b
broken down by dwelling type. Figure 3 was constructed by using NBS
data on house prices. This series is useful because it is available over
longer period and at a more disaggregate geographical level than the

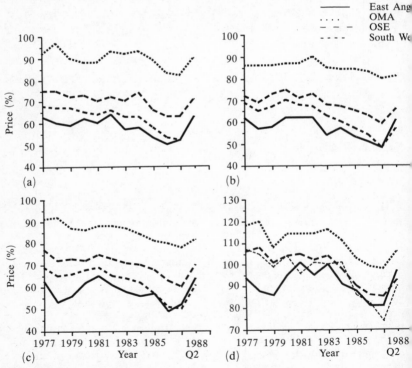

Note: see note to figure 1.

Figure 3. The percentage of London prices for (a) detached houses, (b) semi-detached houses, (c) terraced houses, and (d) other dwellings. Source: NBS, various years.

Halifax Building Society series. It is, however, based on a smaller share of the market, and variations in dwelling size and quality have not been controlled for, as is the case with the Halifax data. It is important to note, however, that neither series goes back to the inflationary boom in the early 1970s. The measurements therefore begin from a period of relatively low inflation, and the possibility that the trends in the early 1970s were similar to those in the present period remains open.

With these provisos in mind it is possible to detect some clear variations in the price trends between regions and dwelling types. For terraced houses and semi-detached houses there has been a slow long-term decline in prices relative to London. Although this trend is perhaps less distinct for terraced houses in East Anglia and for semi-detached house in the OMA, there does seem to have been a relative decline since the late 1970s. For detached houses, prices in the OMA and outer South East (OSE) have held up better relative to London, whereas in East Anglia and the South West there was a steady decline until 1986. It is when we examine the price changes for 'other dwellings' —flats, maisonettes, and bungalows—that the most striking trends can be seen. A sharp relative decline in the OMA, the OSE, and the South West is evident, although there are also pronounced cycles of convergence. The prices of these dwellings in the OSE had dropped from a level approximately 10% *above* that in London in 1978 to nearly 15% *below* by late 1987. The fall in the South West was even more pronounced. Prices in East Anglia, on the other hand, have remained relatively stable.

We can draw two conclusions from these trends. First, the price of some types of housing outside London seems to have risen at a slower rate than in the capital itself. This is particularly clear for smaller dwellings: terraced houses and flats, maisonettes and bungalows. Although there have been relative declines for larger houses, this is less marked, especially in the OMA. Second, since 1986 there has been an upturn in relative prices for all dwelling types in all regions (except terraced and semi-detached houses in the OMA).

3 Socioeconomic characteristics of house buyers in the south of England
An analysis of broad patterns of house price inflation can only take us so far, though. In order to build up a more detailed picture of trends in owner-occupier housing markets it is necessary to examine the socio-economic characteristics of purchasers, together with any geographical variations that may exist. We can again do this by using data from the NBS (see NBS, 1988a).

Figure 4 shows a selection of characteristics of purchasers in the South of England in 1987. It is clear that there are significant local differences between the type of purchaser. London stands out in its high proportion of first-time buyers, followed by Kent, Bedfordshire,

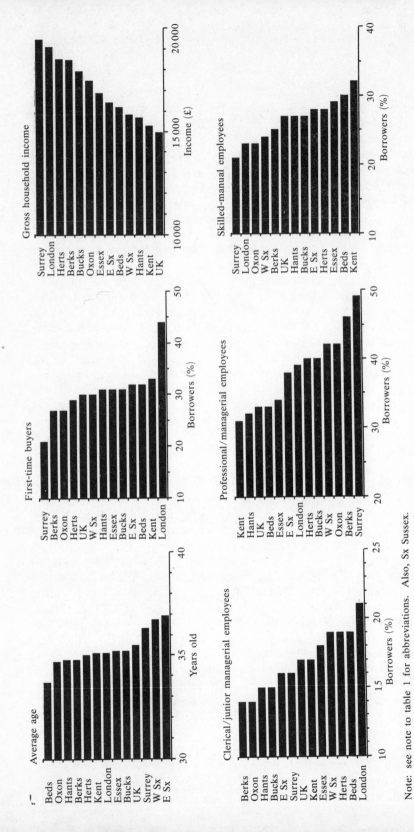

Figure 4. Characteristics of house buyers in the South of England, 1987. Source: NBS, 1988a.

Note: see note to table 1 for abbreviations. Also, Sx Sussex.

and East Sussex. Surrey has by far the lowest proportion of first-time buyers. There are also distinct variations in the average age of purchasers: the youngest buyers are in Bedfordshire and the oldest in East and West Sussex. This is related to the high numbers of retired purchasers on the south coast. In terms of employment status and income it appears that typical buyers in Surrey and Berkshire are the relatively well-paid professionals and managerial employees, whereas in London they are well paid, but more likely to be in junior managerial or clerical positions. Skilled-manual employees form a proportionately larger share of the market in Kent, Bedfordshire, and Essex, and tend to have a lower than average household income.

With use of the NBS data it is also possible to examine the distance moved. The counties with the highest share of movers in the 26 mile – 100 mile range, which takes in the OMA and OSE but excludes short local moves, are East Sussex (23% of purchasers), Oxfordshire, West Sussex, Buckinghamshire, and Kent (15%). Purchasers making short moves (under 10 miles) were proportionately most important in London (87% of purchasers), Hampshire, Hertfordshire, Surrey, and Berkshire (71%).

This information therefore confirms that the owner-occupier housing market in the South East is segmented according to socioeconomic status. Purchasers in certain areas tend to be younger and to have moved further. These purchasers are also more likely to be in less well-paid, lower-status jobs. Tables 1(a) to 1(d) indicate the relative position of different counties in terms of employment status, age, earnings, distance moved, and previous tenure of owner-occupiers. From these tables we can see that purchasers in Berkshire, Hertfordshire, Oxfordshire, and Buckinghamshire are frequently younger, professional, or managerial employees in well-paid jobs. These purchasers are also less likely to be first-time buyers. At the opposite pole, purchasers in Kent, Hampshire, and Bedfordshire tend to be young, less well-paid clerical or junior managerial employees, who are first-time buyers. Both London and Surrey stand out, albeit for different reasons. As we have seen, London purchasers are commonly first-time buyers in high-earning junior managerial or clerical jobs. These owner-occupiers also tend to be slightly older than average. In Surrey, however, buyers are most likely to be highly-paid professional and managerial previous owner-occupiers.

The geography of owner-occupation in the South East therefore seems to have three important features. First, there is a 'wedge' of relatively high-priced housing, with more affluent purchasers, extending from west and northwest from London. It is likely that this 'wedge' extends beyond the boundaries of the South East: in 1987 two of the seven most expensive districts[4] for three-bedroomed semi-detached

[4] These were South Cambridgeshire, Christchurch, Wimborne, Bath, West Dorset, West Norfolk, and Kennet.

houses outside the region were on the 'M4 Corridor' (Bath and Kennet) (NBS, 1988b). The existence of such a wedge is clear from analysis of the *Census 1981 Regional Migration* tables. These show that over 45% of migrants moving from London to this area were in professional and managerial socioeconomic groups (figure 5). Second, a group of counties to the east and south of the capital—Kent, Essex, East Sussex—appear to be dominated by lower-paid purchasers, often first-time buyers. Third, there is London itself, characterised by well-paid first-time buyers, probably at an early stage in their careers.

Table 1. (a) Age and managerial status [professional/managerial (prof./mgrl) to clerical/junior managerial (clerical/jr mgrl)], (b) age and previous ownership characteristics, (c) pay and age status, and (d) distance moved and previous tenure. Source: NBS, 1988a.

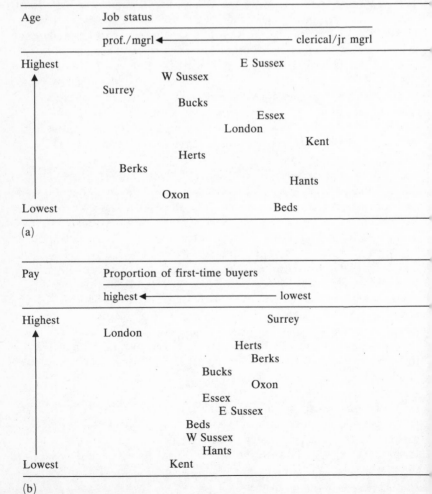

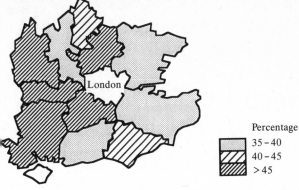

Percentage
	35 – 40
	40 – 45
	> 45

Figure 5. Professional/managerial migrants originating from London (SEG 1 – 5.1, all migrants). Source: OPCS, 1981.

Table 1 (continued)

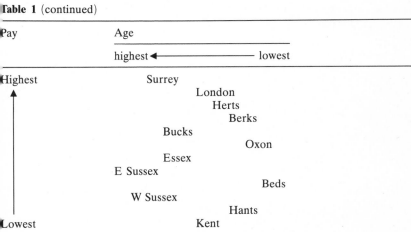

Pay	Age
	highest ◄——————— lowest
Highest	Surrey
↑	London
	Herts
	Berks
	Bucks
	Oxon
	Essex
	E Sussex
	Beds
	W Sussex
	Hants
Lowest	Kent

(c)

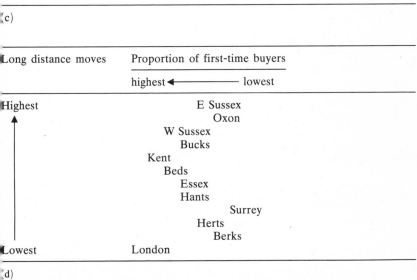

Long distance moves	Proportion of first-time buyers
	highest ◄——————— lowest
Highest	E Sussex
↑	Oxon
	W Sussex
	Bucks
	Kent
	Beds
	Essex
	Hants
	Surrey
	Herts
	Berks
Lowest	London

(d)

4 First-time buyers in the London housing market

The special features of the London housing market deserve more attention, particularly given its dominance by first-time buyers. This group of purchasers plays a key role in the owner-occupier market because they represent an addition to the total demand for housing, without a commensurate increase in supply (that is, through creation of vacancies on moving). The mobility patterns of first-time buyers are therefore of crucial importance in explaining wider trends within the housing market.

Since 1970 the proportion of first-time buyers in London has fluctuated considerably.[5] Figure 6 shows that during the early 1970s over two-thirds of mortgages granted were to first-time buyers. After the peak years of inflation in 1970–72, this share fell sharply before rising again during the late 1970s. During the second wave of inflation, between 1979 and 1981, the proportion of first-time buyers again fell initially, before rising. Since 1984 the share has dropped. So although there have been fluctuations, there has actually been *no* clear downward trend in the proportion of first-time buyer transactions recorded by building societies.[6] Also, because of the substantial growth in owner-occupier transactions during the 1980s, the *absolute* number of first-time buyer purchases has almost doubled, from about 40 000 in 1979 to over 70 000 in 1986.

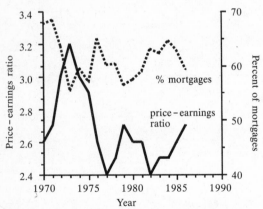

Figure 6. First-time buyers and the London housing market. Source: DoE, 1981; 1987.

[5] Information from DoE *Housing and Construction Statistics*.

[6] It is possible that reliance on information on building society transactions overestimates the scale of the first-time buyer market as these purchasers are less likely to obtain mortgages from other sources.

The question we need to ask, though, is whether there have also been changes in the socioeconomic characteristics of these buyers. Unfortunately, this issue is extremely underresearched. Although the NBS and Halifax data provide a snapshot for 1986 – 87, it is hard to obtain a coherent picture over time. Table 2 shows that the majority of first-time buyers in London today are under thirty-five years old and purchase flats, with a smaller proportion buying terraced houses.

Given the importance of flats in the London first-time buyer market it is pertinent to examine the characteristics of purchasers of this type of housing. The chapter by Hamnett, in this volume, provides a more detailed analysis.

Broadly, purchasers of converted flats are most likely to be in either single-person or two-adult households, without children. First-time buyers dominate the sector, although a not-inconsiderable proportion are previous owner-occupiers. The majority of purchasers are professional and managerial employees, but with lower average incomes than buyers of other types of housing.

Although the incomes of these households tend to be lower than other purchasers, they are nevertheless high when compared with the 'average' household in London. In 1987 buyers of conversions had an average household income of £20 200. In the same year, average annual earnings of all full-time male employees was about £14 600, according to the "New Earnings Survey". The corresponding figure for women was £9600. This would therefore seem to indicate that purchasers of converted flats are paid slightly less than the average for London households in full-time employment: the average earnings of single-person

Table 2. Selected characteristics of first-time buyers in London.

Characteristic	1987		1986 HBS[c]
	NBS[a]	HBS[b]	
Average household income (£)	16 700[d]	20 200	17 000
Age (%)			
< 25	26	na	28
25 – 29	na	na	36
30 – 34	na	na	16
26 – 35	43	na	na
Type of property purchased (%)			
converted flat	22	na	32
purpose-built flat	36	na	27
terraced house	30	na	29

na no data available.
[a] Nationwide Building Society (source: NBS, 1987).
[b] Halifax Building Society (source: LRC, 1988).
[c] Halifax Building Society (source: LRC, 1987).
[d] Average income, second quarter of 1988, £20 500.

households buying conversions, at about £13000, was slightly higher than the overall male–female average.

Although purchasers of converted flats appear to be slightly less well paid than other *purchasers* it is clear that they have substantially higher incomes than the average London household. In 1986, the "Family Expenditure Survey" estimated the average gross income of a London household to be only £12204. Even allowing for a 10% rise in earnings between 1986 and 1987, this would mean that such a household would be earning some £6800 less per annum than conversion buyers. So is the cost of housing in London affecting the ability of nonowners to break into the market? Two points need to be made here. First, the price–earnings ratio for first-time buyers has fluctuated, but there has been no secular upward trend during the 1970s and 1980s (figure 6). In most recent years the ratio has reverted to the level which occurred in 1972–73. Second, although the average price–earnings ratio for first-time buyers has remained relatively stable, since 1983 there seems to have been a growing divergence between average full-time earnings in London and the average income of first-time buyers (figure 7). This could indicate that first-time buyers are being increasingly drawn from a pool of relatively well-paid households. It should be stressed, though, that this trend is fairly recent: since the early 1970s there has actually been a slow *convergence* between average male and female earnings and the average incomes of first-time buyers.

There does, however, seem to be a broad relationship between falls in the proportion of first-time buyers, increases in the price–earnings ratio of such buyers, and an upward drift in the average incomes of first-time buyers: from figures 6 and 7 we can see that this occurred after 1984 and between 1977 and 1979. Unfortunately, the "New Earnings Survey" data is not available for the early 1970s. A similar

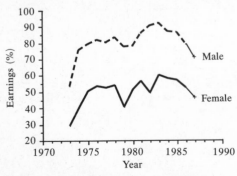

Note: + Halifax Building Society, 1987 figures.

Figure 7. Average male–female earnings as a percentage of the average household income of first-time buyers. Source: DoE, 1984; 1987; HMSO, various years.

relationship can be identified during the 1970-73 bout of inflation, though, by means of income data from the "Family Expenditure Survey". These data suggest that the first-time buyer market in London has been increasingly restricted to better-off purchasers in recent years. However, because of the absence of historic data on the socioeconomic characteristics of this group, it is not possible to say whether this phenomenon is only connected with the current period of rapid inflation in house prices, or whether it has been associated with previous inflationary years. On the other hand, changes to the spatial division of labour and shifts in the pattern of migration lend weight to the idea that London's employment structure has become polarised between a 'service class' of professional and managerial workers, and a group of lower-status occupational groups (Hamnett, 1986; 1987). Much of the rise in owner-occupier households in the 1970s—206 000—was linked to the shift towards these primary nonmanual occupations (Hamnett and Randolph, 1986). Hamnett (1987) also emphasises that there seems to be a concentration of professional and managerial employees in owner-occupation and of the less skilled in council housing.

Although recent calculations by Berge (1988) have disputed that there has been a disproportionate rise in the concentration of professional and managerial employees in London, neither Berge nor Hamnett is able to examine the period after 1981. Since then changes to London's position in the spatial division of labour may have had significant effects. In particular, it is likely that despite a declining share of total national financial employment, London has to some extent consolidated its position as a global financial services centre, with a continued growth in headquarters facilities and an emphasis on activities such as broking, securities, and investment banking. A move towards large centralised-dealing floors has also led to a reduction in support staff (Rajan, 1987). Despite the decentralisation of services, 84% of the largest British firms maintained a London HQ separate from their production plants (GLC, 1985).

It appears, then, that the labour market in London and the South East is becoming more segmented. This has occurred geographically, with London performing 'higher-order' service activities and with fringe areas in the region capturing more routine jobs. This is not to argue that there has been a *strict* spatial division of labour in terms of skill and remuneration levels in the South East, as there has also been a marked trend towards high-status job growth in certain parts of the OMA and OSE. Nevertheless, a degree of geographical restructuring and concentration of selected high-income service jobs appears to have taken place. In terms of the housing market, the effect of this may have been to strengthen the concentration of *relatively* well-paid first-time buyers in London.

5 Population migration, housing markets, and employment decentralisation
We have seen how the market for housing for first-time buyers in London in the 1980s is likely to have become more dominated by relatively high-earning members of the 'service class'. What does this imply for intraregional migration in southern England? Specifically, has there been a 'decentralisation' of lower-earning first-time buyers from the capital to other parts of southern England? In order to examine this it is necessary to recall the characteristics of purchasers in other parts of the South East and to consider recent trends in migration.

It was argued above that there are distinct variations in the relative rate of price inflation for different types of housing in different parts of southern England. Significantly, the price of small dwellings in London has increased faster than in other locations, although since 1986–87 there has been an upturn in the rate of price increase of most housing types in most areas. I would hypothesise that the following may have taken place. As house prices have risen in London, and the representation of higher-income households in the first-time buyer market has grown, a group of potential house purchasers have been 'shut out' of the London housing market. These households do not have sufficient earnings to enter the market in London, but are, nevertheless, able to purchase outside the capital. These geographical differences in market capacity have become especially marked during the most recent inflationary period, although this does not preclude the possibility that a similar process also occurred during previous booms in house prices. Figures 3(a) to 3(d) show how smaller housing units have become relatively cheaper outside London since the early 1980s. It is likely that lower-income first-time buyers have moved out of London in search of cheaper housing in selected parts of the OMA and OSE, and, more recently, in East Anglia. Undoubtedly, other areas within commuting distance have also become desirable for such purchasers. The recent upturn in the price of small dwellings in these areas, relative to London, may be an indication of the growing demand from such purchasers.

Essentially, these households have made a trade-off between lower house prices and higher commuting costs. We have seen how certain parts of the South East—especially to the east and south of the capital— are characterised by towns of younger, less well-paid, first-time buyers. It is possible that this type of purchaser has moved to towns in these areas within reasonable commuting time from central London with lower-cost housing. Places such as Peterborough, Ipswich, the Medway towns, or Portsmouth appear to be performing a role at the lower end of the owner-occupier housing market. In none of the cheapest districts in southern England was the average price of three-bedroomed semi-detached housing more than 86% of the cheapest London borough.

But to what extent is this picture borne out by the migration evidence? Since the 1960s there has been a very substantial decline in the population of Greater London, largely resulting from migration to other parts of the South East. According to Congdon and Champion (1989, table 1) the capital lost over 1 900 000 residents through net migration between 1961 and 1986. They argue, that since the mid-1970s, however, a reduction in total net migration losses and upturn in natural change have resulted in much reduced losses of population in London (compare with Congdon and Champion, 1989). Nevertheless, their figures also show an *increase* in average annual net migration from London to the ROSE: from 93 000 in 1970–71, to 41 000 (1980–81), and increasing to 65 000 in 1986–87 (Congdon and Champion, 1989, table 11.1).[7]

Britton (1986) also believes that there was a slowdown in the rate of population loss in both inner and outer London, and a slightly reduced growth rate in the ROSE in the late 1970s. In the ROSE migration growth rates for the period 1981–85, at 4.0 per 1000 inhabitants, are at their lowest since 1974–77, as is the natural rate of growth. It is possible, therefore, that the trend toward intraregional decentralisation was sustained, albeit at a reduced rate, until the early 1980s. Since then, though, there may have been a return to higher levels of net migration from London to the ROSE.

There is much debate over the precise causes of population decentralisation from London, and especially over the role played by housing and employment factors (see Congdon and Champion, 1989; Gordon, 1987). Early research on the migration flows during the period of maximum net loss show that geographical distribution of jobs in the region was probably only partly responsible. In a study of the period 1966–71, Gordon and Vickerman (1982) found that moves resulting from employment factors accounted for a relatively small proportion of London's population loss (compare with Buck et al, 1986). In the most recent period, Gordon (1987) shows that there is an association between high rates of out-migration, transport costs, and the construction of increased proportions of 'family-sized' dwellings, suggesting that housing and 'environment' factors remain significant.

However, there is other evidence which implies that the relative balance of employment to housing factors is considerably more complex. Congdon and Champion (1989) show that although there is a negative correlation between out-migration from London and the ratio of house prices in London to those elsewhere in the region, the relationship between out-migration and the ratio of housing prices to average incomes

[7] The lack of comparability between migration recorded by the National Health Service Central Register (NHSCR) (1986–87) and Census migration (1970/81 and 1980/81) figures may exaggerate the difference between data for 1980/81 and 1986/87: NHSCR net out-migration figures from London are higher than those in the Census.

in London is *positive*. There also appears to be an important relationship between changes in out-commuting from counties in the OMA/OSE
belt, net in-migration, and levels of job growth. High employment
growth appears to stimulate in-migration and to be associated with
increasing self-containment for a given county. Counties in the western
fringes of London, notably Berkshire, West Sussex, Hampshire, and
Oxfordshire, have all seen growing 'self-containment'. Bedfordshire,
Essex, and Hertfordshire, on the other hand, have seen rates of in-
migration in excess of employment growth rates, and in these counties
there has been a growth of out-commuting.

6 Housing production in the South East
We have seen the complexity of the relationships between migration,
employment, and housing market factors. It is clear that since the early
1980s London and the South East have become a highly attractive target
for housing developers. During the last seven years the region has
experienced something of a building boom. Who are these new dwellings
aimed at?

By 1985 the level of new orders for private housing both in the
ROSE and in Greater London had almost returned to the level of the
previous boom in the early 1970s. The South East as a whole has
captured an ever-increasing share of the national total of new private
building since 1979: up from about 29% to 39% by 1986 (figure 8).
Because these figures exclude the growing market for flat conversions,
overwhelmingly concentrated in London, these figures almost certainly
underestimate the true picture.

These aggregate figures also hide the way the geographical and market
distribution of housebuilding has shifted. There has been a sustained rise
in the share of new orders captured by London. Greater London has

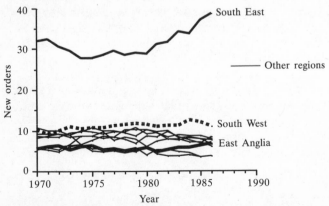

Figure 8. New orders for private housebuilding as a percentage of the national
total. Source: DoE, 1981; 1987.

increased its share of the regional output, from a low of 12.8% in 1977 to a current level of over 20%. Since the mid-1970s, the largest volume of new construction has tended to be in the western half of the region: Berkshire, Buckinghamshire, Oxfordshire, and Hampshire.

In market terms there has, since the 'starter housing' boom of the early 1970s, been a trend towards the construction of more expensive, larger 'trade-up' housing (Ball, 1983)[8]. There are no statistics on the proportion of new houses bought by first-time buyers. However, most volume developers have shifted their production to more 'up-market' and 'niche-market' housing[9]. This has been particularly marked in the 1980s as the market power of previous owner-occupiers has grown with inflation in house prices. The distribution of new housing by price is now almost the direct opposite of the situation in the early 1970s, with the most expensive housing forming the largest share of the market (see Ball, 1983, figure 4.9; DoE, various years, 1986 edition, table 10.13).

To what extent is this new construction related to the migration trends discussed above? Gordon (1987) argues that new housebuilding is important in creating new opportunities for migration to a given area, provided the rate of new building exceeds the local rate of family formation. However, we have already noted the low correlation between migration and new construction. As Congdon and Champion (1989) argue, most moves to new housing are predominantly short-distance moves. I would agree, therefore, that the current housebuilding boom in many parts of the South East is not being fuelled by demand from *lower-income* first-time buyers immigrating from London. Moves by older, wealthier households are probably providing the impetus for much of the growth of housebuilding. From table 1(b) it is clear that purchasers in East and West Sussex, Oxfordshire, and Buckinghamshire are less likely to be first-time buyers and tend to have moved the greatest distance. It is not possible, of course, to determine whether these purchasers are moving primarily for job or for housing related reasons. Berkshire, Surrey, and Hertfordshire, on the other hand, appear to be characterised by higher proportions of short-distance movers, implying that there is more of an 'internal' housing market in these counties.

7 Conclusions

What, then, is the relationship between migration, employment, differential house prices, and new construction in the South East? We can tentatively suggest the following scenario. During the early period of decentralisation, most moves were indeed for 'residential' reasons as Gordon and Vickerman (1982) suggest. Service-sector employment decentralised

[8] Trade-up housing: more expensive housing for second time and successive purchasers, often purchased with a view to further advance up the housing ladder.

[9] Niche-market housing: for specialised socioeconomic submarkets.

from London, to some extent 'following the work force'. Many of the movers during this period were families seeking larger accommodation and/or a better environment. In the 1970s and 1980s, though, firms relocated outside London after rationalisation and structural reorganisation, with workers following or with new labour being recruited in situ. This would have reduced net migration from London during the 1970s, although outward migration of 'service-class' professionals for career purposes continued. However, renewed job growth in London in the 1980s, and a concentration of high-income service-class jobs in the capital have been instrumental in a rapid rise in house prices. House price inflation has outstripped rises in earnings of many *potential* first-time buyers. This group is neither being catered for by new housebuilding outside London, nor by inner London conversions. These new dwellings are largely being built for relatively well-off households, whether first-time buyers or mid-career households trading up. It is *possible*, therefore, that lower-income first-time buyers are now migrating from London in search of cheaper, older housing. However, this may well be a relatively limited phenomenon operating at the margins of the housing market. Without detailed research at the household level in likely areas for this type of migration, this must remain an untested hypothesis.

Whether these trends will be sustained into the 1990s is another matter. The key factor is the balance between house prices in different areas. The regional differentials in house prices now appear to be tailing-off, as parts of East Anglia and the outer South East 'catch-up' with the London inflationary boom. The possible rise in long-distance rail commuter fares, announced in August 1988, may also have a dampening effect on housing-led migration from London. However, it is also clear that average per capita incomes are diverging sharply between London, the ROSE, and the rest of Britain, reflecting the changing spatial division of labour.[10] If this trend is maintained, the 'isolation' of the housing market in London and the ROSE (with its various outliers) vis-à-vis other parts of Britain cannot be ruled out. Given the possible effect of the Single European Market and Channel Tunnel in 'pulling' certain economic sectors to the South East, this may well be the case after 1992.

Acknowledgement. This paper is based on preliminary research for ESRC projects D00232280 on housing provision in European growth regions and D00232198 on the flat conversions market in London.

[10] Since 1979, average gross weekly earnings in London have risen from around 112% to 127% of the British average. The corresponding figures for the ROSE are about 100% to 103%.

References
Ball M, 1983 *Housing Policy and Economic Power* (Methuen, Andover, Hants)
Barlow J, Hamnett C, 1988, "Owner-occupier flat conversions in the London housing market", project technical report, available from authors
Berge E, 1988, "Some comments on C Hamnett's reading of the data on sociotenurial polarisation in South East England" *Environment and Planning A* **20** 973–977
Brennan J, 1988, "Suburbia on the march" *The Observer Magazine* (London edition) 28 February, unpaginated
Britton M, 1986, "Recent population changes in perspective" *Population Trends* **44** 33–41
Buck N, Gordon I, Young K, Ermisch J, Mills L, 1986 *The London Employment Problem* (Clarendon Press, Oxford)
Congdon P, Champion A, 1989, "Trends and structure in London's migration and their relationship to employment and housing markets", in *Advances in Regional Demography* Eds P Congdon, P Batey (Belhaven Press, London) pp 180–204
Craven E, 1969, "Private residential expansion in Kent, 1954–64: a study of pattern and process in urban growth" *Urban Studies* **6**(1) 1–16
DoE, 1980 *Housing and Construction Statistics 1969–1979* Department of the Environment (HMSO, London)
DoE, 1981 *Housing and Construction Statistics 1970–1980* Department of the Environment (HMSO, London)
DoE, 1984 *Housing and Construction Statistics 1973–1983* Department of the Environment (HMSO, London)
DoE, 1986 *Housing and Construction Statistics 1975–1985* Department of the Environment (HMSO, London)
DoE, 1987 *Housing and Construction Statistics 1976–1986* Department of the Environment (HMSO, London)
DoE, 1988 *Housing and Construction Statistics 1977–1987* Department of the Environment (HMSO, London)
GLC, 1985 *The London Industrial Strategy* (Greater London Council, London)
Gordon I, 1987, "Resurrecting counterurbanisation: housing market influences on migration fluctuations from London" *Built Environment* **13**(4) 212–222
Gordon I, Vickerman R, 1982, "Opportunity, preference and constraint. An approach to the analysis of metropolitan migration" *Urban Studies* **19** 247–261
Hamnett C, 1983, "Regional variations in house prices and house price inflation 1969–81" *Area* **13** 189–196
Hamnett C, 1984, "The postwar restructuring of the British housing and labour markets: a critical comment on Thorns" *Environment and Planning A* **16** 147–161
Hamnett C, 1986, "The changing socio-economic structure of London and the South East 1961–81" *Regional Studies* **20** 391–406
Hamnett C, 1987, "A tale of two cities: sociotenurial polarisation in London and the South East, 1961–1981" *Environment and Planning A* **19** 537–556
Hamnett C, Randolph W, 1986, "Labour market restructuring in Greater London 1971–1981: evidence from the OPCS longitudinal survey" WP-44, Social Statistics Research Unit, City University, Northampton Square, London EC1V 0HB
HMSO, various years *New Earnings Survey* (HMSO, London)
LRC, 1987 *London Housing Statistics 1986. London Research Centre Annual Abstract* London Research Centre, 82 Black Prince Road, London SE1 7SZ
LRC, 1988 *Quarterly House Price Bulletin Number 2* Halifax Building Society data; London Research Centre, 82 Black Prince Road, London SE1 7SZ

McGhie C, 1988, "The London effect" *Sunday Times Magazine* 3 January, pages 20–28

NBS, 1988a *Local Area Housing Statistics Number 2. South East England* Nationwide Anglia Building Society, Chesterfield House, Bloomsbury Way, London WC1V 6PW

NBS, 1988b *House Prices: Highs and Lows. A Local View* Nationwide Anglia Building Society, Chesterfield House, Bloomsbury Way, London WC1V 6PW

NBS, 1987 *Local Area Housing Statistics Number 16. London* Nationwide Anglia Building Society, Chesterfield House, Bloomsbury Way, London WC1V 6PW

NBS, various years *House Prices* (quarterly) available from Nationwide Anglia Building Society, Chesterfield House, Bloomsbury Way, London WC1V 6PW

OPCS, 1981 *Census 1981 Regional Migration, South East (Part 2)* Office of Population Censuses and Surveys (HMSO, London)

Rajan A, 1987 *Services—The Second Industrial Revolution? Business and Jobs Outlook for UK Growth Industries* (Butterworth, Sevenoaks, Kent)

The Guardian 1987, "East Anglia is no longer the end of the line", 10 October, page 23

The Independent 1987, "Distance to London the key as house price gap widens", 9 October, page 5

The Observer 1984, "Razzle-dazzle of Romford", 2 September, page 43

The Observer 1986, "Bargain homes in new towns", 16 November

The Observer 1987, "Rethinking the Medway", 30 August, page 46

The Spatial and Social Segmentation of the London Owner-occupied Housing Market: An Analysis of the Flat Conversion Sector

C HAMNETT
The Open University

1 Introduction

In some of my previous work on London and the South East I have examined the social and spatial restructuring of the region and its links with the tenurial restructuring of the housing market (Hamnett, 1983; 1986; 1987). I have argued, amongst other things, that the decline of the private rented sector, particularly in central and inner London, and the growth of the council and owner-occupied sectors over the last twenty-five to thirty years (Hamnett and Randolph, 1983) have led to the development of sociotenurial polarisation, whereby the less skilled, low paid, unemployed, and some minority groups have become concentrated in the council sector whereas the professional and managerial and white-collar groups have become concentrated in the owner-occupied sector. This polarisation process has been associated with the social residualisation of the council sector in inner London (Hamnett and Randolph, 1987). Although Berge (1988) questions the extent to which the professional and managerial workers have become increasingly overconcentrated in owner-occupation, his work clearly shows the crucial role of the housing market in producing sociospatial segregation in the South East (Hamnett, 1989).

It has also been argued (Hamnett and Randolph, 1982) that the changes in the tenure structure of the London housing market have played a crucial role in influencing the population decline and the recent growth in the resident population. In brief, it was argued that replacement of high density, private rented, multioccupied housing in the inner city by lower density, council redevelopment, and single-family owner-occupation played a key part in reducing the population densities during the 1960s and 1970s. Because it reduced the number of household spaces, particularly in sharing households in the inner London private rented sector, housing tenure change was associated with large-scale population decline. But, as we also argued, the slowing down or completion of some of these processes of housing market change, particularly the virtual cessation of council clearance and redevelopment, and the sale of many private rented houses for owner-occupation, meant that the rate of decline of inner London's population was likely to slow down or stabilise during the 1980s, with some areas even showing an increase in the population.

The evidence of the 1980s shows this prediction to have been correct (Champion and Congdon, 1988), although there is considerable dispute over the proper explanation of these changes (Congdon and Champion, 1989; Gordon, 1988).

In this chapter I want to take a different focus and examine the *social and spatial segmentation* of the Greater London private housing market, looking particularly at the characteristics, role, and geographical distribution of an important new source of owner-occupied housing in London, the conversion of larger older houses (sometimes single family, but more often multioccupied) into flats for sale. The social and spatial segmentation of London and its links with the housing market has long been realised (Daly, 1971). Traditionally, central and inner London have had an above average proportion of young, single, or childless people, concentrated in privated rented housing, and outer London has been dominated by single-family owner-occupation. But during the 1960s, 1970s, and 1980s the private rented sector has declined rapidly to be replaced by local authority housing and various forms of owner-occupation

2 The development of the flat conversion market
The development of the flat conversion market in London has to be seen as part of the *tenurial transformation* of inner London. Until the mid-1960s, inner London was dominantly privately rented. In 1961 64% of households in inner London rented privately, only 17% were owner-occupiers, and 19% were council tenants. In central London the proportion of private renters was even higher at 80%. Outer London, by contrast, was largely developed as suburban owner-occupation and in 1961 52% of households were owners compared with 30% in private renting and 18% in council renting. By 1981 the tenure structure of inner London had been completely transformed. The proportion of households renting privately had fallen to 30%, owner-occupation grew to 27%, and council renting was the single largest tenure at 43%. In several boroughs to the north, east, and south of central London, council renting exceeded 50% (Hamnett and Randolph, 1983). In the process, the social structure of inner London became sharply polarised between council tenants and owner-occupiers (Hamnett, 1983; 1986; 1987; Hamnett and Randolph, 1987).

The growth of owner-occupation in inner London occurred as a result of sales of privately rented housing for owner-occupation rather than new building. This tenure transformation from renting to owning has taken *three* major forms. *First*, the sale of private rented houses, often in multiple occupation, into single-family ownership. This process is generally termed gentrification and was dependent on building societies granting mortgages on older inner-city property (Hamnett and Williams, 1980; Williams, 1976; 1978). *Second*, there were sales of purpose-built privately rented blocks of flats (Hamnett and Randolph, 1984;

1985; 1988). The *third* and most recent manifestation has been that of flat conversions, and again, this was largely dependent on the willingness of building societies to lend on converted flats—which they were reluctant to do until the early 1970s. Conversions are a product of rapidly rising house prices in London which have progressively pushed single-family owner-occupation out of the reach of first-time buyers.

The flat conversion market has only emerged in the last twenty years, and conversions are very highly concentrated in central and inner London and some other towns in the South East and South West where they play a major role in catering for young, single, childless, professional, and managerial first-time buyers. It will be shown that the geographical distribution and the physical and social characteristics of flat conversions are quite distinctive from the rest of the owner-occupied housing market. First, however, it is important to examine the important, but often over-looked, role of conversions in changing the urban housing stock.

3 Conversions and processes of change in the urban housing stock

The housing stock of most cities is built up slowly over time as part of a gradual process of development. But, as Bourne (1981) has suggested, a city's housing stock can be changed in *three* key ways; by new construction, by renewal or redevelopment, and by the modification of the existing stock. In the literature on housing and urban change in Britain, most attention has been focused on the first two of these processes—the growth of owner-occupied suburbia and inner-city council redevelopment. Little attention has been given to forms of adjustment within the standing housing stock. This is a major deficiency, not least because the standing stock accounts for the overwhelming majority of dwellings.

Bourne identifies four broad types of change within the existing stock. These are: (1) changes in the relative quality or value of housing units or areas (filtering), (2) changes in occupancy and population density, (3) changes in tenure from rental to owning or vice versa, and (4) changes in numbers and size of dwellings. This last category includes the conversion of residential stock to nonresidential uses, the conversion of nonresidential uses to residential uses, and *residential conversions* "where existing housing units are subdivided or merged". Bourne argues that:

"The process of sub-division and merger is the principal mechanism through which new units may be created from the existing stock, or the size of existing units altered in the short term. Often, but not necessarily, it is accompanied by changes in housing quality and tenure" (page 27).

As we shall show, Bourne is correct in his assessment of the key role played by residential conversions, at least where the London private housing market is concerned. There is also evidence that a high proportion of housing association completions in London have involved flat conversions, though neither these nor council conversions are included in this discussion. In the remainder of the chapter we examine the numbers, geographical distribution, and the physical and social characteristics of the private converted flat sector in London, making comparisons with the characteristics of other sectors of the London owner-occupied market.

4 The size of the flat conversion market in London and the South East
Flat conversions are very much a product of the twenty years since the late 1960s and early 1970s. In 1960 a survey of dwellings in Greater London based on valuation office data (Gray and Russell, 1962) showed that out of a sample of 1291 owner-occupied rateable units, 2.4% were flats in converted houses. Grossing this up gave a total of 24 500 flats in London. A special tabulation prepared for the GLC (Greater London Council) from the 1966 10% sample census showed that there were some 163 390 household spaces in converted dwellings in Greater London. Of these, 23 170 households were in owner-occupied flats—2.3% of owner-occupied households. Unfortunately neither the 1971 or the 1981 census included converted flats as a specific dwelling type. But, working on the very restrictive definition of "households with shared entrance from outside the building within self-contained accommodation' —a definition which excludes those households living in a self-contained basement or ground-floor flat with a separate entrance from outside the building—some 121 600 freehold and leasehold flats were enumerated in England and Wales in 1981. Of these no fewer than 58 100 or 48% were found in London where they comprised almost 5% of owner-occupied households. This represents an increase of exactly 150% on the 1966 figure, and the real number of households may be almost half as large again. Also, many inner London boroughs have recorded conversion gains of 500 to 1000 units a year since the early 1980s, and figures from SERPLAN (1988) based on a London Research Centre study of borough level estimates indicate that Greater London could generate a net gain of 6300 converted units a year in the period 1987-91, or 30% of London's net housing gains. Inner London would yield 5200 units—no less than 43% of the net gain in dwelling units in inner London. As these are net figures and deduct the single-family dwelling units lost, the real gross gain of converted units is higher by some 60%. The London Research Centre (LRC, 1987) estimated that the total net gain from conversions in 1987 was 5912 units, but we identified 8500 new units from conversions in just fourteen boroughs in 1987. On these figures, conversions are the single largest source of new housing gains in inner London and, for many boroughs, they represent the only significant source of new dwelling units.

The geographical concentration of such flats in London and the South East is shown by the fact that 7851 households (6.5%) were found in the OMA (outer metropolitan area) and 16 633 (13.7%) in the OSE (outer South East). Overall the South East had 68% of conversions in England and Wales, and the South West another 11.3%. By comparison the total number of conversions in Greater Manchester was 1757, 2343 in the West Midlands, and 1367 in West Yorkshire (OPCS, 1983, Housing and Households, England and Wales, table 10). These data are paralleled by mortgage data supplied to me by the Nationwide Building Society (NBS). In 1985 the NBS granted almost 100 000 new mortgages nationally. Of these, 3500 or 3.5% of the total were for converted flats. But 72% of the loans were in Greater London (where they accounted for 15% of all loans) and a further 18% were in the rest of the South East (ROSE). Overall, 90% of mortgages for flat conversions were in London and the South East. Although current mortgage lending data do not, of course, reflect the overall distribution of conversions, they do provide a useful insight into change at the margin. Comparison of NBS lending data for 1978 with those for 1985 reveals that the number of mortgages given on conversions increased from 1132 to 2513 and that the proportion of all London mortgages given for flat conversions rose from 21.6% in 1978 to 24.2% in 1985. Over the same period, the proportion of all inner London mortgages given for flat conversions rose from 41% to 51%. Flat conversions are clearly playing an increasingly important role within mortgage lending in inner London.

The reason for the geographical concentration of conversions in London and other towns and cities such as Hove, Brighton, Bristol and Bournemouth is largely one of differences in the supply and demand for housing and in house prices. Conversions are likely to be found in areas where there is a large proportion of one-person and two-person households, where the stock is suitable for conversion and where high prices make conversions profitable. There will be very few conversions in regions where terraced houses can still be bought for under £30 000. Given that even cheap conversions will cost several thousand pounds per unit it is totally uneconomic to convert existing houses into flats in those parts of the country where buyers can obtain older terraced houses relatively cheaply.

5 The geographical differentiation of the private housing market and the distribution of flat conversions in London

The London owner-occupied housing market is very geographically differentiated by type of property. Looking at the distribution of flat conversions in London, the 1981 census figures show that inner London accounted for over 35 000 or 61% of the London total, and the three central boroughs of Camden, Kensington, and Westminster contained almost 14 000 or 25% of London's total. In inner London as a whole, household spaces in owner-occupied flat conversions accounted for over 13% of all owner-occupied spaces, and in the three central boroughs the figure was 28% (OPCS, 1982, table 20). In outer London, by comparison, the figure was just 2.4% and the London average was 4.8%. Figures 1(a),

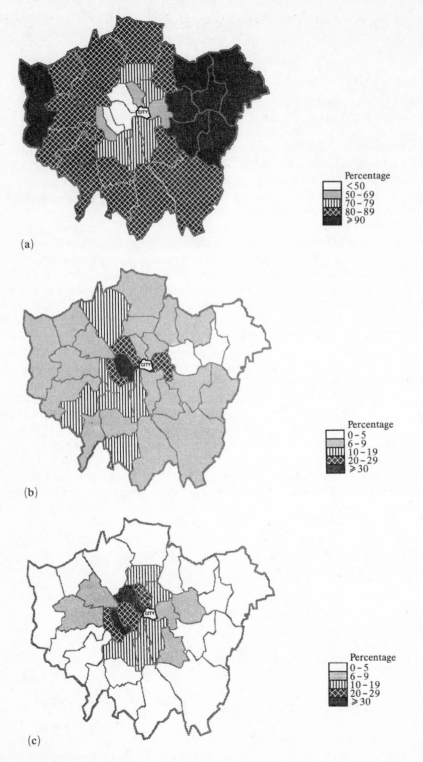

Figure 1. Percentage of private housing stock (a) single-family dwellings, (b) purpose built flats, and (c) conversions.

1(b), and 1(c) show, respectively, the distribution by borough of single-family dwellings (household spaces with a separate entrance from outside the building), purpose-built flats, and conversions, given as a proportion of the total number of owner-occupied household spaces by means of 1981 census data. They show that although single-family housing is highly concentrated in the outer London boroughs, purpose-built flats and flat conversions are concentrated in inner London (for a discussion of reasons for concentration of purpose-built flats in central and inner London, see Hamnett and Randolph, 1988).

Mortgage-lending data from the NBS for 1986 provides a more up-to-date picture of the distribution of mortgages by property type. It should be remembered, however, that this gives a cross-sectional picture of change at the margin, in which young, moving households are likely to be overrepresented. Table 1 shows the spatial differentiation of Nationwide mortgage lending in London in 1986. It can be seen that although flat conversions accounted for an average of 16% of all new mortgages in Greater London in 1986, they accounted for under 5% in several outer London boroughs compared with over 50% in the central London boroughs of Camden, Kensington, and Westminster. The proportions were also high in the inner London boroughs of Islington (57%), Hammersmith (48%), Lambeth (35%), Hackney (34%), Haringey (33%), Wandsworth (28%), Southwark (24%), and Lewisham (20%). When these figures are added to those for purpose-built flats, flats comprise between 86% and 95% of all mortgages in the three central London boroughs, 79% in Islington, 77% in Hammersmith, 64% in Wandsworth, 57% in Lambeth, and 52% in Haringey. Figure 2 shows

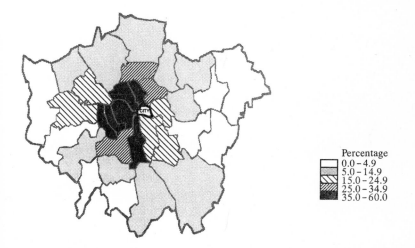

Figure 2. Type of property purchased in London—converted flats as a percentage of all purchases, 1986. Source: NBS, 1986.

the distribution of Nationwide mortgage lending for conversions in London in 1985.

These figures are not atypical. Halifax mortgage-lending data for 1986 reveal a very similar borough distribution of mortgages by property type. In fact, whereas the Nationwide gave 14% of its mortgages to flat conversions in 1987, the equivalent 1986 Halifax figure was 23%, and in Camden, Islington, and Kensington, over 60% of Halifax mortgages

Table 1. Percentage of different types of property purchased in London by borough. Source: NBS, 1986.

London borough	House type					
	det.	semi-det.	ter.	bung.	PB	conv.
Barking and Dagenham	0.5	9.3	80.4	0.5	6.4	2.9
Barnet	8.8	26.7	22.5	1.3	27.4	13.3
Bexley	4.7	40.3	35.6	3.6	13.7	2.1
Brent	3.9	24.6	25.1	0.6	27.4	18.4
Bromley	14.8	26.1	26.3	3.1	19.8	9.9
Camden	1.5	1.9	10.9	0.0	36.5	49.2
Croydon	10.8	24.9	32.8	2.0	18.5	11.0
Ealing	1.8	22.1	35.3	0.5	23.8	16.5
Enfield	2.8	18.2	48.0	0.6	19.0	11.4
Greenwich	2.9	22.8	51.2	1.6	12.6	8.9
Hackney	1.0	1.9	43.2	0.0	19.4	34.5
Hammersmith and Fulham	1.0	3.7	18.1	0.0	28.9	48.3
Haringey	0.6	5.7	40.8	0.0	20.2	32.7
Harrow	10.0	37.7	25.2	0.7	16.1	10.3
Havering	7.5	41.0	35.6	5.9	9.1	0.9
Hillingdon	8.7	33.3	32.7	4.5	18.3	2.5
Hounslow	4.4	34.6	32.0	1.3	23.3	4.4
Islington	0.0	1.7	19.4	0.0	21.4	57.5
Kensington and Chelsea	1.2	1.2	8.4	0.0	28.9	60.3
Kingston	10.0	35.3	25.8	0.7	21.6	6.6
Lambeth	0.8	10.8	25.7	0.4	26.9	35.4
Lewisham	2.2	17.3	41.5	0.0	18.9	20.1
Merton	2.5	15.4	50.2	1.7	22.5	7.7
Newham/Tower Hamlets	0.9	6.4	73.7	0.2	10.4	8.4
Redbridge	3.8	20.3	52.3	1.5	13.1	9.0
Richmond	4.8	25.7	33.5	0.7	23.8	11.5
Southwark	3.4	16.4	35.1	0.4	20.5	24.2
Sutton	10.9	28.0	24.7	1.9	30.9	3.6
Waltham Forest	2.0	9.6	49.2	0.5	26.6	12.1
Wandsworth	1.2	5.6	28.8	0.0	36.8	27.6
Westminster	0.0	1.0	4.0	0.0	44.2	50.8
Greater London total	5.2	21.2	35.0	1.4	21.6	15.6
United Kingdom	20.4	28.4	29.2	8.8	9.6	3.6

Note: det. detached houses, semi-det. semi-detached houses, ter. terraced houses, bung. bungalows, PB purpose-built flats, conv. converted flats.

were for flat conversions. It is clear from these figures that London's owner-occupied housing market is very strongly geographically differentiated by property type. Whereas the current inner London owner-occupied market is predominantly a flat market, outer London is predominantly a house market with a limited number of purpose-built blocks of flats.

The geographical concentration of flat conversions in inner London is partly a reflection of the concentration of older terraced 3–4 floor houses in the inner city. As Donnison (1967) has observed:

"The lateral conversions that can be made in Victorian and Georgian terraces are usually impossible in ... modern semi-detached houses ... the greater economy of their design means that halls and passages are smaller, ceilings lower and walls thinner than those provided in the more durable middle class housing built before the First World War" (page 222).

But although spatial distribution of the older housing stock may be a necessary condition for conversions to occur, it is not a sufficient condition. As already suggested, the growing number of one-person and two-person households, the rapid rise of house prices, and developers' profits from conversions are also important factors. If the conversion market were not profitable, conversions would not occur on anything like the scale they have done. The availability of the stock provides the material but not the motive to convert.

6 The physical characteristics of the stock

We have shown the geographical concentration of conversions in the London housing market and have tried to establish its geographical segmentation by property type. The next stage is to illustrate the distinctive physical characteristics of converted properties vis-à-vis other property types. The tabulations of NBS mortgage lending for 1985 is very useful. Conversions are generally much smaller than other types of property. Figure 3 shows that 94% of all conversions had a total floor area of less than 1000 square feet, with a mean of 660 square feet, and a median of 622 square feet. This is in contrast to a mean of 957 square feet for terraced houses, 1071 square feet for semi-detached houses, and 1251 square feet for detached houses. The floor area of houses was some 50%–100% greater than that of converted and purpose-built flats.

The small size of conversions and purpose-built flats is reflected in the number of rooms they possess. Table 2 shows that 91% of conversions and purpose-built flats had only one reception room, whereas 52% of terraced houses and 65% of semi-detached houses had two or more reception rooms. Table 3 also shows that 54% of conversions only had one bedroom and another 40% had two bedrooms. These figures are very similar to those for purpose-built flats, although the proportions of one-bedroomed and two-bedroomed flats were reversed (38% and 55%, respectively). The major difference is between flats and houses. Scarcely any houses only had one bedroom, and very few had only two bedrooms (25% of terraced houses, 9% of semi-detached, and 3% of detached). The great majority of houses had three or more bedrooms.

Table 2. Number of reception rooms, by property type (%), London, 1985.

Property type	Reception rooms				
	0	1	2	3	4
Conv.	0.6	91.0	8.0	0.0	0.0
PB	1.4	90.0	7.3	0.0	0.0
Ter.	0.0	47.4	45.1	7.0	0.0
Semi-det.	0.0	32.5	58.0	8.4	1.1
Det.	0.0	19.7	57.8	18.2	4.3

Note: Conv. converted flats, PB purpose-built flats, Ter. terraced houses, Semi-det. semi-detached houses, Det. detached houses.

Table 3. Number of bedrooms, by property type (%), London, 1985.

Property type	Bedrooms					
	1	2	3	4	5	5+
Conv.	53.7	39.8	5.8	0.5	0.0	0.0
PB	37.6	54.6	7.4	0.3	0.0	0.0
Ter.	2.8	25.4	62.8	7.3	1.4	0.3
Semi-det.	1.4	9.4	73.3	12.7	2.2	0.9
Det.	0.6	3.3	44.1	40.1	10.0	1.9

Note: see table 2 for abbreviations.

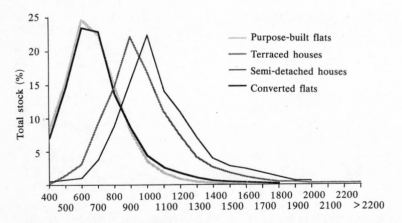

Figure 3. Superficial floor area (in square feet) of property, London, 1985.

7 The price distribution of different property types

Not surprisingly, the small size of flats is reflected in their price. Nationwide data for 1986 show that the average price of conversions and purpose-built flats was £45000–£46000, compared with £56000 for terraced houses, £69000 for semi-detached houses, and £99000 for detached houses. These differences have been long standing (see table 4). Although some large luxury conversions or those in central London are very expensive, Nationwide data from 1984 (figure 4) show that the price distribution of conversions was more tightly bunched than that for either terraced or semi-detached houses. Exactly 50% of conversions were priced in the range £30000–£39000 and another 26% were in the range £25000–£29000 or £40000–£44000.

But, as table 5 shows, the price per square foot both for flat conversions and for purpose-built flats was higher than that for terraced and semi-detached houses. In terms of pounds per square foot, flats are not a

Table 4. Average price (in pounds) of property in London, by property type (%), 1979–86.

Property type	1979	1980	1981	1982	1983	1984	1985	1986
Conv.	19902	23641	24134	25166	28401	33489	39709	45834
PB	20011	23720	24335	25740	28518	33472	38375	45213
Ter.	23453	27545	28658	30387	34625	41345	48287	56036
Semi-det.	28828	34161	35850	37756	43866	51647	59130	68991
Det.	41991	52864	50703	54004	62563	73774	84305	99194
Average	24524	28788	29383	31198	35890	42566	48785	55905

Note: see table 2 for abbreviations.

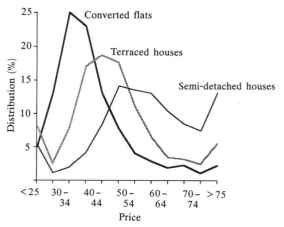

Figure 4. Price distribution of property, by type, London, 1985. (Prices are given in thousands of pounds.)

cheap option. What they offer is a relatively cheap form of entry into the expensive owner-occupied housing market in central and inner London.

Table 5. Price per square foot (in pounds), by property type, 1979–86.

Property type	1979	1980	1981	1982	1983	1984	1985	1986
Conv.	29.4	35.9	36.9	38.3	43.1	50.2	60.7	73.5
PB	31.1	37.5	38.7	40.7	44.4	51.8	61.6	70.0
Ter.	24.6	29.4	30.4	32.6	36.7	43.3	51.1	61.3
Semi-det.	28.0	33.4	34.9	36.6	41.7	48.2	56.4	66.5
Det.	34.0	40.8	41.2	44.1	49.9	56.7	66.9	78.6

Note: see table 2 for abbreviations.

8 The characteristics of buyers of converted flats

The distinctive price and geographical characteristics of the converted flat sector is paralleled by the equally distinctive characteristics of its residents. They are overwhelmingly young, single, childless, first-time buyers, with lower incomes than the older, family buyers of houses. Looking first at household type, Nationwide data (table 6) shows that no fewer than 80% of buyers of conversions were single, and only 7% had children. This is in contrast to figures of 28% of single buyers and 50% with children for the buyers of semi-detached houses at the other end of the spectrum. Conversions are equally distinctive in terms of the age of the main borrower, and table 7 shows that 59% of buyers were aged between twenty and twenty-nine, compared with just 37% of buyers of terraced houses and 25% of buyers of semi-detached houses. Very few (9%) buyers of converted flats were aged forty years or over.

Given the age and household characteristics of buyers of converted flats, it is not surprising to discover that 80% of them are first-time buyers (table 8), compared with 50% of those buying terraced houses, 28% buying semi-detached houses, and 12% buying detached houses. Some 32% of people buying converted flats had previously rented privately and 38% had lived with friends and relatives. It is clear that

Table 6. The household characteristics (including number of children) of people taking out mortgages with the Nationwide Building Society, London, 1985.

Property type	Single (%)		Married (%)			
	0	children	0	1	2	3
Conv.	77.3	3.1	15.7	2.3	1.5	2.1
PB	70.1	4.0	19.5	3.5	2.3	2.9
Ter.	35.9	7.1	29.0	11.2	12.3	4.5
Semi-det.	21.3	6.3	29.0	15.4	21.2	6.7
Det.	14.0	7.1	24.3	17.3	25.3	11.6

Note: see table 2 for abbreviations.

conversions and purpose-built flats (78% of first-time buyers) function as a first step on the owner-occupied housing ladder in London. It also appears, though it cannot be directly shown from the data, that with increasing age, marriage, and children, many owners move out of flats and into houses.

The role of London's converted and purpose-built flat sectors as a first step on the owner-occupied housing ladder for younger buyers is shown from the data on average incomes in table 9. Both mean and median incomes for flat buyers are considerably lower than those for house buyers. The median income of flat buyers was £240 per week in

Table 7. Age of main borrower, for three property types (%), London, 1985.

Property type	20–24	25–29	30–34	35–39	40–44	45–49	50–54	55–59	60+
Conv.	18.4	40.9	21.4	9.6	4.2	2.2	1.2	1.2	0.4
Ter.	10.9	26.5	23.3	15.9	9.4	6.0	3.5	2.4	2.0
Semi-det.	5.8	19.3	25.4	20.3	12.6	7.5	4.6	2.6	1.9

Note: see table 2 for abbreviations.

Table 8. Previous tenure of buyers in London, by property type (%), 1985.

Property type	Own.-occ.	Priv. rent	Council	H. Assoc.	Emp.	Friend/rels
Conv.	20.2	32.1	5.6	0.9	3.2	37.8
PB	22.1	22.9	7.6	1.1	2.6	43.4
Ter.	49.6	11.3	12.0	2.4	1.5	22.9
Semi-det.	71.8	5.7	6.6	1.1	1.1	13.5
Det.	88.5	3.7	1.1	–	1.0	5.7

Note: Own.-occ. owner-occupied, Priv. rent private rented, H. Assoc. Housing Association, Emp. provided by employer, rels relatives. For other abbreviations, see table 2.

Table 9. Distribution, by property type (%), of average weekly household income (in pounds), 1985.

Property type	50–140	150–190	200–240	250–290	300–340	350+	Median income	Mean income
Conv.	5.0	14.8	26.0	18.2	13.8	22.3	241	279
PB	6.8	15.3	24.5	19.3	14.6	19.6	239	271
Ter.	5.3	9.2	17.5	18.3	17.2	32.4	279	307
Semi-det.	3.6	7.0	14.0	18.1	17.1	39.2	298	330
Det.	2.2	2.6	6.7	11.7	14.6	62.4	342	449

Note: see table 2 for abbreviations.

1985 compared with £280 for buyers of terraced houses, £300 for those of semi-detached houses, and £340 for people buying detached houses. The mean income figures display similar differences. But as table 10 shows, these income differences are not the result of the lower occupational status of flat buyers compared with house buyers. On the contrary, the reverse is true. The proportion of professional and managerial workers is higher (46%) among buyers of converted flats than it is for terraced (34%) or semi-detached (42%) buyers. Only buyers of detached houses (66%) have a higher proportion of such workers. The proportion of junior managerial and clerical buyers is also considerably higher in the flat sector (27%) than in that of terraced (20%), semi-detached (17%), or detached (11%) houses.

These data can be interpreted in a number of different ways. They could indicate that flat buyers earn less because they are younger and at a lower stage in their white-collar careers. They could indicate that because of house price inflation, today's buyers are increasingly forced into this cheaper sector than those who got into owner-occupation some years earlier, or they could reflect the fact that a very high proportion of flat buyers are single and have lower household incomes than older, married couples living in houses.

In the absence of other evidence it is difficult to assess the relative merits of these explanations, but on the face of it, it would seem that all three contain an element of truth. We know that buyers of converted flats are younger than house buyers, and that the households are predominantly of single people. This would support the first and third explanations. But we also know that house prices have risen very sharply since 1983 and that house price to income ratios have also risen sharply. Other things being equal, it can be expected that this would push first-time buyers down market towards cheaper, and hence more affordable, properties. It can also be argued that the supply of cheap, single-family housing in inner London has been reduced as a result of the activities of developers in buying up poor-quality housing for conversion. This is more speculative, however, as developers are generally attracted to the

Table 10. Employment status.

Status	Conv.	PB	Ter.	Semi-det.	Det.
Professional and managerial	46.5	39.3	34.3	42.5	65.9
Junior managerial and clerical	26.6	26.6	19.6	17.0	10.8
Skilled manual	13.4	17.7	24.5	22.8	13.3
Semi-skilled manual	3.1	5.5	8.7	6.7	3.2
Retired/widow	0.6	1.8	2.2	2.3	0.8
Unskilled manual and armed forces	8.5	7.7	9.2	7.6	5.1
Total	99.7	99.6	99.5	98.9	99.1

Note: see table 2 for abbreviations.

larger houses which offer potential for conversion into three or more flats. First-time buyers are unlikely to be in this market, although they were able to purchase such houses in inner London in the late 1960s and early 1970s before prices pushed them out of reach to all but a small minority of affluent buyers.

9 Summary and conclusions

It has been argued that London's owner-occupied housing market is socially and spatially segmented. Whereas outer London is dominated by single-family housing, particularly semi-detached and detached housing, inner London is dominated by terraced housing and by converted and purpose-built flats. Where the distribution of current mortgages is concerned, the split is even more marked, with flats accounting for over two-thirds of all mortgages in many central and inner London boroughs.

The geographical differentiation of the market is paralleled by differentiation in terms of size and price and by differentiation of the social characteristics of residents. Residents of converted flats are typically young, single, childless, and most of them are first-time buyers. They tend to have lower incomes than house buyers even though their occupational composition is heavily white-collar. It is concluded that converted flats play a key role as a first step on the owner-occupied ladder in inner London for young, single, white-collar workers who would, twenty years ago, have probably remained in private renting until they bought a house. But, with the virtual disappearance of private renting, flat conversions are playing a rather similar role in the private market. The key difference is that today it is necessary to buy a flat to live in inner London, as little rented property remains.

Acknowledgements. I am grateful to the ESRC who funded the research on conversions, to James Barlow who was the research fellow on the project, and to John Hunt for drawing the figures.

References

Berge E, 1988, "Some comments on C Hamnett's reading of the data on socio-tenurial polarisation in South East England" *Environment and Planning A* **20** 973–977

Bourne L, 1981 *The Geography of Housing* (Edward Arnold, London)

Champion A, Congdon P, 1988, "Recent trends in Greater London's population" *Population Trends* **53** 7–17

Champion A, Congdon P, 1989, "Trends and structure in London migration and their relation to employment and housing markets", in *Advances in Regional Demography* Eds P Congdon, P Batey (Belhaven, London) pp 180–204

Daly M, 1971, "Characteristics of 12 clusters of wards in Greater London", RR-13, Department of Planning and Transport, Greater London Council

Donnison D, 1967 *The Government of Housing* (Penguin Books, Harmondsworth, Middx)

Gordon I, 1988, "Resurrecting counter-urbanisation: housing market influences on migration fluctuations from London" *Built Environment* **13** 212–222

Gray P G, Russell R, 1962 *The Housing Situation in 1960* Social Survey (Central Statistical Office, London)

Hamnett C, 1983, "Split city: socio-tenurial polarisation in London, 1966–81" *Roof* (July/August) 13–14

Hamnett C, 1986, "Socio-economic change in London and the South East, 1961–81" *Regional Studies* **20** 391–406

Hamnett C, 1987, "A tale of two cities: sociotenurial polarisation in London and the South East, 1966–81" *Environment and Planning A* **19** 537–556

Hamnett C, 1989, "Sociotenurial polarisation in London and the South East: a reply to Berge's comments" *Environment and Planning A* **21** 545–548

Hamnett C, Randolph W, 1982, "How far will London's population fall? A commentary on the 1981 census" *The London Journal* **8**(1) 95–100

Hamnett C, Randolph W, 1983, "The changing tenure structure of the Greater London housing market" *The London Journal* **9**(1) 153–164

Hamnett C, Randolph W, 1984, "The role of landlord disinvestment in housing market transformation: an analysis of the flat break-up market in central London" *Institute of British Geographers, Transactions: New Series* **9** 259–279

Hamnett C, Randolph W, 1985, "The rise and fall of the purpose-built block of privately rented flats in London, 1880–1980" *The London Journal* **11**(2) 160–175

Hamnett C, Randolph W, 1987, "The residualisation of council housing in inner London", in *Public Housing: Current Trends and Future Developments* Eds D Clapham, J English (Croom Helm, Andover, Hants) pp 32–50

Hamnett C, Randolph W, 1988 *Cities, Housing and Profits: Flat Break Up and the Decline of Private Renting* (Hutchinson, London)

Hamnett C, Williams P, 1980, "Social change in London: a study of gentrification" *Urban Affairs Quarterly* **15** 469–487

LRC, 1987, "London's housing capacity: a report to the London Planning Advisory Committee", London Research Centre, Parliament House, 81 Black Prince Road, London SE1 7SZ

NBS, 1986 *Nationwide Building Society (1986): Local Area Housing Statistics— London Boroughs* Nationwide Anglia Building Society, Chesterfield House, Bloomsbury Way, London WC1V 6PW

OPCS, 1982 *County Report for Greater London, Part 1* Office of Population Censuses and Surveys (HMSO, London)

OPCS, 1983 *Census 1981: England and Wales. Housing and Households* Office of Population Censuses and Surveys (HMSO, London)

SERPLAN, 1988, "Regional trends in the South East" *SERPLAN Monitor 1987–88* RPC 1060, London and South East Regional Planning Conference, 50–64 Broadway, London SW1H 0DB

Williams P, 1976, "The role of institutions in the inner London housing market: the case of Islington" *Institute of British Geographers, Transactions: New Series* 72–82

Williams P, 1978, "Building Societies and the inner city" *Institute of British Geographers, Transactions: New Series* **3** 23–34

The Death of Strategic Planning: Murder, Suicide, or Euthanasia?

M BREHENY, D HART
University of Reading

If current reports are to be believed, strategic planning in Britain is not merely dead, but buried deeply and virtually forgotten. But, rather like Mark Twain's comment when he read his own obituary—rumours of its demise might have been exaggerated.

For the purpose of this paper strategic planning can be defined simply as public land-use-based planning which is large-scale, and long-term in character. That is: it is concerned with development issues which affect several local authority areas—which can be as large as a major metropolitan area, or even an entire standard region—over the period of a decade or longer (Hart, 1976).

Certainly, strategic planning of this description was very much alive only a few years ago. In fact, two major *types* of public-sector-led strategic planning can be identified in the recent past. The first—and arguably the purest—strand consisted of dozens of regional reports, studies, and strategies, which had been prepared by central and local government planners from the mid-1960s to the mid-1970s. The second—more recent and smaller-scale—component reached its peak during the late 1970s through until the mid-1980s when scores of structure plans (subsequently updated) were produced by the county councils.

Today, strategic planning under both of these headings has evidently either ceased to exist entirely or now consists largely of marginal revisions and alterations. Regional plans have disappeared entirely, structure plans are about to be abolished, the metropolitan authorities have gone, and the whole tenor of planning has become increasingly pragmatic and localised. Why, then, has this once healthy and robust movement either passed away—virtually without trace and certainly with very few mourners —or become weakened to the point of death?

In this chapter we seek to address these questions. It takes the form of a preliminary inquest—a pathology of strategic planning policy over the past few years. In it, an investigation will be carried out regarding the causes of the demise of strategic planning. There is, however, a certain irony about the timing of this exercise. It could well be argued that genuinely strategic issues are currently proliferating: including, for example, the economic and environmental implications of the Channel Tunnel; the expansion of Stansted Airport; the proposals for regional shopping centres and private new towns; the growing congestion of motorways, airports, and trains—particularly in the southern half of Britain; and the long-recognised need to promote new economic activity in the north. At the same time, major economic and demographic trends, including industrial and residential decentralisation from the urban areas in both the north and the south, are rapidly changing the character both of inner cities and of formerly rural areas. Yet nowhere is there any systematic attempt to coordinate these activities, to redress unhealthy imbalances, or even to deal with the inevitable cumulative consequences of these components of strategic change (Breheny et al, 1987). Our contention is, therefore, that the time is now ripe for reconsidering whether an obituary for strategic planning might not have been premature and whether a need for this planning still exists.

First, however, it is important to find out what precisely happened before strategic planning's hasty decline, and demise. In particular it is important to determine *how, why, and at whose hand* it died. Inevitably, in using an analogy-based approach there is a danger of becoming too anthropomorphic, but equally, such an approach could be illuminating for policy analytical purposes. Our concern at this preliminary stage in the research is less to apportion blame in a literal fashion, but more to ascertain whether a prima facie case can be made for strategic planning or whether the case for strategic planning can now be finally closed.

2 The inquest
We dismiss at the outset the possibility that strategic planning died of natural causes. A good case can be made in arguing that the model of strategic planning that was born in the 1960s was a sickly child, with various congenital defects. The regional level of activity never had statutory backing; the structure plan system was designed for single-tier authorities not the two-tier system that transpired; the whole was out of tune with the practical and intellectual context; and so on. However, these defects were not sufficient to cause death. They may be contributory in the sense that it is easier to overpower a weakling than a strongman, but not the cause. The system could have been maintained, with or without changes. A verdict of natural causes might also be more plausible if it were not so obvious that various groups had a vested interest in seeing the demise of strategic planning.

Three causes of homicide will be considered in this paper which will explore the demise of strategic planning in Britain in detail. The examination will ask, firstly, was it *murdered* by one or more parties ideologically committed to the dismantling of land-use planning—often for quite different reasons—and if so, was the murder deliberate? The reasoning behind this possible commitment will be examined. In particular the assertion that the private-sector benefits from deregulation of planning controls will be assessed in relation to the strategic context.

Secondly, the possibility will also be examined that strategic planning committed *suicide*. In particular, the very process of carrying out strategic planning with its alleged attendant delays and excessive collection of detail will be briefly considered to determine whether it inevitably carries with it some type of death wish.

A related consideration under this heading is that the planning profession itself changed direction so dramatically in the late 1970s— switching from a genuine concern with strategic issues to an obsession with local planning and individual sites—that it willingly or unwillingly helped to force the death of strategic planning. Further it could be contended that the demise of strategic planning was, in part at least, a case of professional suicide.

A final view that needs examination is the possibility that by a general, but largely unspoken consensus of parts of central government, local government, the planning profession, and the private sector, strategic planning needed to be put to rest because the movement was old, feeble, and unsustainable, and an obvious candidate for *euthanasia*. According to this view the world had changed so much that public strategic planning was no longer either required or possible during the late 1980s and it was systematically starved of resources and then quietly put to sleep.

3 The 'murder of strategic planning'

There is a widespread, but far from conclusively substantiated, view within the planning profession as well as outside of it, that strategic planning was murdered. Our investigation will begin by considering critically the evidence on this subject. As in any inquest, if death other than by natural causes is suspected, then three main factors have to be addressed: method, motive, and opportunity. That is: what caused the death, why did it happen, and how did the situation come to arise? Under this particular heading, we can also add a fourth set of considerations, if indeed a murder was committed: who was the guilty party?

3.1 Strategic planning and the public sector

A number of witnesses have reported that during the late 1960s and the early 1970s strategic planning was alive and not merely well, but rapidly expanding its domain. One important component of strategic planning mentioned earlier—regional planning—was particularly active during this period. Practitioners in Britain and abroad had no doubt about its then-current importance, and its ultimate significance. In a document published in 1968, entitled "Regional planning: a European problem", one of the pioneers of regional planning and for many years the French Minister for Reconstruction, Claudius Petit, stated "regional planning really means the planning of our society" (Council of Europe, 1968, quoted in Glasson, 1974, page 16).

During this period, five major regional planning strategies and reviews were commissioned in Britain directly by central government ministries, including the Ministry of Housing and Local Government, and subsequently by the Department of the Environment. These documents consisted of: the *Strategic Plan for the South East* (*SPSE*) (SEJPT, 1970); the *Strategic Plan for the North West* (*SPNW*) (NWRST, 1974); *Strategic Choice for East Anglia* (*SCEA*) (EARST, 1974); the *Development of the Strategic Plan for the South East* (*DPSE*) (SEJPT, 1976); and the *Northern Regional Strategy* (*NRS*) (NRST, 1977). By the time that the *DPSE* and the *NRS* actually appeared, however, it was already clear that regional planning was faltering. Particularly in the case of the *Northern Regional Strategy*—the document was never formally adopted by government, still less was it implemented. It was, in fact, quietly abandoned and no new regional strategies for the remainder of the country were commissioned by the DoE.

It is, then, really from the late 1970s onwards that we must look to establish the time of death. In a surprisingly brief period of time, regional strategic planning had disappeared. What began as a retreat turned into a route and the route became a massacre. But how and, more importantly still, *why* did this occur?

The circumstantial evidence is strong and a key suspect quickly emerges. After the election victory of the Conservatives in 1979, strategic planning immediately received a number of grievous blows. The regional economic planning councils—the only agencies that could be said to represent regional interests in terms of planning and development—were abolished as part of the 'quango-hunt' instigated by Michael Heseltine, then the new Secretary of State for the Environment.

Regional strategies have now been replaced by terse regional advice given by the Secretary of State for the Environment in letters a few paragraphs long to the Chairman of the Standing Conference of Local Authorities in the South East (SERPLAN), at irregular intervals. There is a sharp contrast between the five substantial volumes of the *Strategic Plan for the South East* and the six pages of the latest letter from the Secretary of State to the Chairman of SERPLAN concerning the provision of housing land for the South East. But perhaps the very difference in length provides some kind of clue about what happened to strategic planning.

In the late 1970s and early 1980s other things were happening on the strategic planning front as well. The Centre for Environmental Studies (CES)—the principle research centre for studies of urban and regional development and planning issues in Britain—was abolished early on in the life of the current government. More recently still, the Greater London Council (GLC) and the six metropolitan counties have all been abolished by central government—for reasons at least partly related to the perceived inadequacies of strategic planning.

The present government's (in 1988) disenchantment with the strategic planning approach pioneered in the late 1960s and the early 1970s became increasingly plain. The government's White Paper, *Streamlining the Cities* (1983), for example, which presaged the abolition of the GLC and the metropolitan counties, disparagingly suggested that this period marked

"... the heyday of a certain fashion for strategic planning, the confidence in which now appears exaggerated. It is perhaps not surprising that, in this climate, structural reform was approached with too little regard for economy and that the structures created in that era tend sometimes to give inadequate weight to the need to obtain value for money" (White Paper, 1983, paragraph 1.3).

The government went on to state that not merely was strategic planning and the organisations associated with it expensive, they were unnecessary as well. The White Paper suggested that they exemplified a "search for a 'strategic' role which may have little basis in real needs" (White Paper, 1983, paragraph 1.11). It therefore logically followed, as night follows day, that strategic planning and the organisations supporting it should be swept away—and to a large extent they were.

During the early 1980s, both planning at the strategic level and many of the administrative structures which were designed to support it—the regional economic councils and the GLC and the metropolitan counties— have been largely dismantled as part of a continuing process of what the government calls 'streamlining' the administrative procedures surrounding land-use planning. This 'streamlining' is, in turn, part of a twin move on the part of central government towards both more 'localised' planning of land and the environment, and more centralised control of resource allocation.

After having briefly reviewed the evidence available, and considered some of the opportunities and methods that could have been employed to murder strategic planning, it is difficult to avoid pointing the finger for the death of strategic planning at the present government which took office in 1979 and has now held power for a decade. But why? We still lack that most vital of components in an alleged murder: a sufficiently strong motive.

Given the absence of an actual murder confession, it is possible to build up a case based on a deeper examination of the psychology behind the events which have been reviewed above. One persuasive explanation is that the sequence of events, which have left us with the corpse of strategic planning, arise from an ideological commitment on the part of powerful elements within the government to as near a free market in land and development as possible. Thus, according to this view, every opportunity has been taken to reduce planning delays and to deregulate development in order to create a laissez-faire economy.

This view, of course, suggests that the unfettered market will resolve virtually all development issues in time and that private business is satisfied with a planning system that has no strategic guidance. If this were the case, the government's actions would be consistent with its own political commitments, the best interests of business and therefore, according to its beliefs, of society as a whole. But is it?

3.2 Strategic planning and the private sector

In principle, we might expect private-sector interests to welcome the current strategic nonplan regime, and to flourish as this type of planning wanes. Businessmen should have been, according to this view, ready accessories—both before and after the fact—to the murder of strategic planning. There is some limited and largely inconclusive evidence that this is the case.

For example, the cynical view is that it is no coincidence that the recent spate of proposals for regional shopping centres occurred just as the metropolitan authorities disappeared, and that house builders welcomed the opportunity of a laxer planning regime to seek planning permissions for private 'country villages' in rural areas by fighting appeals at, for example, Tillingham Hall in Essex and Foxley Wood in Hampshire. And yet a moment's reflection suggests that this approach—development by appeal—is a random, risky, time-consuming, and expensive way of proceeding for the private sector. Appeals can be lost, as Tillingham Hall demonstrated, as well as won, and 'development by lottery' is clearly unsatisfactory at both the local and the strategic level.

There is, however, quite a different view of the attitude of the business community to strategic planning. It might be described as the 'strategic certainty' perspective and in summary, it runs like this: there is considerable evidence that large private corporations—including multinational firms, major retailers, and volume house builders—are not only practicing techniques and approaches of strategic planning within their own organisations, but also wish to operate in a strategically planned environment which reduces uncertainty (Friend and Jessop, 1977). Far from wanting a market free-for-all, as certain sections of the government apparently assume, many businesses would welcome as close to a 'surprise free' an environment as it is possible to obtain.

At the moment there seems to be a fundamental ambiguity—an internal contradiction—between the public expressed attitudes of certain types of large firms—which supports both deregulation in principle and the government's deregulation policies in practice—and their own private, practical business interests which favour strategic planning guidance as means of increasing the certainty about the future. These large firms mentioned own tens of thousands of acres of land in Britain; employ millions of people; and earn billions of pounds in profits. They have

major interest in reducing the risk and uncertainty elements in the
development process.

But it sometimes seems that the government's desire for deregulation
in planning arises from a concern with one part of the private sector—
small businesses and small businesspeople. It is often the small firms
which feel restricted unreasonably by planning controls from expanding
or changing the use of their premises. The views of small businesspeople
appear to be confused in land and development policy terms with the
attitudes of the private sector generally.

Ironically, what has happened is that planning regulations at the very
local level have remained virtually intact, whilst strategic planning—
which many managing directors of large corporations appear to support—is
disappearing rapidly. Thus, the support for deregulation of local planning
controls (where deregulation has not occurred) has been assumed to
extend to support for the deregulation of the *strategic* planning framework—
where it has succeeded.

Those companies with a direct interest in development issues, such as
the developers of high-street stores and regional shopping centres or
volume housebuilders, want to be confident that their investment decisions
will not be undermined by later unforseen events; or unwelcome nearby
neighbours; or inadequate infrastructural provision. The response of
the powerful House Builders Federation (HBF) to the government's
proposals for the alternative use of agricultural land was instructive in
this regard. The HBF expressed not unalloyed joy—as the nonplan
perspective would suggest—but a cry of 'chaos' and a call for coordinated
planning (*The Guardian*, 10 February 1987).

More recently, the Federation has complained specifically to the
Secretary of State for the Environment about the general lack of strategic
guidance and has argued that the government is not meeting its most
basic responsibility in the field of development, *the need to govern*.
They have stated:

"It is the responsibility of government to ensure that the pressure of
economic growth in the South East which is creating not only jobs but
also a matching demand for housing, are adequately met. For if they
are not, that crucial economic recovery will be jeopardised. It has to
be said that the government is not currently fulfilling that responsibility"
(HBF statement quoted in *The Planner*, 1987).

In addition, another influential private-sector grouping, the 'Oxford
Group' of major retailers has also felt the need to present a joint
approach to government about the lack of strategic guidance on retail
development. These views of major private-sector developers represent
a far cry from the view that there is no real need in the private sector
for strategic planning.

Even for some companies with only an indirect interest in development,
the spatial issues nevertheless remain important. It is very clear from the

current concentrations of 'high-tech' industry around airports and motorway corridors that public infrastructure provision is an important factor in business efficiency for many such companies. Presumably these companies would benefit from the planned rather than accidental provision of such infrastructure benefits. They want to know how they can take advantage of, say, Stansted Airport or the Channel Tunnel or the east coast ports. (On this, see Breheny et al, 1986; Hall et al, 1987.)

In recent years the South East has had economic success in spite of virtually nonexistent strategic planning. The success of the 'Western Crescent' has resulted from the fortuitous coincidence of a number of positive factors, *many of them directly funded and separately planned by public-sector agencies*: the development of Heathrow Airport; the opening of the M4 motorway; the introduction of high-speed 125 British Rail trains; and the presence of defence research establishments at Farnborough and Aldermaston, for example, linked with major private suppliers such as Ferranti and Racal—all directly financially supported by the Ministry of Defence (Hall et al, 1987). The belief that the M4 Corridor is a shameless triumph of unplanned, unfettered private-sector free enterprise is demonstrably false.

In passing, it is worth reflecting on how much greater might this particular success, and the general success of the region, have been if these factors had been publicly and properly planned for? And how much greater might have been the possibility of deliberately replicating it, at least in part, in other regions if conscious foresight had been employed to coordinate public investment in partnership with the private sector? This line of reasoning raises a final important issue: perhaps there are different *forms* of strategic planning which can be designed to suit different conditions; different points in time; and even different ideological persuasions.

We must, however, return to the inquest. Clearly, the chief suspect in the murder of strategic planning must be the present government. Indeed, it—or at least some of its more radical supporters—might willingly plead guilty. But perhaps this is too simplistic. The government itself pleads not guilty to the charge, despite all the evidence which has been so far adduced. At least an important ministry, the DoE, claims its hands are clean.

In a recent speech, for example, to the annual conference of the Royal Town Planning Institute, William Waldegrave, then Minister for Planning, stated that planning had never been seen by the government as similar to those constraints on enterprise that it had sought to remove. It had merely worked to simplify it and improve its efficiency—the system itself was not in question (*The Planner*, 1988, page 13). Having said this, however, it is still apparently the case that 'streamlining' the system began, contrary to good practice in aerodynamics, by slicing the top off the planning structure and then locally grounding it.

4 The suicide of strategic planning

There is, of course, another view of what happened—or what *is* happening—to strategic planning. It is, that the activity was not murdered but perished as a result of its own actions instead, as a result of a series of 'own goals' based on its clearly evident suicidal tendencies.

Seemingly, the government's current proposals to 'localise' planning could be seen not as a deliberate, premeditated act but simply as a reflection of what was, sadly, already happening in practice any way. To put matters in a slightly different way: it was simply making a virtue of a necessity. According to this view, the two major forms of strategic planning documents, first, regional strategies and, now, structure plans have singularly failed to achieve what might be termed 'policy credibility', and have, to further extend the anthropomorphic analogy, in effect lost any purpose in living and have done away with themselves. They have, in other words, committed public policy suicide.

But, once again, how and why has this happened? According to some observers, there is some kind of 'iron law of strategic planning' which says that however far-sighted the original conception of a particular type of strategic planning was, it becomes increasing choked by detail and delay until it is hopelessly outdated and unworkable in practice. In short, on more than one occasion, strategic planning has begun to develop a death wish. Eventually, it succeeded in realising its ambition.

It takes time, however, for a full-blown death wish to take effect. The Department of the Environment discussion document, *The Future of Development Plans*, for example, published in 1986, demonstrates how the process started with "the type of large-scale regional planning which was attempted in the 1960's and 70's" (DoE, 1986, paragraph 44). Regional planning, the document states, "proved largely ineffective and implied a degree of central direction and control that would not be compatible with today's conditions or with public opinion" (paragraph 44). In effect not only was this process incapable of sustaining itself, but it was also both unpopular and unrealistic in terms of the basic assumptions it was based upon.

It is perhaps worth noting that, ironically, the 1986 *Future of Development Plans* is the second government planning report with precisely the same title. The first, produced by the Planning Advisory Group and published in 1965, was responsible for *establishing* the structure plan system in Britain (PAG, 1965). There is, therefore, with regard to this issue and others in the strategic context, not so much a feeling of moving forward, but a feeling of déjà vu and a concern that strategic planning is, by its very nature, incapable of sustaining its own existence.

Currently, the DoE is arguing that the same unhealthy pathology that led to the demise of regional strategies can now be found in what is arguably the last remaining vestige of a strategic planning approach—structure planning. According to the DoE, structure planning is also on the road to committing suicide—for related reasons. In the discussion document *The Future of Development Plans* (mark two)—confirmed legislatively in January 1989 in a White Paper (Cmnd 569) of the same title—the government proposed the abolition of structure planning on th grounds that structure plans are too lengthy and too detailed and that they have taken too long to prepare (DoE, 1986, paragraph 34). Very similar arguments were used to justify the abandonment of the old-style development plans and the introduction of structure plans in *The Future of Development Plans* (mark one) twenty-three years earlier (PAG, 1965).

This danger has been apparent more recently as well. In 1977 the House of Commons Expenditure Committee, reviewing the operation of the then decade-old structure planning system, stated:

"A serious cause for concern about the planning system is the time which is being taken to prepare the full coverage of plans. Nearly ten years after the new system was introduced regional strategies have been approved for only five of the eight planning regions in England and none in Wales. Only seven structure plans have been approved and it will be 1979 before most of the country is covered" (House of Commons Expenditure Committee, 1977; quoted in DoE, 1986, paragraph 15).

In the event this estimate proved to be optimistic. As noted earlier, the last regional plan, *The Northern Regional Strategy*, was published in the same year that the Expenditure Committee reported. Curiously, the Committee was apparently unaware that no further regional strategies would be commissioned by the Department of the Environment althoug they and their advisors must have worked closely with representatives from the DoE. The regional coverage of the country in planning terms was, therefore, apparently not merely slow, as the Committee suggested, but fatally flawed, because it was to remain forever unfinished.

The structure planning system, it was also argued by the DoE, was flawed in other important ways as well. The length of time involved from initiating the plan to having it finally approved, for example, was considerable. The first complete round of structure plans for all of the counties in England and Wales took fourteen years to complete. Some observers have suggested that the lengthy time involved was caused by the relative newness of the system and unfamiliarity both for members and for officers. However, as the DoE have pointed out, *in terms of completion times alone* recent events are not encouraging.

During the period 1981–85 the average length of time from the submission of a plan, or a major alteration of an existing plan, to the Examination in Public (EIP) Panel to final approval was twenty-four months. Table 1 gives an indication by year about how this time was divided up.

Rather than accelerating as local authorities became more familiar with the system, the government indicated that, if anything, the length of time involved in processing the structure plans was increasing. The *average* length of time from the beginning of the public participation exercise to final approval was three and a half years. The continued relevance of the plan was clearly called into question.

Nor was this the only suicidal tendency displayed by structure planning. The length and level of detail involved in at least some of the plans was considerable. According to the DoE, many of the first round of structure plans were over 100 000 words long and one (unnamed) document was 185 000 words long. In the second round, several of the plans contained well over a hundred and fifty separate policies and in at least one case over two hundred, in spite of frequent government advice to concentrate on key issues (DoE, 1986, paragraphs 20–23).

These problems of excessively lengthy production times and degree of detail contribute to our evidence of strategic suicide which occurs because of the very nature of the process itself, but we cannot regard them as conscious attempts by planners to undermine structure and, hence, strategic planning. However, we can find more conscious attempts in the changing attitudes of the profession in the late 1970s and into the 1980s. During this period there was a shift of power in the profession from the strategic county planners to the pragmatic district planners (Breheny and Hall, 1984). This shift in power resulted from a number of changes coinciding at this time. Given a decade of structure planning and the intended detailing of such plans via local plans, a focus on local planning was inevitable. By this time also, some of the disenchantment with structure plans—as discussed above—began to set in, with a consequent call to 'get things done' on the ground. Implementation became all important.

Table 1. Time from submission to approval of structure plan proposals, England and Wales. Source: DoE, 1986, paragraph 17.

Year	Number of approvals	Average time (months)			Total
		submission to EIP (start)	EIP to publication of proposed modifications	publication of modifications to approval	
1981	10	6	10	5	21
1982	8	7	14	6	27
1983	6	9	13	11	33
1984	4	9	16	5	30
1985	4	8	12	9	29
Average 1981–85 (32 approvals)		8	13	7	28

By this time, district planning officers—created as recently as 1974, of course—had begun to organise themselves and gain confidence in their collective strength. This increasing strength is reflected in the rise of the District Planning Officers Society and the increasing dominance of district officers in the Royal Town Planning Institute. The election of the first district planning officers to the presidency of the Institute occurred in the late 1970s.

This change of emphasis within the profession was aided at this time by the 1980 Planning and Land Act which significantly cut many of the links which had hitherto bound local plans to structure plans. Now local plans did not have to conform directly to structure plans. According to McAuslan, "a determined district planning authority can now flout the wishes of the county planning authority ... without the county being able to do very much about it" (McAuslan, 1981, page 245). The result was to undermine structure plans and to strengthen the hand of local planners.

The prevailing disenchantment with structure/strategic planning in the late 1970s was therefore taken advantage of by the newly-confident local planners, who changed the focus of planning away from strategic and conscious forward planning to local, pragmatically addressed problem-solving; all under the banner of implementation.

Breheny (1983) has argued that this switch of emphasis in the planning profession was unconsciously aided by the changing attitudes of planning academics at the time. Up to the mid-1970s in the United Kingdom, planning academics were closely associated with planning practice, and in particular with structure planning. In turn, planning practitioners were happy to take on board many of the ideas put forward by these academics. In the mid-1970s, planning academics started to criticise the practice of structure planning and began to embrace philosophies which challenged any involvement with capitalist state intervention. Consequently the new pragmatists in local government became at best indifferent and at worst hostile to planning theory.

The overall result was an increasing gulf between planning academics and practitioners. Thus, one source of energy for the profession—the injection of new ideas—simply dried up. As many of these ideas had previously been aimed at strategic planning, it was that level of planning that was the main loser (Breheny and Hall, 1984, page 97).

If we are to conclude that the demise of strategic planning can be attributed to professional suicide, then we have to be clear that there were no accomplices involved. In this case we would have to assume that central government in particular, and the Department of the Environment specifically, were neutral on the issue. Clearly, given what we know from our consideration of the possibility of murder, this assumption is difficult to sustain.

The Conservative government of 1979 clearly did have a conscious policy of reducing if not actually killing strategic planning. In some ways this is reminiscent of the codicil to the Hippocratic Oath, "Thou shalt not kill, nor strive officiously to keep alive". Therefore, we have to conclude that the planning profession was aided and abetted in killing off strategic planning, *at the very least by a lack of government support.*

Given that the process of strategic planning itself, and also independent agencies, contributed to the end to strategic planning, perhaps a verdict of simple murder is questionable. Possibly this coincidence of responses suggests that strategic planning was really a very sick patient, with the prospect of nothing but a slow, lingering, and painful demise, and was best put out of its misery. A case, in fact, of euthanasia.

5 Strategic planning put out of its misery: euthanasia

On the face of it the evidence for euthanasia is strong. Strategic planning in the 1960s and 1970s had not delivered what was expected. Regional plans were only ever indicative and they never had the force required to ensure that they would be implemented—particularly the force of law. The failings of structure plans have been considered in detail earlier. Certainly in the form and status allowed to it, strategic planning during this period was a great disappointment. Towards the late 1970s, with the onset of recession, this failure seemed harder and harder to condone. Strategic planning at this time was sickly and ineffectual; perhaps a genuine candidate for euthanasia.

But let us be a little more careful. Euthanasia assumes that those responsible for actually putting down the patient have no vested interest in the death, have nothing to gain from the patient's demise. If we assume that central government and the planning profession were jointly responsible for finally killing off strategic planning, we must be suspicious of their motives. As we have seen, the government had a clear ideological opposition to strategic planning on the grounds that it hinders enterprise. Likewise, at least some elements of the planning profession, following disenchantment with the practice of structure planning, had deliberately attempted to boost the role of local, pragmatic planning. Clearly, it has been to their advantage to undermine strategic planning.

Given these motives, the killing off of the sickly patient was not as altruistic as it might seem; certainly not a genuine case of euthanasia.

6 Conclusion

Clearly, in trying to determine the nature of death, the motive, and possibly any guilty parties, we have a difficult case. We do have a corpse: to all intents and purposes strategic planning of the kind envisaged in the 1960s is dead. Given its relatively sudden demise from the late 1970s, we cannot assume death by natural causes. In some way, death has been hastened. The question is, in what way, by whom, and for what motive?

We have rehearsed the evidence for *murder*. There is considerable evidence that the Conservative governments from 1979 onwards have consciously and deliberately killed off strategic planning. The motive would appear to be that strategic planning stifles enterprise. Although the logic of this thinking has been challenged, a motive for murder does not have to make sense: it is sufficient for it to exist. The DoE has pleaded not guilty, but other powerful views and organisations, including the Department of Trade and Industry, are no friend of strategic planning or of planning generally.

On the face of it the case for murder is strong. If this evidence stood alone, it might be sufficient to indict elements within the government. However, as we look at other possible causes of death, alternatives to murder begin to emerge. There is considerable evidence that the way in which strategic planning was conducted and the attitude of the planning profession deliberately encouraged its suicidal tendencies, and in effect played into the government's hands. It was a case of professional *suicide* in the most profound sense of that term. But this verdict is undermined by the fact that several accomplices completely outside planning also appear to have been involved.

The apparent existence of accomplices to the murder—and accomplices with supposedly independent views—implies that *euthanasia* should possibly be considered. Perhaps strategic planning was so frail and sickly that the kindest response from both central government and the planning profession was to put it out of its misery. However, this verdict is itself brought into question by the knowledge that both of these groups had vested interests in its death.

Possibly, the most realistic verdict is one that we have not considered in detail, but is the nearest to a hybrid of those that we have considered: *manslaughter*. Strategic planning was, in effect, set upon by various parties—including central government departments, some local authorities, small businesses, and powerful elements within the planning profession—who intended harm but who did not deliberately intend to kill with malice aforethought.

Initially, the perpetrators of the crime showed no remorse. Although they did not intend to kill off strategic planning, they did not mourn its demise. The suspicion is that after time to reflect on their actions, and as the context changes, several of the parties involved do show some regrets. The planners now appear to support the idea of some resurrection of strategic planning; witness the report 'Strategic planning for regional potential' (RTPI, 1986). The government, perhaps more cynically, shows some softening of attitude. As yet, no legal or procedural changes have been made, but faced with a backlash from Tory backbenchers over growth in the outer South East—particularly in the Green Belt—ministers may be forced to think again. However, the immediate portents are not good. Just as this backlash gathers force, the government has issued, in January 1989, its White Paper formalising the abolition of structure plans. This inquiry has found that strategic planning is to all intents and purposes dead in the public sector. However, a close relative can be found living in exile in the private sector, with powerful patrons including major developers, volume house builders, airport authorities, and large-scale retailers. The seeds of a new form of strategic planning could be found within this sector, which would combine planning and development capability at the strategic level. Some form of strategic planning must occur because it is the only real alternative to a constant series of clashes between the cumulative NIMBY—not in my backyard—response and the development imperative, TINA—there is no alternative. New developments *must* take place; new houses *must* be built; new facilities both public and private *must* be appropriately sited. A case has to be made for the resurrection of genuine strategic planning.

References
Breheny M, 1983, "A practical view of planning theory" *Planning and Design* **10** 101–115
Breheny M, Hall P, 1984, "The strange death of strategic planning and the victory of the know-nothing school" *Built Environment* **10** 95–99
Breheny M, Hall P, Hart D, 1987 *Northern Lights: A Development Agenda for the North* (Derrick Wade and Waters, London)
Breheny M, Hart D, Hall P, 1986 *Eastern Promise?: Development Prospects for the M11 Corridor* (Derrick Wade and Waters, London)
DoE, 1986, "The future of development plans", Department of the Environment, discussion document (HMSO, London)
EARST, 1974 *Strategic Choice for East Anglia* East Anglian Regional Strategy Team (HMSO, London)
Friend J, Jessop W, 1977 *Local Government and Strategic Choice* (second edition) (Pergamon Press, Oxford)
Glasson J, 1974 *An Introduction to Regional Planning* (Hutchinson Educational, London)
Hall P, Breheny M, McQuaid R, Hart D, 1987 *Western Sunrise: The Genesis and Growth of Britain's Major High Tech Corridor* (Unwin Hyman, Hemel Hempstead, Herts)
Hart D, 1976 *Strategic Planning in London: The Rise and Fall of the Primary Road Network* (Pergamon Press, Oxford)
Local Government Planning and Land Act, 1980 *Public General Acts—Elizabeth II* chapter 65 (HMSO, London)
McAuslan P, 1981, "Local government and resource allocation in England: changing ideology and unchanging law" *Urban Law and Policy* **4** 215–268
NWRST, 1974 *Strategic Plan for the North West* North West Regional Strategy Team (HMSO, London)
NRST, 1977 *Northern Regional Strategy* Northern Regional Strategy Team (HMSO, London)
PAG, 1965 *The Future of Development Plans* Planning Advisory Group (HMSO, London)

RTPI, 1986, "Strategic planning for regional potential—a discussion document", Royal Town Planning Institute, 26 Portland Place, London W1N 4BE

SEJPT, 1970 *Strategic Plan for the South East* (five volumes) South East Joint Planning Team (HMSO, London)

SEJPT, 1976 *Development of the Strategic Plan for the South East* South East Joint Planning Team (HMSO, London)

The Planner 1987, "South-east regional guidance inadequate, says HBF", *The Planner Mid Month Supplement* May, page 3

The Planner 1988, "Conference report: contributions from the politicians", July, page 13

White Paper, 1983, "Streamlining the cities", Cmnd 9063 (HMSO, London)

White Paper, 1989 *The Future of Development Plans* Cmnd 569 (HMSO, London)

Strategic Issues in the Fourth Report on Physical Planning in the Netherlands

G A VAN DER KNAAP
Erasmus University of Rotterdam
A VAN DELFT
National Physical Planning Agency

1 Introduction

The main issue in the debate on planning theory is how planning practice reponds or should respond to changing circumstances. Planning methods and issues in physical planning are changing over time. The Netherlands has a strong tradition in the field of physical planning (see table 1). We set the most recent report of the central government on physical planning in this dynamic field: the Fourth report, published in 1988, proposing the outline of spatial policy over the coming decades.

In section 2 of the paper we give a short historical introduction to the various factors involved in the process of the changing planning methodology up to the Fourth report. The reports on physical planning of the Dutch central government are seen as the codifications of these phenomena. Of course, the focus is on the Dutch case, but most of the themes will be recognisable in other countries too.

In sections 3 and 4 we outline the main issues in the Fourth report from the points of view of continuity in Dutch physical planning and of new themes, respectively.

Section 5 is devoted to issues in the field of spatial management and spatial decisionmaking in their legal and planning methodological setting.

Table 1. Reports on physical planning in the Netherlands.

Year	Description
1956	Report on the Western part of the country
1960	First report on physical planning
1966	Second report on physical planning
1973	Outlook on future planning ⎫
1976	Report on urbanisation ⎬ Third report
1986	Report on rural areas ⎭
1986	New spatial trends
1988	Fourth report on physical planning

2 An historical overview

Planning can be defined as anticipatory decisionmaking, so physical planning as the shaping of spatial conditions for the future. However, planning methods are conditioned by the social, political, and economic environment of the period in which plans have been constituted.

Society is a dynamic complex of opinions and standards. Emancipation and individualism have changed Dutch society from a corporate state clearly organised along lines of religious or political convictions after World War Two (Goudsbloem, 1967) into a more pluralistic society in the 1980s. The consensus on social goals which existed in the 1950s and the 1960s has ceased to exist since the 1970s.

Expectations for future developments—optimistic or pessimistic—are different in different eras; and the belief in social engineering and so the belief in shaping the future also fluctuate. The treatment of uncertainty over future developments has become more and more an element of planning methods. The evolution from discrete and integrative planning methods (blueprint planning) to more continuous and cyclical planning (process planning) is well known, but the change from detailed planning to more selective, strategic planning is a recent trend (see Friend and Hickling, 1987).

Political coalitions and the associated opinions on planning also change over time. The socialist-led political coalitions in the first period after World War Two implemented the socialist planning traditions of the interwar period, based on ideas about centralised coordination in an overall national plan. Todays liberal democratic coalitions emphasise coordination by market forces and thus the deregulation and simplification of the administrative planning system. The amendments of 1986 made to the Physical Planning Act (1965) aimed at shortening procedures and increasing the flexibility of the different physical planning instruments. The decentralised nature of the administrative organisation in the Netherlands (see figure 1) is also reflected in the Physical Planning Act. This decentralised setting is one of the reasons why the spatial plans exhibit a diminishing measure of abstraction and why they become more concrete down the line of levels of administration (MHPPE, 1987). It is particularly in the municipalities that the various policies are transformed into regulations which are directly binding upon the citizen.

The legitimation of the government as the dominant planning authority has been subjected to criticism for some time. This led to discussion of theoretical planning concepts such as planning by negotiation and communicative planning. Variation in the issues with which physical planning is concerned is another way in which the changes in planning environment are reflected. First, the priority given to an individual topic—in politics and in physical planning—is not constant over time. Although the rate of change is not the same for the various topics, the general nature of this shift in priority can be illustrated by the concept of the policy life-cycle (see figure 2).

In the first stage of such a policy cycle the debate on a topic is rather confusing. There is little consensus on the nature of a problem, and planning is devoted to the research on empirical facts and to the operationalising of concepts. In the second and third stages—the stages

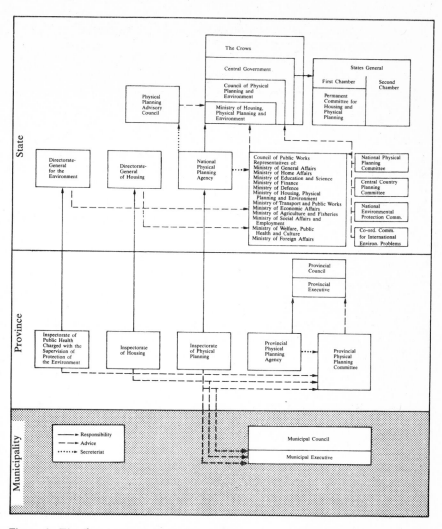

Figure 1. The Dutch physical planning system.

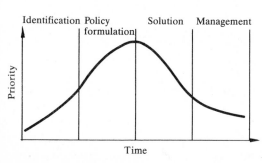

Figure 2. Policy life-cycle.

of policy formulation and solution—the role of planning is dominant. The topic becomes firmly established on the political agenda. In the second stage the discussion is focused on planning methods, and in the third stage planning can be concentrated on the definition of policy instruments for specific cases or for well defined areas. In the last stage—the stage of managing problems and policies—the priority of a topic in planning terms diminishes.

The changing priorities which are attached to individual topics, the nonsynchronous scheme of different policy life-cycles for different issues, and the rise of new topics lead to changes in the mix of themes in physical planning over time. Analogous to the policy life-cycle, the variation over time in the mix of topics in Dutch physical planning can be characterised by a cyclical movement. Highly simplified, a trade-off in dominance between two sets of issues can be noted (see figure 3). The first set consists of issues related to the spatial conditions of economic growth. The second set is composed of issues which are related to environmental quality, involving ecological factors and living conditions.

Obviously, the detailed composition of both sets varies over time. In the reconstruction period between the end of World War Two and the mid-1950s, the main issue was the transformation of the (wrecked) Dutch agricultural and commercial economy into a modern industrialised state. Subsequently, high priority was given to policies related to the spatial consequences of a rapid growth in population. In the 1960s, priority slowly shifted to regional imbalances in population and welfare in a period of economic prosperity. Towards the end of the 1960s and in the first half of the 1970s the depletion of natural resources and problems of pollution seemed to set limits to economic growth (Dutt and Costa, 1985). The increasing interest in the natural environment was reflected in the definition of physical planning which has been used since the Second report: "the search for, and establishment of, the best possible mutual adaptation of space, and society for the benefit of society" (Second Report, 1966, page 6). After the oil crisis of 1973 and the economic depression over the period 1980–82 priority has once again shifted towards the stimulating of economic growth.

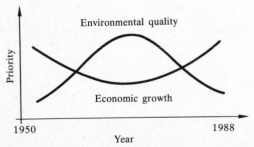

Figure 3. Issues in physical planning, 1950–88.

3 The Fourth report

In summary, the planning environment in which the Fourth report was produced can be characterised by two key concepts: uncertainty and retreat of government. Uncertainty is related to both the developing pluralistic nature of Dutch society and the future economic, technological, and social trends. Retreat by the government from its earlier role as the dominant planning actor fits into the liberal tradition of restrained intervention in social and economic processes. It has also been strongly enforced by the retrenchment of government budgets in an era of weak economic growth. These two elements explain to a high degree the nature of the Fourth report.

The planning methodology of the Fourth report can be labelled as strategic, but not in the traditional sense of clearly defined goals and elaborated policy strategies as, for example, in the 1976 report on urbanisation. Consensus and priority on spatial goals seem to be too low, and uncertainty about future trends too high. The strategic nature of the Fourth report lies more in its long-term approach to the spatial organisation of the Dutch society, and in defining the responsibilities to be taken by the central government in guiding future developments in cooperation with other actors in the field of physical planning. The philosophy expressed in the Fourth report on strategic planning implies selectivity over policy issues and in policy actions. An integrated vision of the spatial organisation of the Dutch society in the twenty-first century is not given, but the major trends are explored. Not every future spatial problem is discussed, but rather those about which the central government can make an essential contribution to solving.

The planning horizon of the report is the year 2015. This, however, is an expression of the long-term nature of physical planning rather than a precisely defined period for forecasts and policy actions.

For a good understanding of the status and the nature of the Fourth report it is necessary to keep in mind that it represents the opinion of the central government in a decentralised physical planning system. The primary actors in decisionmaking are the provincial and local authorities. However, strong emphasis is also placed on the role and responsibilities of private investors. Most of the policy actions announced in the Fourth report have to be seen as actions which will either initiate or support the steps to be taken by the other participants in physical planning.

The main themes in the Fourth report are presented in figure 4 (see over). In the tradition of physical planning in the Netherlands the Fourth report opens with an analysis of future trends. This is an explanatory survey of major changes and possible trends rather than a set of (quantified) forecasts.

In the outline of spatial policy for the next decades two points of view are taken in the report. One is from the perspective of the individual citizen in respect of changes and adaptations in the daily living environment, both rural and urban. The other is from a national point of view and the focus is mainly on the spatial conditions for the revitalisation of the Dutch economy in an international (European) setting

From this evaluation of future trends it is concluded that society is becoming ever more varied. This puts major demands on the way the spatial setting is organised. Most of the decisions on daily living conditions are taken by the public itself, and the state's role is confined to ensuring that certain basic qualities are maintained. In this respect local authorities and provinces have the first responsibility. The role of central government is confined to a supportive policy with respect to local initiatives.

A characteristic of the Fourth report to be mentioned here is the shift in the focus of planning, from the problem of expansion in land use to the quality of the spatial settings in which future social activities will be organised. This shift is expressed in the emphasis on spatial quality.

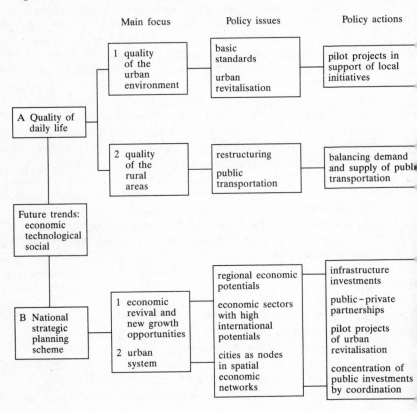

Figure 4. Main themes in the Fourth report.

Although it is not clearly defined, spatial quality is seen as the surplus value of physical planning which results from the (spatial) integration of other policy actions. The cohesion of the functions within living and working environments, the variety in architecture and landscapes, and the flexibility to meet changes in requirements are elements of the spatial quality of areas.

4 New themes and new responses

The need to anticipate future international, economic, and technological developments was the main reason for the publication of the Fourth report on physical planning. *Internationalisation* is a special theme in the Fourth report. It is stated that the report should be considered as the first outline of regional development in a future Europe without frontiers. Traditionally the Dutch economy has a very pronounced international orientation.

International transportation and trade have been important sectors. The ongoing international integration of production, services, and capital markets has been leading to new economic challenges (and risks) for the Netherlands. From 1992 on, the European Community should be a single market without economic barriers and tariffs. The transportation infrastructure of the Netherlands has to be integrated into the European networks in order to secure the outstanding international position of the Dutch distribution sector for the future. The growing importance of internationally-orientated producer services leads to competition between urban areas in Europe.

Economic prosperity is the main issue in the governmental policy of today; and so it will remain in the foreseeable future, as economic forecasts indicate only moderate economic growth in the coming decades. Nevertheless, even with a moderate economic growth a substantial increase in prosperity can be expected. Income per capita may rise by at least some 40% by 2010. As prosperity rises, the demand for spatial quality will also rise. On the other hand, the upgrading tendencies in the Dutch production structure (high-technology industries, top-level services) stress the importance of production environments of high quality.

Technological innovation will have a major impact on spatial organisation. Application of new technologies in agriculture, manufacturing and services allow for changes as well as for reductions in land use. Developments in communication technology will give less importance to geographical distance as a factor in physical planning. Even in small country like the Netherlands the scope for spatial interactions will increase.

The strategic national planning scheme outlines the contribution of physical planning in safeguarding the economic position of the Netherlands in this changing international and technological context.

The scheme is based on three principles:
1 variety in and quality of residential and business areas as stimuli to economic development,
2 a focus on economic activities which have high international potentials, and
3 reinforcement of the individual spatial and economic potentials of the various parts of the country.

In these basic principles changes in the approach to physical planning are clearly reflected. First, the strong emphasis on economic aspects of development is obvious. In the previous governmental reports on physical planning and regional economic policy an equitable spatial distribution of economic activity and prosperity was the guiding principle in order to ensure a filtering down of economic activity from the densely populated urban area (Randstad Holland) in the western part of the country to intermediate and more peripheral parts of the country. This filtering-down concept is abandoned in the Fourth report. The classical trade-off between equity and efficiency in regional economic policy has been compromised by a focus on the opportunities of all individual regions and on a select number of economic sectors with a high international potential as well. Those strong points of the Dutch economy are transport and distribution of goods, trade and producer services, high-value agricultural industry, and assembly and high-technology manufacturing. Most of the activity in those international sectors is and will be located in the core area of the Dutch economy. The core area is, incidentally, no longer defined only as the Randstad Holland. It also includes the adjacent parts of the provinces of Gelderland and North-Brabant.

The emphasis on regional economic efficiency has led to a shift in focus from the areas which have problems in economic development to those areas which have a development potential. This may have the consequence that some of the areas which were assisted areas in the regional development policy are again incorporated, but now on the basis of their assets instead of their problems.

The regional economic analysis of the Fourth report is based on an analysis of the distribution and information potential of regions and their technological potentials (see Van der Knaap and Louter, 1988). The first has been approached by the regional share in high-quality commercial-service activities and the second by the spatial distribution of R&D activities and promising industrial activities in the high-technology processing and production sectors. When these two elements are combined with the level of regional welfare, a picture emerges which describes the economic health of a region.

However, these three elements are in turn also influenced by other factors, such as the international position of the Netherlands or regional variations in external economies expressed by differences in agglomeration costs and benefits. The international position is of importance within the context of the strong position of the Netherlands in distribution and transport. In this context the role of the Randstad within Western Europe should be a point of special consideration. The future economic development of this region means that it can compete with other main European cities. Therefore it must secure and improve its position within the European city system. This is of course not only relevant regarding its position in the transport and distributive trade but also in terms of its relative position with respect to other European centres of high-grade economic (industrial) activity.

The relative differences in cost structure are also reflected in the factors which contribute to the production environment of a region. These include the availability of commercial services, skilled labour, good residential environment, good access to markets for intermediate goods, and markets for final products. These factors produce potential regional variations in economic performance.

The relation between technological potential, distribution, and information potential and the level of regional welfare has been measured with the use of a causal model in which the relations are estimated on the basis of partial least squares. The results of this procedure are a set of regional scores on each of the three main features. These scores reflect the relative position of a region within the national context (figure 5, see over).

The technological potential has two points of regional concentration: one is a strong concentration in the southeast and the second is a more dispersed pattern in the west with some small areas of concentration. In general the part of the country south of a line from The Hague to Arnhem has a higher concentration. What emerges clearly from this pattern is that the cities, not only the largest ones, occupy a prominent position. Hence, there is little evidence of where new national centres of growth are located.

The distribution and information potential exhibits a strong concentration in the Randstad region. This is caused by the large number of wholesale and computer software firms. In addition to this there is a concentration of internationally-oriented commercial services located near the airport of Schipol and the port of Rotterdam. These elements support the quality of the economic environment in the Randstad. In combination with the level of welfare there emerges a picture with a strong focus on the west and south of the country. However, one should not jump to this conclusion too rapidly as, for comparative purposes, the three elements should not be dealt with in a simple additive way. When the regions are clustered on the basis of the similarity of their scores a more complex but better picture can be given of the relative position of a region.

The second main element in the strategic planning scheme is the basic urban structure of the Netherlands. In the Fourth report nine urban centres are selected as the nodal points in the future spatial organisation of the country (see figure 6). The selection, of course, includes the four largest urban agglomerations of the Randstad Holland, but also include five medium-sized cities in the other parts of the country. The selection emerges from evidence of a bundling of high-quality facilities such as universities, telecommunication facilities, and other producer services, together with access to the fast and efficient national and international transportation infrastructure in order for their production environments to serve the whole country as well as the individual regions.

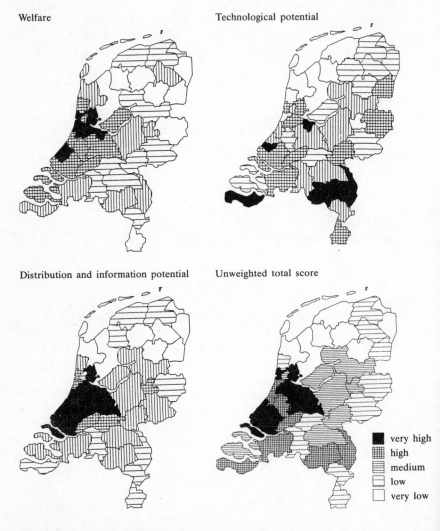

Figure 5. Indicators for regional economic potential.

The concept of a main urban structure related to economic development is a new element in Dutch physical planning. It includes a hierarchy of three types of nodal urban centres. The three periphally situated nodal points—Groningen in the north, Enschede and its twin city Hengelo in

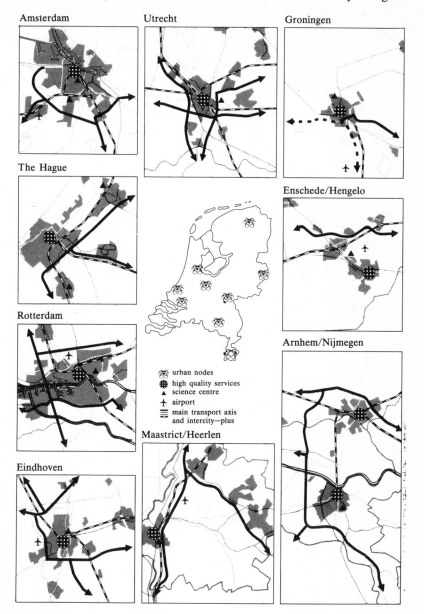

Figure 6. Nodal urban centres.

the east, and Maastricht/Heerlen in the south—have mainly a regional function in light of the economic potentials of the regions they serve.

The Randstad cities—Amsterdam, Rotterdam, The Hague, and Utrecht—together with Arnhem/Nijmegen and Eindhoven (headquarters of Philips) constitute the main urban structure—an urban ring—on which the further economic development of the economic core area is based. This core area offers a large variety of production environments suitable for the needs of the whole set of economic activities of a high international potential.

The three largest urban agglomerations in the western part of the Randstad Holland—Amsterdam, Rotterdam, and The Hague—are seen as a conurbation which offers an internationally competitive production environment for producer services with an international status. It is not the large metropolitan areas of Europe—London and Paris—but rather cities like Brussels, Frankfurt, and Düsseldorf which are the competitors with which the western part of the Randstad has to cope.

The concept of nodal points in the national urban structure can be considered as a first step towards spatial network planning (see Van der Knaap and Van Delft, 1988). However, the layout and geographic scale of functional networks within the urban structure has not been clearly elaborated in the Fourth report. The selection of the nodal points is based mainly on the characteristics of the individual cities and on the strategy of a wide distribution of nodal points over the national territory. Obviously, on the international scale the position of Rotterdam and Amsterdam as main ports in a European distribution network has been recognised. The conurbation of Randstad Holland, offering an internationally competitive production environment, can itself be considerd as a spatial network, but the interrelations and complementarity between the individual cities of Amsterdam, Rotterdam, and The Hague have not been defined. The same holds for the functional interrelations within the urban ring of the economic core region.

In this context the policy implications for the central government are confined mainly to transportation infrastructure questions and to the regional position of the nodal points. This implies actions for:
(a) Removing bottlenecks in the international and national transportation axes. Priority is to be given to the hinterland links of the port of Rotterdam and the airport Schiphol, to the infrastructure connecting the nodal points within the core area, and to infrastructure linking the other nodal points to the economic core regions (see figure 7). Special attention is to be paid to the transportation infrastructure within the Randstad.
(b) Reinforcement of the internationally relevant features of the three major cities and strengthening the spatial structure of the open space—the Green Heart—in the Randstad Holland.
(c) Reinforcing the functioning of the nodal points as regional centres, by improving the production environment.

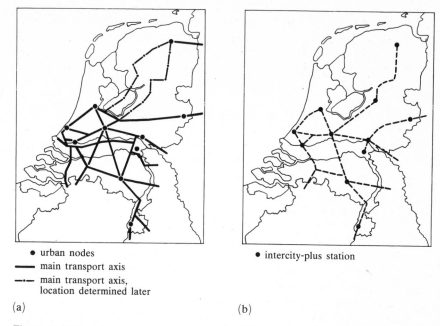

● urban nodes
—— main transport axis
—·— main transport axis,
    location determined later

● intercity-plus station

(a)   (b)

Figure 7. Main transport axes: (a) road, (b) intercity-plus.

5 Spatial management and spatial decisionmaking
Spatial policy is not only concerned with sectoral policy but also with
the nature of the social and economic processes themselves. Therefore,
when the features of a spatial policy are discussed from a physical
planning perspective, these should be related to the following four
characteristics:
1 the spatial impacts of the policy both direct and indirect,
2 the spatial processes leading to spatial quality,
3 spatial quality, as the synergetic effect of the policy, and
4 the evaluation of this policy.
The spatial impacts aspect is based upon the direct involvement of
government using its available instruments. This relates to legislation
and control at different levels of government. The spatial process is a
complex interplay between spatial design, allocation of the functional
structure, and the geographical space in which these events occur. They
can all be characterised by their own dynamics and this may lead to
changing relations over time.
   The nature of these variations can be illustrated by the different types
of spatially relevant cooperation between different levels of governments
and the private sector. As was pointed out in section 2 of this paper,
physical planning is closely related to the social context and to time-
dependent policy actions (see also Bussink, 1988). The role of the
various actors in this game, as well as their mutual relations, vary

over time. Therefore the intensity and the nature of the cooperation
between government(s) and private enterprise is changing over time. In the
case of real estate and infrastructure development in the Netherlands,
three distinctly different periods from the point of view of the nature of
the cooperation can be identified: 1945-68, 1968-78, and 1978-88
(see Prins, 1986).

The first period was characterised by a considerable willingness of
public and private organisations to cooperate, private investment paving
the way for this cooperation. The planning process in the early period
can be characterised as 'top down'. In the second period there was a
boom of public investment, and various types of public-public cooperation
emerged, and problems of vertical coordination appeared. This public
investment was separate from investment activities in the private sector.
The dominant mode in the planning process in this period was also top
down. In the third period, the most recent, there is again a development
of different forms of public-private cooperation in which neither of the
partners occupies a dominant position. The planning mode in this period
can thus be described as horizontal. Obviously, when one considers the
variation in the role of government, the variation in different types of
cooperation shows an inverse relationship to economic development.
When this development peaked, public-public cooperation was the
dominant mode.

Associated with these changes in cooperation are the changes in
spatial strategies and in the role of planning and thus of the plan itself.
In the planning process a shift in emphasis can be observed from the
Third to the Fourth report. In the Third report there was a more direct
concern for the characteristics of geographical space and spatial allocation.
In marked contrast to this is the more abstract view of the Fourth report
in which there is a dominance of general (predominantly economic)
trends, and a strong emphasis on spatial design.

These changes should also be understood in terms of the changing
views on the role of the plan during the 1970s. At least three different
lines can be identified in this period. The plan was intended to serve
as a tool for spatial coordination, spatial decisionmaking, and spatial
management. The spatial coordination approach was the dominant mode
in this period and a considerable effort was put into its implementation.
This led to various forms of vertical and horizontal coordination, such
as the emergence of city-region administrations or regional administrations
for a well-defined set of problems. Simultaneously there was the
reorganisation of local government to create larger units. Today very
little remains of this complex structure of mutual relations in which
responsibilities were shared.

The second line was to regard the role of the plan as an instrument
for spatial decisionmaking (Faludi, 1973). This is a rather complex
issue as it raises directly questions about the nature of the free or

available decision space (which is usually rather restricted), the role of the actors, and the legislation to support the appropriate actions. The discussion is often put in the perspective of the role of the structure plan in relation to the detailed and restrictive land-use planning of local authorities (see also Mastop, 1984). However, because of the nature of the particular questions being raised, it involves the position of the national plan as well. The demand for a plan as a tool for spatial decisionmaking is at the same time a demand for an increase in the decision space of a lower-level of government. This also requires a formal legal structure to enable provincial and municipal authorities to act effectively to support the decisions by legal means. Therefore it will increase the powers of local government. At this stage of discussion two basic issues emerge: the first is the question about the dualistic structure of government, and the second relates to the degree to which a decision-orientated planning approach can contribute to an effective planning system. There is still very little knowledge, however, about the relation between policy development and spatial planning. Galle (1988), using the Fourth report as an example, argues that the policy practice has not been the development of a plan based upon policy development, but rather that the development of the plan in itself generated the development of a particular policy. Related to the first point (the dualistic structure of the government) is the issue of the devolution of power to local levels of government. The question which arises immediately is: power for what? Power for the development, management, or execution of a plan require entirely different supporting legal frames. This relates directly to the third line mentioned above: the plan as a tool for spatial management. The experience with the 1965 law on physical planning has led during the 1970s to some criticisms about its effectiveness as a tool for managing uncertainty. Two types of criticism were dominant: one was related to the length of the procedures and the second was related to the problem of vertical coordination and the role of the structure plan: that is, to the possibility of having decision powers at a lower spatial level. In order to solve these problems the Minister of Physical Planning considered a revision of the 1965 Act.

During this revision it was suggested not only that a formal legal structure might be developed, but also a procedural structure which would guarantee the legal position of the citizens to protect their rights, as well as the execution of the spatial plan. This would, it was argued, also contribute to the resolving of conflict in situations in which coordination between authorities could not be reached by mutual agreement. Two proposals in particular must be mentioned (Koningh et al, 1985): (1) the operational area assignment, and (2) the binding project decision. These suggestions relate to the problems which have emerged from the coordination of the various laws concerning the ownership of property. The development of these laws has been independent and each has a history of its own. This has led to a legal body which is incoherent from the point of view both of the spatial allocation of functional properties and of spatial management. Given the growing interest in urban renewal associated with functional structural change and urban revitalisation, the demand for improved tools to facilitate effective urban management has increased. In particular, the operational area assignment was thought to be a possible tool for the coordination of large-scale projects, in which a number of partners from outside the field of physical planning was involved. In cases where the possibility of conflict resolution was low and the Physical Planning Act did not provide sufficient tools, the binding project decision could, it was thought, solve any problems that might arise. Ultimately the different proposals led to a revision of the 1965 Act in the new act on physical planning in 1985 and the associated Rules of Physical Planning in 1987. One of the main characteristics of this act, not surprisingly now, is the increased flexibility of the planning system, especially with respect to the structure plan and to the shortening of the planning procedures.

The increased flexibility has been also reflected in the proposals in the Fourth report. However, it is not only a reflection of the discussion on the structure of the planning system in the last decade, but also an indication of increased uncertainty concerning future spatial development. One important decision has been taken: that is, the emphasis on selectivity. The challenge is to keep open the options within the framework presented. The leading theme of the Report is 'choose your lane for the next century'. Until now only a first choice has been made, but a large number has still to follow.

6 Conclusion
The Fourth report thus appears to mark a new era in Dutch physical planning. The three main characteristics of the new approach have been mentioned in this paper:
1 selectivity in issues and policy actions,
2 flexibility in planning methods and procedures, and
3 an emphasis on spatial conditions for economic development.

Although the Fourth report has been criticised in detail, these basic principles nevertheless seem to be accepted. In defining the leading issues in future spatial development and the responsibilities of the (central) government, the report provides a long-term framework for the decision of the other actors in the field of physical planning.

The need for physical planning in consultation and cooperation with the private sector is the main message contained in the Fourth report. Public investments have to provide leverage for private investments in the spatial organisation of the future Dutch society. This seems to imply a planning system of public–private partnership in which the government no longer is the dominant actor. In this sense, the Fourth report introduces strategic planning not only as a planning methodology, but also as a reconsideration of the role of the public sector.

Acknowledgements. The authors wish to thank Professor P R Odell, Director of Eurices, for his critical comments on an earlier draft of this paper.

References
Bussink F L, 1988 *Samenwerken bij het Ruimtelijk Beleid* (Cooperation in Physical Planning) (Samson, Alphen aan den Rijn)
Dutt A K, Costa F J (Eds), 1985 *Public Planning in the Netherlands* (Oxford University Press, Oxford)
Faludi A, 1973 *Planning Theory* (Pergamon Press, Oxford)
Fourth Report, 1988, Staatsuitgeverij, The Hague
Friend J, Hickling A, 1987 *Planning under Pressure, The Strategic Choice Approach* (Pergamon Press, Elmsford, NY)
Galle M M A, 1988, "Constructie van beleidstheorie van direct nut voor de beleidspraktijk?", (Policy theory of use for policy practice?) *Beleid en maatschappij* **15** 45-55
Goudsbloem J, 1967 *Dutch Society* (Random House, New York)
Koningh Th de, Van der Knaap J W M, Leemeijer B W, Schoonveld R, Lubach D A, Oosting M, 1985 *Ordening van Besluitvorming over de Ruimte* (Organising Spatial Decisionmaking) (Kluwer, Deventer)
Mastop J M M, 1984 *Besluitvorming, Handelen en Normeren* (Decisionmaking, Action, and Standards) PhD thesis, Department of Planning and Demography, University of Amsterdam
MHPPE, 1987 *The Rules of Physical Planning 1986* Ministry of Housing, Physical Planning and Environment The Hague
Physical Planning Act, 1965 *Wet op de Ruimtelijke Ordening* staatsblad; number 340, 24 July
Physical Planning Act, 1985 *Wijziging op de Wet op de Ruimtelijke Ordening* (revision) staatsblad; numbers 623, 624, and 625, 21 November
Prins E J, 1986 *Public-private partnerships vanuit de Optiek van de Ontwikkelaar/ Risicodrager* (Public-private Partnerships from the View of the Private Sector) AMRO Bank, Apeldoorn
Second report, 1966, "Second report on physical planning", abbreviated version, Staatsuitgeverij, The Hague
Van der Knaap G A, Van Delft A, 1988, "Ruimtelijke Netwerken in Ontwikkeling", (Spatial Networks in Flux) WP-88-15, available from author at Economisch Geografisch Institut, Erasmus University of Rotterdam, Rotterdam
Van der Knaap G A, Louter P J, 1988, "Technologische ontwikkeling en ruimtelijke specialisatie in de Randstad", (Technological development and spatial specialisation in the Randstad Holland) *Geografisch Tijdschrift* **1** 3-14

London 2001

P HALL
University of Reading, University of California

An academic observer of London in the late 1980s might well come to believe in a cyclical theory of history. Just as in the early 1960s, the British media are again full of the problems of London and the South East: population growth and spread, escalating land and house prices, traffic congestion, overcrowding on the tubes and British Rail, fights about development in the home counties. Some of the current scenes of battle, like Hook in Hampshire, are the same now as then. Once again, we are in a period and under a government devoted to the principle of setting the people free. And everywhere, voices are being raised that it is not good enough; that something must be done. In other words, regional planning has reached its nadir, and is just about to come back into fashion.

Perhaps it is all a manifestation of half a Kondratieff long wave, or (better) a Kuznets construction cycle. Perhaps, as Schlesinger (1987) has recently suggested, political issues really do recycle at roughtly twenty-five-year intervals. Whatever the explanation, it may be useful to ask whether history is truly repeating itself.

In reality there seem to be uncanny similarities, and also some significant differences. Twenty-five years ago, at the end of a book called *London 2000* (Hall, 1963), I made some predictions of the future. In preparing a sequel, to be called *London 2001*, I reexamined them. Some prove to have been reasonably on target, some wildly off the mark. Almost everyone in the 1960s wildly overestimated the growth of population and employment in the London region. Obsessed with problems of a buoyant economy, no one could have predicted that there would be fewer jobs in the London metropolitan area in the late 1980s than in the early 1960s. On the other hand, almost everyone then seems to have been right in accepting the fact of massive decentralisation of the population from core to periphery, and in predicting its continuation. In fact the only mistake we made was to underestimate the scale of the movement.

In the intervening quarter century there have, I think, been at least two huge changes in the socioeconomic landscape of the South East and in our perception of it. The first, known to everyone, is what could be called the progressive polarisation of the economy, which David Eversley was the first to identify and predict nearly twenty years ago (Donnison and Eversley, 1973, page 27). Above all, in London itself, we now witness an extraordinary set of contrasts: on the one hand, the over-heated 'Yuppie' economy; on the other, minutes away, a society with no jobs and no prospects. It is most poignantly expressed by the almost unbelievable variations that now exist in residential unemployment rates across a few miles: from less than 9% in Redbridge to over 24% in Hackney, or from 6% in Sutton to 20% in Lambeth (SERPLAN, 1987, page 91). It is encapsulated in the conclusion of Buck and Gordon, in their ESRC-funded study of local employment, that an unqualified, unmarried, black worker, aged 16–19, in an unskilled manual occupation, living on a council estate, is thirty times more likely to become unemployed than their statistical 'standard male' (Buck and Gordon, 1987, page 99).

We all know why; these reasons have been explored in meticulous detail in the ESRC study. We might well differ about some of the prescriptions that follow. Basically, there are three underlying structural causes. The first is that the whole base of unskilled manual work has dramatically collapsed. The second is that this base was particularly concentrated in inner east and inner south London, which only a quarter of a century ago contained a mass of factories and workshops as well as the Port of London. I do not think it is generally appreciated, even now, that behind the hype, the London economy actually performed less well during the 1960s and 1970s than that of any other major city in Britain; worse even than Liverpool, that archetypal case of economic failure. The ESRC study has confirmed just how catastrophic was the destruction of the London job base in those years: a loss of nearly 750 000 jobs between 1966 and 1984; more than 600 000 lost in manufacturing alone (Buck et al, 1986, page 66). In comparison, the growth in the so-called information sector was negligible. It may have improved very recently, but the latest evidence we have gives no proof of this.

As a result, in these working-class districts of east and south London we now find a kind of ghettoised society, reproducing itself through the failures of the education system; hence the ESRC conclusion that anyone in this or a similar society would have better prospects almost anywhere else. The third, special factor is race prejudice, which reinforces the poor performance of some ethnic groups (but not others) in the London schools—a performance that may itself be related to self-reinforcing racial stereotypes (ILEA, 1987).

This is not uniquely a British problem. On the contrary, the key features have been analysed for a long time in North American cities, and—as the comparative work of John Kasarda and Jürgen Friedrichs has shown—are now observable in West German cities also (Kasarda and Friedrichs, 1986). As they show, the most important single cause is what, twenty years ago, the American economist Charles Killingworth identified as 'job twist': a structural decline in demand for unskilled work coupled with a rapid escalation in the qualifications required to enter almost any job at all (Killingworth, 1968).

However, the interesting point is that this is no longer the aspect that interests the media. It is a 1970s issue, not a 1980s one. In the middle-class view of London life, which is now the view of 80% of the population, it is of interest only in terms of a high crime rate, the distant possibility of a riot, and the indirect impact on the package of services provided by the local borough (support for community groups versus fixing the cracks in the pavements). For this average consumer of the media, the problems of London are not those of economic failure but of explosive economic success: escalating house prices, the return of gazumping, overcrowded tube trains, difficulty in finding a good builder, etc. The underclass are of interest only when, by accident, they physically impinge on the gracious but harried life of 'Yuppiedom'.

Tom Wolfe's *The Bonfire of the Vanities* might thus equally be a parable for contemprary London as for New York. Nevertheless I share the view of Ian Begg et al, in the conclusion of their ESRC study: that the possible consequences of prolonged deprivation might be "severe alienation, crime and violence, extreme and widespread poverty, large-scale vandalism and physical dereliction, the eventual removal of the private sector from such areas, and a gradual deterioration and breakdown of law and order and any sense of community" (Begg et al, 1986, page 12) It sounds uncannily like Wolfe's New York. Surely no Londoner who had seen the reality of the South Bronx would relish the prospect.

But let us go back to the middle class. The other dominant feature is that they are escaping from London, and that they are going ever further afield. It is true that Tony Champion has identified a break in trend in terms of a reversal of London's long population decline during 1984 and 1985 (Champion, 1987). The gain was concentrated in outer London, but in inner London the population stabilised after years of loss. There are good reasons: the high birth rate among certain immigrant groups, and the bonus from housing completions in Docklands and elsewhere. Time alone will show whether the reversal will be maintained the 1987 figures again showed a fall in London's population, and out-migration is continuing at a high rate.

Meanwhile, the very important news is that the wave of really rapid growth is moving steadily farther and farther out. Martin Mogridge's analysis, indeed, suggests that the process has been occurring at a very steady rate since 1861, come war come peace, with plans or without (Mogridge, 1985). It crossed the boundaries of Greater London in the 1950s or earlier; it leapt over the limits of the outer metropolitan area during the 1960s; during this decade, it has rolled on outward beyond the boundaries of the South East region. The really significant growth now is occurring in a zone that has no name: you can call it the 'Golden Belt' or the 'Sunbelt' or, more pedantically, the 'Rest of the Greater South East'. It consists of a belt of counties from Dorset, through Wiltshire, Northamptonshire and Cambridgeshire, to Suffolk; by the 1990s, according to the OPCS projections, it may embrace Lincolnshire OPCS, 1986). Within it, the growth is strongly concentrated in a few major city regions:

Bournemouth – Poole (which, unnoticed, has become one of the most dynamic places in Britain in the 1980s), Swindon, Milton Keynes – Northampton, the belt that stretches through the Fenland border from north of Cambridge to Peterborough, and Ipswich.

What is happening in this belt? Did the people get pushed there, or were they pulled, or is it some combination of the two? What is the economic base that keeps these places running? As there is presently no research on the causes, let me hazard some speculations. Some, the younger ones in the family building cycle, are doing so because only down the lines can they find the single-family housing they need, at a price they can afford: an exact repetition of the 1960s story. Others, the older ones, may be cashing in their accumulated housing gains while the going is good.

As to jobs: there is some long-distance commuting via British Rail's Intercity 125 services, though not as much as the media suggests. There is much more growth of irregular commuting on the part of people who do not have fixed 9-to-5 Monday-to-Friday patterns of employment, like professional consultants, TV cameramen, or academics. There is retirement and semi-retirement and anticipation of retirement on the part of people who have decided to cash in their London house values, sometimes investing the difference in small businesses. There is also a local economy, in the form of high-tech and decentralised office employment along the M4 corridor. There is the development of certain places in the eighty to hundred mile range from London as strong regional service-centres. All these can interact, as in the case of the older professional who retires early and starts up a business or a consultancy from a small town in Dorset or Suffolk, catering to the demands of the buoyant local economy.

There is scope for much research here. One approach is to try to establish exactly how the economy of such places is growing. I hope that the current ESRC research on the urban system may throw light on this question. Another is to disentangle the effects on commuting patterns. For all the media attention to the plight of long-distance straphangers, now as twenty-five years ago, there is next to no evidence of a long-term growth in London's commuter field; rather the reverse. The explanation again comes from the ESRC Inner Cities study. When people move out, at first they join the army of commuters. But then, at the rate of about 7% – 10% a year, they find local jobs. After ten years, something like three-quarters work locally. The indirect result of population movement is to reinforce the local economies of the towns of the fringe. This mechanism has worked very well, and it is the reason for a major paradox revealed in the ESRC research: though the London economy has performed so terribly, the fact has not led to higher unemployment there: the out-movers eventually release jobs for those who stay behind (Buck et al, 1986, pages 45 and 97).

Further, as they do so, they cease to be long-distance commuters.
It could well be that we are now witnessing a temporary transitional
phenomenon which will subside. But there may be a different problem
in the making: a tangle of shorter-length and medium-length journeys
into the towns of the fringe, almost all made by car, leading to the
condition which in the United States Robert Cervero has labelled
'Suburban Gridlock' (Cervero, 1986). It is now abundantly clear that i
the USA, decentralisation of office functions has reached such an
advanced stage—northern New Jersey for instance has more office spac
than downtown Chicago and Los Angeles combined—the traditional
dominance of radial journeys is being completely overlain by this new
pattern of daily movement. And everywhere—Orange County south of
Los Angeles, Silicon Valley, the so-called 'I-680 Corridor' in the San
Francisco Bay Area, and the New Jersey and Connecticut suburbs of
New York—the result is an increasing paralysis, to which conventional
transportation planning has no solution. I do not think that the greate
South East has yet reached that point, but some parts are approaching
it. Martin Boddy and his colleagues are studying the patterns on the
western end of the M4 Corridor; but we need more analysis closer to
London, around such major recipients of office decentralisation as Readi
and Basingstoke.

But it is not the commuters who have provided the biggest stories f
the media during recent months. It is the house buyers—or, more
precisely, the people who want to build houses for them, in the form (
the House Builders Federation and also Consortium Developments,
arrayed on one side of the battlefield, and the planners, in the form of
the districts and counties and SERPLAN, the standing conference of t
South East planning authorities, on the other. They have been locked
in conflict, with the statistical departments of the major building societi
providing cannon balls in the form of regular analyses showing South
East house prices increasing at a dizzying rate: according to one muc
quoted account in mid-1987, by £53 a day. They have not risen as
spectacularly this year, but that is because the zone of maximum grow
has now moved out into the South West and East Anglia.

Both sides have engaged their professional experts to bolster their
cases (Evans, 1987; Grigson, 1986). They seem to agree on one poi
that house prices have risen roughly in line with incomes. They have
probably risen much faster than the Retail Price Index. The proportic
of house price represented by land has risen, though no faster than in
the rest of the country. The builders interviewed quote land availabili
as the main constraint in their achievement of their plans, but they ha
always tended to say that.

The arithmetic, which applies only to the South East standard regic
is simple. SERPLAN has for a long time stuck with a figure of a nee
for 460000 homes in the 1990s. It thinks one third of these can and

should be built within Greater London. The house builders say that the real figure is much higher, perhaps 800 000 or more. Nicholas Ridley, after some dithering, has recently settled on a figure between 560 000 and 580 000.

Predictably, no one is satisfied. The house builders paint a picture of continued shortages. The protestors paint a rival picture of the concreting over of the South East. That is rather far from the mark: Robin Best's estimate, twenty years ago, was that between 17% and 19% of the region was urbanised; a more recent estimate from Margaret Anderson gives only 16%, rising to 17% by the year 2000 (Best, 1981, page 65; HBF, 1987, page 32). The one almost indisputable fact is that there is likely to be a very large surplus of farmland by the end of the century, as a result of subsidy reductions to farmers. The Countryside Commission in 1987 estimated that on the most likely set of assumptions farmland could be as much as one quarter of the present agricultural area of the country, though clearly this might be lower in a relatively fertile region like the South East (CC, 1987). So, as in the 1930s, farmers may once again discover that their most profitable crop is of bungalows.

The critical questions clearly are: 'How much?' and 'Where?' The latter question really splits into two parts: 'How concentrated or how spread at the regional scale?' and 'How much at a local scale?' At one extreme, as in the *Strategic Plan for the South East* of 1970, we could seek to concentrate a large part of the total growth into a few well-sited growth areas (SEJPT, 1970). That strategy did not work very well, for the population figures show that three of the five so-called major growth areas failed to grow very much at all; but that, perhaps, was because the local planners were not trying very hard to provide for growth, or were even trying to stop it. One irony is that the people who seem to believe in the 1970s plan are the volume builders. A very substantial part of all the twenty or more new communities now proposed for the South East are in the major or medium growth-zones designated in the Plan. If all of their proposals for the Reading – Wokingham – Aldershot – Basingstoke quadrilateral came to pass, for instance, we should get an urban structure for that area very similar to what the 1970 plan team had in mind. The contrary irony concerns the SERPLAN planners: apart from wanting to crowd one third of their calculated need into London, they wish to spread the other two thirds quite evenly across the region, arguing that the demand will come mainly from locals and must therefore be met locally. The strategic planners have completely rejected the strategic planning orthodoxy of eighteen years ago. No wonder that the government can dismiss strategic planning as an outdated notion from the 1960s.

My personal opinion—it can be no more—is that they are about 50% right, 50% wrong. Much of the demand will arise locally, but a lot will also arise from footloose households, and it would be right—as argued in the 1970 report—to concentrate this in places which offered easy commutes to central London, and which also had a sufficiently large and varied economic base to provide for subsequent commuter drawback. The Reading–Wokingham–Aldershot–Basingstoke area is an outstanding example. Milton Keynes–Northampton, Crawley–Gatwick, and South Essex are others. Notice that they are 'neatly' placed roughly at the four compass points, on major transportation corridors. Cambridge–Peterborough–Huntingdon might well be added to them, because of the access offered by the newly electrified East Coast main line and the M11–A604 corridor.

Further, it would also make sense to try to develop these locations in association with the commercial regeneration of selected accessible locations in the inner and middle rings of London, along the same transportation corridors, which could attract the necessary mix of skills by intercepting the commuters, but which could also provide jobs suitable for the local unemployed work force. It is interesting that, just before *London 2001* went to press, the London Planning Advisory Committee published its strategic planning advice for Greater London, with a similar policy for selected sites in East London, notably Stratford Broadway (LPAC, 1988). I had also identified that site, but I disagree with the LPAC that the policy should concentrate solely on East London. There are extraordinarily accessible sites elsewhere in the inner and middle rings, some of which are almost completely undeveloped because the accessibility has never been exploited. Among them, perhaps the most outstanding are Deptford Park near the Millwall football ground in southeast London, and the Old Oak Triangle in west London. There are also developed sites ripe for redevelopment, like the Finsbury Park–Wood Green corridor, which could fulfill exactly the same role.

There is a final element in this strategy. It is to enhance accessibility within the South East by a balanced programme of rail and road investment. Planning in the region, over the last quarter century, has been bedevilled by starvation funding and by the fact that transportation planning has become a political football: one lot of people all pro-road, the other all pro-rail. The right solution, surely, would be to concentrate on rail investment for the job that rail is good at—intercity and commuter services—and accept that the rest of the region will ride on the roads.

This means selective investment in new and improved roads, with more orbital capacity both in south London and in the outer metropolitan area (OMA), at roughly forty miles from central London, together with new radials into congested OMA centres like Reading, Luton, Chelmsford, and Maidstone; both should provide for priority for buses and other high occupancy vehicles. But it also means, as top priority, the creation of a new regional express rail system, on the model of the Parisian RER or the new S-Bahn systems of German cities, which would bring long-distance commuters into and under the centre of London. A first element

distance commuters into and under the centre of London. A first element
of such a system has been in place since May this year: Thameslink, which
connects Bedford and Luton directly via King's Cross, and Blackfriars
with Sevenoaks, Orpington, Gatwick, and Brighton. A first step should
be to complement it by an east – west line, linking Reading and Heathrow
with Docklands and Southend. Later would come a line joining
Northampton and Milton Keynes with Basingstoke and Tonbridge. Such
a system would be a key element in linking the major growth centres
with the zones of regeneration within London.

Does this sound over impressive, even fantastic? As a twenty-year
plan, it is the reverse. Much of it will be needed, come what may. A
joint study by London Regional Transport and British Rail, published
early in 1988, evaluated a rail package along these lines. Much of the
investment could and should come from the private sector, which has
shown itself willing and eager to put money into new road and rail
schemes as well as into new communities. It needs a modicum of
imagination plus political will. Above all, it needs a commitment to a
notion of public planning and private investment working hand in hand.
It is a mixture that has worked brilliantly in Paris, Tokyo, and Singapore.
It could work well in London too.

References
Begg I, Moore B, Rhodes J, 1986, "Economic and social change in urban Britain
  and the inner cities", in *Critical Issues in Urban Economic Development. Volume 1*
  Ed. V A Hausner (Oxford University Press, Oxford) pp 10 – 49
Best R H, 1981 *Land Use and Living Space* (Methuen, Andover, Hants)
Buck N, Gordon I, Young K, 1986 *The London Employment Problem* (Oxford
  University Press, Oxford)
Buck N, Gordon I, 1987, "The beneficiaries of employment growth: an analysis
  of the experience of disadvantaged groups in expanding labour markets", in
  Critical Issues in Urban Economic Development. Volume 2 Ed. V A Hausner
  (Oxford University Press, Oxford) pp 77 – 115
CC, 1987, "New opportunities for the countryside: the report of the Countryside
  Policy Review Panel", CCP-224 (Countryside Commission Publications,
  19 – 23 Albert Road, Manchester M19 2EQ)
Cervero R, 1986 *Suburban Gridlock* (Center for Urban Policy Research, Rutgers
  University, New Brunswick, NJ)
Champion A, 1987, "Momentous revival in London's population" *Town and
  Country Planning* **56** 80 – 82
Donnison D, Eversley D E C, 1973 *London: Urban Patterns, Problems and
  Policies* (Sage, London)
Evans A W, 1987 *House Prices and Land Prices in the South East—A Review* H/12
  (BEC Publications, Federation House, 2309 Coventry Road, Sheldon, Birmingham
  B26 3PL)
Grigson W S, 1986 *House Prices in Perspective: A Review of South East Evidence*
  RPC 572, for the London and South East Regional Planning Conference,
  50 – 64 Broadway, London SW1H 0DB
Hall P, 1963 *London 2000* first edition (1969, second edition) (Faber and Faber,
  London)

HBF, 1987 *Private Housebuilding in the Inner Cities: A Report by an Independent Commission Prepared for the House Builders Federation* The House Builders Federation (BEC Publications, Federation House, 2309 Coventry Road, Sheldon, Birmingham B26 3PL)

ILEA, 1987 *Ethnic Background and Examination Results 1985 and 1986* RS 1120/87, Inner London Education Authority (ILEA Publications, Centre for Learning Resources, 275 Kennington Lane, London SE11)

Kasarda J D, Friedrichs J, 1986, "Comparative demographic-employment mismatches in U.S. and West Germany", in *The Future of the Metropolis: Economic Aspects* Eds H-J Ewers, H Matzerath, J B Goddard (De Gruyter, Berlin) pp 221–249

Killingworth C M, 1968, "The continuing labor market twist" *Monthly Labor Review* **91**(9) 12–17

LPAC, 1988, "Strategic planning advice for London: policies for the 1990's: draft document for discussion", London Planning Advisory Committee, Eastern House, 8–10 Eastern Road, Romford RM1 3PN, Essex

Mogridge M, 1985, "Strategic population forecasting for a conurbation using the negative exponential density model" *Transportation Research A* **19** 189–206

OPCS, 1986 *Population Projections: Area* series PP3 number 6, Office of Population Censuses and Surveys (HMSO, London)

Schlesinger A M, 1987 *Cycles of American History* (Deutsch, London)

SEJPT, 1970 *Strategic Plan for the South East: A Framework* South East Joint Plan Team (HMSO, London)

SERPLAN, 1987 *Regional Trends in the South East: The South East Regional Monitor 1986–87* RPC 800, the London and South East Regional Planning Conference, 50–64 Broadway, London SW1H 0DB